EPICTETUS

EPICTETUS

A STOIC AND SOCRATIC
GUIDE TO LIFE

A. A. Long

CLARENDON PRESS · OXFORD

OXFORD
UNIVERSITY PRESS

Great Clarendon Street, Oxford OX2 6DP

Oxford University Press is a department of the University of Oxford.
It furthers the University's objective of excellence in research, scholarship,
and education by publishing worldwide in

Oxford New York

Auckland Cape Town Dar es Salaam Hong Kong Karachi
Kuala Lumpur Madrid Melbourne Mexico City Nairobi
New Delhi Shanghai Taipei Toronto

With offices in

Argentina Austria Brazil Chile Czech Republic France Greece
Guatemala Hungary Italy Japan South Korea Poland Portugal
Singapore Switzerland Thailand Turkey Ukraine Vietnam

Oxford is a registered trade mark of Oxford University Press
in the UK and in certain other countries

Published in the United States
by Oxford University Press Inc., New York

© A. A. Long 2002

The moral rights of the author have been asserted

Database right Oxford University Press (maker)

First published 2002
First published in paperback 2004

British Library Cataloguing in Publication Data
Data available

Library of Congress Cataloging in Publication Data
Long, A. A.
Epictetus: a Stoic and Socratic guide to life / A. A. Long.
p. cm.
Includes bibliographical references and index.
1. Epictetus. I. Title.
B563.L66 2002   188–dc21   2001052070

ISBN 0–19–924556–8 (hbk.)
ISBN 0–19–926885–1 (pbk.)

Typeset by Hope Services (Abingdon) Ltd.
Printed in Great Britain
on acid-free paper by
Biddles Ltd., King's Lynn, Norfolk

For Monique

CONTENTS

PREFACE

The idea of writing this book began to crystallize while I was teaching a graduate seminar on Epictetus at Berkeley in the spring of 1999. My students were far more responsive to his Stoic discourses than I had dared to hope, and by the end of the semester I myself was thinking about little else. By a happy coincidence, I was about to begin a sabbatical year of research leave, generously assisted by grants from my university. My official project for this leave had not been a study of Epictetus, but now I knew that this was what I wanted to write, and so I set to work.

Although the idea of this book arose only recently, Epictetus has been on or near my desk for more years than I care to recall. I have been fascinated by him ever since I began to work on Hellenistic philosophy, and I have incorporated him in much that I have previously published. But I had never devoted a whole course to Epictetus before, and I had never immersed myself in him completely. Like many others, I tended to read him piecemeal, concentrating on passages that bore on my general interests in Stoicism rather than trying to engage with his singular mind and arresting style for their own sake. Now, instead, I read him through in entirety several times.

In doing so, I became especially interested in his educational strategies and his devotion to Socrates, and I also found myself increasingly impressed by the distinctive stamp of his Stoicism and by his remarkable personality. Quite coincidentally, excerpts of Epictetus were beginning to reach a large public through Tom Wolfe's brilliant novel *A Man in Full*. Reactions to that book in newspapers had shown that Epictetus' text, just by itself, was capable of touching modern nerves. Yet, there was no up-to-date and comprehensive introduction to Epictetus. All the more reason, I thought, to write a book that would offer a sufficiently in-depth treatment in a manner that could attract new readers to him as well as those to whom he needs no introduction.

That is what I have tried to do, with the strong encouragement of Peter Momtchiloff of Oxford University Press and his anonymous advisers, for whose advice at the planning and later stages I am most grateful. I do not presume any prior knowledge of Epictetus or Stoic philosophy, and I have liberally included my own translations of numerous passages, using these as the basis for all my detailed discussions. These excerpts are the most important part of the book, because its main purpose is to provide sufficient background and analysis to enable Epictetus to speak for himself. What he says, however, often stands in need of clarification and interpretation. Research on Epictetus has a long way to go. I hope I have contributed a number of fresh ideas, but it would defeat the purpose of this book if I defended them in the main text with a barrage of scholarship. At the end of chapters I append bibliographical details and provide guidelines on various details and points of controversy.

My warm thanks are due to numerous people. First, I am delighted to mention all those who attended my seminar on Epictetus: Chris Brooke, Tamara Chin, Luca Castagnoli, James Ker, Erin Orzel, Miguel Pizarro, Walter Roberts, Tricia Slatin, Belle Waring, and two visiting scholars, Antonio Bravo Garcia and Bill Stephens. I learnt a lot from them all, and I especially thank Chris Brooke, whose seminar paper on Epictetus in early modern Europe introduced me to some references I have gratefully incorporated in my Epilogue. I have been wonderfully served by Christopher Gill, Brad Inwood, Vicky Kahn, and David Sedley. They read the entire first draft of the book and gave me extremely helpful comments. Peter Momtchiloff has been a splendid editor, not only through his publishing expertise but also by acting as the book's model reader. Our e-mail correspondence over the past year has been a great stimulus and pleasure to me.

The final product is appreciably better as a result of all this advice. I have benefited from the publications of scholars too numerous to acknowledge completely, but among my contemporaries I especially thank Rob Dobbin, Christopher Gill, Rachana Kamtekar, Susanne Bobzien, Michael Frede, David Sedley,

Pierre and Ilsetraut Hadot, Brad Inwood, Julia Annas, Jonathan Barnes, and Robin Hard. James Ker, a graduate student at Berkeley, has earned my gratitude not only by assembling data and checking references but also by vetting my translations and suggesting other improvements. I am also very grateful to Hilary Walford for her care and courtesy as my copy-editor and to Charlotte Jenkins for her fine management of the book's production.

I presented some of the material in Chapters 3 and 4 as Corbett Lecturer at the University of Cambridge, and this is now published in my article, 'Epictetus as Socratic Mentor', *Proceedings of the Cambridge Philological Society*, 45 (2000), 79–98. I also gave related talks to the Loemker Conference on Stoicism, at Emory University, Atlanta, the Stoicism seminar at the Centre Léon Robin of the University of Paris Sorbonne, the Philosophy Department of the State University of Milan, and the Philosophy and Classics Departments of the University of Iowa. I am very grateful for these invitations, especially to Steve Strange, Jean-Baptiste Gourinat, Fernanda Decleva Caizzi, and John Finnamore, and for the feedback I received in discussions following the lectures. When my typescript was in its final stages, I delivered some of the material in a series of seminars at the École Normale Supérieure of Paris under the kind auspices of Claude Imbert. My French colleagues and students were a wonderful audience, and their comments enabled me to make several last-minute corrections and additions. Finally I thank the University of California Berkeley for the Humanities Research Fellowship I was given and also the Office of the President of the University of California for the award of a President's Research Fellowship in the Humanities.

I dedicate this book to my wife, Monique Elias. With her artistry, beauty, and spontaneity, she has seen me through all the dry days, and she has been a magnificent companion at every stage of composition.

A.A.L.

Berkeley
June 2001

CITATIONS AND ABBREVIATIONS

References to ancient authors are generally given in full. For citations in the form Frede (1999), see the References. The following abbreviations are used:

ANRW   *Aufstieg und Niedergang der römischen Welt*
DL   Diogenes Laertius
Ench.   Epictetus' *Encheiridion* or *Manual*, compiled by Arrian
EN   Aristotle, *Nicomachean Ethics*
In Ench. Simplicus' commentary on the *Encheiridion*
LS   A. A. Long and D. N. Sedley, *The Hellenistic Philosophers*, 2 vols. (Cambridge, 1987). Volume i includes translations of the principal sources, with philosophical commentary, and volume ii gives the corresponding Greek and Latin texts, with notes and bibliography. A reference in the form LS 61A refers to the chapter number of either volume and the corresponding letter entry.
SVF   *Stoicorum Veterum Fragmenta*, ed. H. von Arnim, 3 vols. (Leipzig, 1903–5). This is the standard collection of evidence for early Stoicism.

ANTHOLOGY OF EXCERPTS

Introduction

Epictetus is a thinker we cannot forget, once we have encountered him, because he gets under our skin. He provokes and he irritates, but he deals so trenchantly with life's everyday challenges that no one who knows his work can simply dismiss it as theoretically invalid or practically useless. In times of stress, as modern Epictetans have attested, his recommendations make their presence felt.

Living as an emancipated slave and Stoic teacher in the Roman Empire, Epictetus inhabited a world that is radically different from the modern West. Yet, in spite of everything that distances him from us—especially *our* material security, medical science, and political rights, and *his* fervent deism—Epictetus scarcely needs updating as an analyst of the psyche's strengths or weaknesses, and as a spokesman for human dignity, autonomy, and integrity. His principal project is to assure his listeners that nothing lies completely in their power except their judgements and desires and goals. Even our bodily frame and its movements are not entirely ours or up to us. The corollary is that nothing outside the mind or volition can, of its own nature, constrain or frustrate us unless we choose to let it do so. Happiness and a praiseworthy life require us to monitor our mental selves at every waking moment, making them and nothing external or material responsible for all the goodness or badness we experience. In the final analysis, everything that affects us for good or ill depends on our own judgements and on how we respond to the circumstances that befall us.

Epictetus expounds these ideas in numerous ways, but he is chiefly concerned with the training and contexts for their implementation, and with rebutting objections to them. The contexts range over the whole gamut of human experience—tyrannical threats to life and limb and political freedom, loss of property, jealousy and resentment, anxiety, family squabbles and affections, sexual allure, dinner-table manners, bereavement, friendship, dress, hygiene, and much more. This guide to life is as demanding as it is comprehensive; for it is central to Epictetus' philosophy that no occasion is so trivial that his salient doctrines do not apply.

His cultural and historical significance have never been in doubt. He was revered by many of his contemporaries and by those, including the Emperor Marcus Aurelius, who knew him later through his student Arrian's record of his teaching. Early Christian writers mentioned him approvingly, and Simplicius, the great Neoplatonist commentator on Aristotle, wrote a commentary on the *Manual*. Translations of this abridgement of Epictetus were so familiar during the seventeenth and eighteenth centuries that Epictetus became virtually a household name for the European and early American intelligentsia. William Congreve starts his play *Love for Love* with a penniless young man reading Epictetus in his garret. Elizabeth Carter, a prominent member of the Bluestocking Circle, was the first person to translate the whole of Epictetus into English. Her near contemporaries, Shaftesbury and Butler, are two of the British moralists who invoked him during the eighteenth century, and in America his later admirers included Thomas Jefferson, Walt Whitman, and Henry James.

For much of the nineteenth and twentieth centuries, however, Epictetus was not a central figure. He was largely treated as a Stoic popularizer, lacking depth and creativity. Since about 1970 Epictetus has begun to regain his former status as a powerful thinker on ethics and education, worthy of discussion alongside Socrates and Plato, but he still tends to be read selectively, either as the author of maxims preaching self-reliance or simply as a spokesman for Stoic philosophy or for life under the Roman Empire. Happily that situation is changing, as this book's References section shows. Yet, there is no modern book that presents Epictetus in the round as author, stylist, educator, and thinker. That is the gap I hope to fill by publishing this volume. Epictetus can be explored from many different perspectives. These include intellectual and social history, the interpretation of Stoicism, ethics and psychology, both ancient and modern, the theory and practice of education, rhetoric, and religion. As a historian of ancient philosophy by profession, I have concentrated on the analysis of Epictetus' main ideas, but all the perspectives I listed are relevant to my goal—which is to provide an accessible guide to reading Epictetus, both as a remarkable historical figure and as a thinker whose recipe for a free and satisfying life can engage our modern selves, in spite of our cultural distance from him. I have given a lot of space to translated excerpts, building my discussion of many details around these, and I have also included the full text of several of the shorter discourses. All these passages are numbered throughout the book, and I have collected the main ones at the beginning in an Anthology of Excerpts, where they are briefly described for ease of reference.

I start from the assumption that Epictetus is deceptively simple to read, or, rather, that he is a complex author with patterns of thought and intention, including irony, that have been scarcely appreciated. When he is read rapidly and selectively, Epictetus can appear hectoring, sententious, or even repellent. I do not maintain that these qualities simply disappear under analysis. His work contains passages I prefer not to read, which have even on occasion deterred me from writing this book. Yet I am also convinced that a good many candidates for such passages are ironical or at least rhetorically motivated by reference to cultural conventions, his educational programme, and its youthful audience.

Epictetus has also been misunderstood because his appeals to theology, which are ubiquitous, have been consciously or unconsciously read in the light of Christianity. In my opinion, Epictetus' deepest ideas are remote from the main Christian message, notwithstanding notable parallels between some things he says and the New Testament. His ethical outlook includes stark appeals to self-interest, which ask persons to value their individual selves over everything else. Yet, Epictetus *is* a moralist, an advocate of uncompromising integrity in human relationships and a forerunner of Kant in his stance that material considerations and contingencies have no bearing on the rightness of a right action. How his theology, egoism, and social commitments tie together is a major question, and one that has been little addressed up to the present. I try to answer it in the second half of this book.

A further source of misunderstanding has been the description of his teachings as *diatribes* or sermons, with the implication that he is a preacher to human beings, or at least men, in general. I prefer to call the surviving record of his work dialectical lessons, in order both to call attention to his persistently conversational idiom and to register his deliberate affiliation to Socratic dialectic. Socrates, rather than any Stoic philosopher or even the Cynic Diogenes, is Epictetus' favoured paradigm, not only as a model for life but also as a practitioner of philosophical conversation. The point is not that Epictetus refrains from sermonizing or haranguing; that is one of his styles. But it is a style he adopts in response to a specific audience.

Our Epictetus is only what his pupil Arrian chose to record, edit, and then publish. Like Socrates, Epictetus did not compose for publication, but Arrian's reports put us in the position of being a fly on the wall in his private classes, and on occasions when he was visited and consulted by someone passing through. Taking account of this auditory context, which quite often focuses upon a single, generally anonymous individual, is indispensable if we want to evaluate the tone and purpose of numerous discourses. Epictetus is typically addressing precisely the people—young men—who have opted to study with him. Recognition of this audience aids appreciation of the hyperbole, irony, and repetitiousness that are characteristic of his teaching.

I have tried to make this book as accessible as possible by sparing use of footnotes and by largely confining bibliographical and other scholarly matters to appendices at the end of chapters. To the extent that seemed essential I have explained Epictetus' relation to his Stoic authorities and tradition, and I have sometimes compared him with the other Roman Stoics. But I have been concerned throughout to keep the focus on Epictetus as author, letting him speak for himself rather than reducing him to the status of one among other Stoic philosophers. Much more could be said than I have offered by way of positioning him within the Stoic tradition. My excuses for playing this history down are simple—such a treatment would not only have turned this into a lengthy and technical book, which I was keen to avoid; it would also have detracted from the distinctive power of Epictetus' voice. Readers who are eager to compare Epictetus with other Stoics will find ample material in the sections of Further Readings and Notes that I have appended to the chapters.

The book is designed to be read in the sequence of the chapters, but each of these can also be approached independently. Those who are interested in first sampling Epictetus' discourses could consult the Anthology of Excerpts or begin with Chapter 5, where I translate two short discourses in full and give a detailed analysis of their style and thought. Chapters 1–4 are chiefly concerned with placing Epictetus in his intellectual and cultural context and with the methodology of the discourses. In Chapters 6–9 I focus on the themes and concepts that I find central to his thought and its fundamental unity. However, this division is by no means hard and fast. The reader who reaches Chapter 6 after proceeding through all the earlier chapters will have already seen most of Epictetus' principal concepts at work. What I offer in Chapter 6 onward is a more sustained treatment of his philosophy, topic by topic. This procedure involves some unavoidable repetition, but any account of Epictetus that disguised his repetitiousness would be quite misleading. In an Epilogue I give a selective account of Epictetus' afterlife in Europe and America, and I also ask what we can make of him today.

A final word about my translations. I have naturally striven for accuracy, and by that I include respect for the tone and rhetoric of the original rather than a literalness that could jar or misrepresent the effect of Epictetus' Greek. For example, Epictetus often uses the vocative *anthrôpe*, literally '(O) human being' or '(O) man'; but neither of these translations works in modern English. So I have preferred to write 'friend' or 'my friend'; and I occasionally use a modern colloquialism such as 'wow!', where that seems just right to capture the feel of the original. Because the discourses are largely composed as conversations, I have tried to reproduce that effect by having my excerpts printed accordingly, with the interventions of Epictetus' generally fictive interlocutors, or his responses to his own questions, presented in italics. The original text lacks most modern devices of punctuation, and it can be difficult to decide how to distribute its questions and answers. When in doubt, I have adopted continuous paragraphs, so readers can be confident that whatever appears in the book as dialogue is so in the original.

FURTHER READING AND NOTES

Texts and translations
The most accessible Greek text of Epictetus, together with English translation, is the two-volume Loeb edition of Oldfather (1925–8). This includes the four books of discourses, the *Manual*, and fragments (short excerpts quoted by various ancient authors from works that have not otherwise survived). The major edition of the Greek text of the discourses is Schenkl (1916), and there is also an excellent four-volume edition, together with French translation and detailed introduction, by Souilhé (1948–65). Boter (1999) is the best edition of the *Manual*. His book includes a remarkable account of that work's manuscript tradition, and Boter has also edited Greek versions of the *Manual* that were adapted to monastic use; see p. 261 below.

There is no modern commentary on the whole of Epictetus, but Dobbin (1998) is an outstanding commentary on book 1 of the discourses, together with translation. Gourinat (1996) is a French translation of the *Manual* with a fine introduction to Epictetus and his Stoicism. Hadot (2000) is a further French version of the *Manual* with an excellent analysis of the work's structure. For commentary on 3.22 (on the ideal Cynic), see Billerbeck (1978), and for commentary on Epictetus' discourses that deal with logic, Barnes (1997).

The best English translation of Epictetus in entirety is Hard in Gill (1995). For the *Manual* on its own, see White (1983).

CHAPTER I

Epictetus in his Time and Place

What else am I, a lame old man, capable of except singing hymns to God? If I were a nightingale, I would do the nightingale's thing, and if I were a swan, the swan's. Well, I am a rational creature; so I must sing hymns to God. This is my task; I do it, and I will not abandon this position as long as it is granted me, and I urge you to sing this same song.

(1.16.20–1)

I.I ORIENTATION

In the early years of the second century AD, with the Roman Empire under Trajan, its most effective ruler since Augustus, a group of young men were to be found studying together in the city of Nicopolis, situated immediately north of the modern Greek port of Préveza on the Ionian Sea. They were the students of Epictetus. One of them, Arrian, made a detailed record of his master's teaching, and it is these *Discourses* that enable us to read Epictetus today and to treat him as a virtual author in his own right.

Epictetus was a Stoic philosopher, one of many to be found in Rome and other cities of its vast empire. The essence of his teaching went back to Zeno, Cleanthes, and Chrysippus, the founding fathers of Stoicism in the third century BC at Athens. Their original writings are lost, and, although some of what they contained is recoverable through accounts by later authors, Epictetus is the Stoic teacher we are in a position to read most extensively.

For that alone his work would be important, but its value and interest go far beyond what it tells us about the doctrines and rationale of Stoicism. In Epictetus' work that philosophy is not so much expounded as lived, made urgent and even disturbing by his remarkable personality and powers of expression. He has an inimitable way of specifying and interpreting Stoicism for his students, and he appropriates Socrates more deeply than any other philosopher after Plato. These things, together with much else that will be explored in this book, make Epictetus one of the most memorable and influential figures of Graeco-Roman antiquity.

Epictetus needs no defence concerning his capacity to interest and challenge modern readers. Thanks to the celebrated *Manual*, a summary set of rules and doctrines that Arrian extracted from Epictetus' discourses, he has never gone out of print.[1] He has even been copiously quoted in Tom Wolfe's best-selling novel *A Man in Full*, where the character who encounters a book containing translations of Epictetus finds his life transformed accordingly, and converts another character to Stoicism. The popularity of self-help books and therapy sessions has its ancient prototype in the *Manual*, where one finds such thoughts as these:

1   Don't ask that events should happen as you wish; but wish them to happen as they do, and you will go on well.   (*Ench.* 8)

2   Sickness is an impediment to the body, but not to the will unless the will consents. Lameness is an impediment to the leg, but not to the will. Tell yourself this at each eventuality; for you will find the thing to be an impediment to something else, but not to yourself.   (*Ench.* 9)

---

[1] 'Manual' translates the Greek *encheiridion* (abb. *Ench.*), sometimes rendered as 'handbook'.

3 If someone handed your body over to a passerby, you would be annoyed. Aren't you ashamed that you hand over your mind to anyone around, for it to be upset and confused if the person insults you?

(*Ench.* 28)

Packaged in this way, Epictetus has his appeal, but if this were all we would scarcely call him a major precursor of our modern *philosophical* tradition. We would relate him rather (and I do not mean disparagingly so) to the rule books of Christian monasticism or to the Wisdom literature of Buddhism and Confucianism. Those contexts and their meditative practices are appropriate up to a point; Epictetus recommended his students to concentrate on such thoughts as those excerpted above, and some of his work has a mantra-like quality. The excerpts of the *Manual*, however, are only that—passages Arrian organized, selected, and compressed from the full record in order to present Epictetus' teaching in a more accessible and memorable form. They give a limited and somewhat grim impression of his thinking and speaking in his actual *Discourses*.

There, rather than advancing maxims and potted doctrines, he chiefly tries to show why the prescriptions of the *Manual* are grounded in truths he thinks he can prove concerning the nature of the world at large, human nature, and a rational mind's dialogue with itself. In addition, he addresses this instruction quite specifically to his student audience, relating it to questions and problems they face as would-be Stoics and as persons engaged in social life, with aspiration to various careers including the teaching of philosophy. To engage their attention, he intersperses quiet reflections with histrionic wit, hyperbole, and Swiftian pungency. The *Discourses* represent a unique blend of philosophy, pedagogy, satire, exhortation, and uninhibited dialogue.

In this book, therefore, my focus will be on the Epictetus of the *Discourses* rather than the potted excerpts of the *Manual*.

I.2 BIOGRAPHY

Little is known of the details of Epictetus' life. He was born probably in the years AD 50–60 at Hierapolis, a major Graeco-Roman city in what today is south-western Turkey, 100 miles due east of Ephesus, and connected with that great centre by a Roman road. Probably a slave by birth rather than seizure, he was acquired by Epaphroditus, a famous freedman and the secretary of the Emperor Nero. This may have happened after Nero's death in AD 68, but Epaphroditus resumed his secretarial career under Domitian (accession AD 81). We can infer, then, that the young Epictetus had direct experience of the imperial court. This is confirmed by his vivid references to persons soliciting emperors, hoping for favours from people like Epaphroditus who had the emperor's ear, and by his anecdotes about the fate of those who had incurred imperial displeasure.

In the *Discourses* Epictetus speaks of himself as a lame old man (1.16.20). His lameness may have developed only in later life, but Christian sources attribute it to the cruelty of a master, though not to Epaphroditus specifically; and in fact Epictetus mentions his former owner in ways that, though not complimentary, are far from savage (1.1.20; 1.19.19; 1.26.11). He was permitted, while still a slave (1.9.29), to attend lectures by Musonius Rufus, a prominent Stoic teacher, and Epaphroditus may have freed him soon after this began. Under the patronage of Musonius, Epictetus probably began his teaching career in Rome. In AD 95 Domitian banished all philosophers not only from the capital but also from Italy itself. It was presumably at this time that Epictetus moved to Nicopolis with a reputation sufficiently assured to enable him to attract students there and to live simply off payments he received from them.

Nicopolis, founded by Augustus to commemorate his victory over Marc Antony at nearby Actium (31 BC), was a large and resplendent city, as its modern remains still show. It became the political and economic centre for Roman rule in western Greece, while its coastal location made it the stopping place for numerous persons travelling between Greece and Italy. In choosing Nicopolis as the site for his school, Epictetus was no doubt influenced by the city's metropolitan status and facilities. His students will have found good lodgings there, and the resources of Nicopolis will have been reassuring to their parents. There, apart perhaps from short visits to Athens and Olympia, he appears to have stayed until his death in around the year AD 135. He is reputed to have been visited by the Emperor Hadrian, and the *Discourses* indicate that other prominent figures sought conversations with him. In the main, though, young students seem to have been the centre of his life until old age, when he adopted an infant that would otherwise have been exposed to death, and after years of celibacy took a wife (or live-in female servant) to support the child.

Not a strikingly eventful life, but yet a memorable one, especially in the context of elite Roman society and its conventional members' jockeying for position over wealth, repute, and status. Former slaves, as the career of Epaphroditus shows, could rise well up the social ladder, but Epictetus without any of that achieved renown simply by being a dedicated teacher, impervious to all external marks of success. In this he contrasts radically with the immensely wealthy and powerful Seneca, who was not a practising teacher and whose Stoicism, though certainly sincere, was fully tested only in old age when Nero forced him to commit suicide. Epictetus escaped that end, but his slavish origins, chronic ill health, exile, and probably precarious income are experiences to keep in mind as one reads his often severe comments on the inability of more materially fortunate people to handle themselves with dignity and equanimity.

Threats to life, torture, exile, and bodily infirmities all figure prominently in Epictetus' discourses, but slavery versus freedom is more than one of his themes. The contrast between a mental freedom available in principle to anyone and self-inflicted slavery encapsulates his chief message throughout. Freedom and slavery had long been metaphors for states of mind and attitudes pertaining to people irrespective of their social status. Yet when, as often, Epictetus calls one of his free-born students, 'slave', his words are charged with a resonance that goes well beyond either this convention or the Stoic paradox that only the wise man is free. As a person who knew the indignity of slavery from direct experience and who had also lived under the tyrannical regime of Domitian, Epictetus' philosophy acquires an experiential dimension that removes from it any vestige of mere theorizing or posturing. Marcus Aurelius, who ascended the imperial throne in AD 161, probably never met Epictetus, but the *Discourses*, or at least a written account of Epictetus' teaching (see p. 41), were a profound influence on the emperor's Stoic *Meditations*. That an ex-slave actually shaped a Roman emperor's deepest thoughts is one of the most remarkable testimonies to the power and applicability of Epictetus' words.

1.3 INTELLECTUAL AND CULTURAL CONTEXT

We can make only guesses about Epictetus' early education and first acquaintance with philosophy. Intelligent masters were quick to spot talented slaves, so it is likely that Epaphroditus encouraged him and helped him to get access to books, but his formal training as a teenager was probably rudimentary in comparison with the students he subsequently taught at Nicopolis. In a conversation with a self-important man, who had visited him on his way to Rome, Epictetus pulls no punches in exposing the person's trivial interests in philosophy:

4 You will say:
> *Meeting Epictetus was like meeting a stone or a statue.*

I agree—You took one look at me, that's all. But the person who really encounters another is one who gets to know the other's judgements and reveals his own in turn. Get to know my judgements, show me your own, and then say you have met me. Let's examine one another, and if I have a bad judgement, remove it; if you have one, bring it out into the open. That's meeting a philosopher. But that's not your way:
> *We're passing by, and while we're renting the boat we can also look in on Epictetus; let's take a look at what he's saying.*

Then you leave:
> *Epictetus was zero; his language was quite ungrammatical and unidiomatic.*

What else could you assess when you came with that attitude?

(3.9.12–14)

Epictetus likes to exaggerate and play himself down. Although he has no time for discourse that is merely elegant and flowery, he is a virtuoso user of colloquial Greek. Unlike his students, however, he probably did not have the elaborate training in schoolbook rhetoric that was the staple of Roman education. While his discourses are replete with allusions to Greek myths, he draws on figures and situations familiar to anyone with a smattering of culture—especially Homer's Achilles, Ajax, Agamemnon, and Odysseus, and Medea, Oedipus, Eteocles, and Polyneices. Likewise, his examples of historical figures, such as Croesus, Demosthenes, Philip and Alexander, and Lycurgus. All the names of this incomplete list are likely to have figured in the books by earlier Stoics that he read. His literary and cultural allusions are quite limited in comparison with the displays of learning characteristic of such contemporaries as Plutarch, Aulus Gellius, Philostratus, and Dio Chrysostom. By further contrast with them, he specializes in homely and sometimes shocking illustrations—chamber pots, greasy fingers, wobbly legs, dunghills, cracked saucepans, and the like. He must have known Latin, but the language has left only superficial traces on his text, and his references to Rome and Roman persons pertain either to his own time or to the recent past.

As with his self-deprecating remarks about language, we should not simply assess Epictetus' level of education from what he chose to exhibit in his discourses. He makes it a point to distinguish his role as a teacher of philosophy from literary interpreter or 'grammarian' (*Ench.* 49). His disdain for mere learning is one of his ways of stating the incomparably greater importance of training oneself to live well; in the words he uses to inculcate that project he is as artful as the rhetoricians from whom he officially distances himself. Still, Epictetus was probably not widely read as compared with Cicero, Seneca, and his own erudite contemporaries.

The most important influence on Epictetus from a living person was almost certainly his Stoic teacher, Musonius Rufus. A knight or member of the equestrian order, Musonius was one of a number of upper-class Romans whose Stoicism and resolute character displeased the paranoid emperor Nero. During the latter's reign

(AD 54–68) Musonius along with Cornutus, another famous Stoic, was banished to the small Greek island Gyara, which became a byword for exile (Epictetus 1.25.20; 2.6.22). Musonius was able to return to Rome after Nero's death, but may have suffered exile again under Vespasian. With the accession of Titus (AD 79), he was certainly back in Rome, and it is to this period that we can probably date the beginning of Epictetus' association with him.

As a would-be Stoic, he found the right teacher. Musonius' pupils may have included Euphrates, whose undemonstrative excellence is singled out by Epictetus (3.15.8; 4.8.17), while Musonius himself was widely heralded as an exemplar of Stoic fortitude and contentment. Although he did not publish, we have a record of some twenty of his lectures and also a collection of sayings. His themes include such (by then) standard topics as the endurance of pain, exile, and old age, but his work is most noteworthy for its treatment of more specific questions—for instance, the income appropriate to a philosopher, whether a philosopher should marry, and, most interestingly, the education of girls who, he argues, should be trained no differently from boys and regarded as no less suitable to practise philosophy.

In their transmitted form, made by an auditor, Musonius' lectures hardly live up to the promise of his enlightened themes. They are a dull read by comparison with Arrian's record of Epictetus. Perhaps Epictetus would always have overshadowed his teacher, but the impression Musonius made on him was unforgettable, and something that plainly influenced not only his Stoicism but also his teaching style. Take the following passage, where Epictetus cajoles his students for not working hard enough:

5   Why are we still idle, lazy, and sluggish, looking for excuses to avoid making efforts and staying awake as we work at improving our own rationality?
    Well, if I go astray in this, I haven't killed my father, have I?
    No, you slave, your father wasn't there for you to kill.
    So, what have I done (you ask)?
    You have made the one mistake you could have made in this case. I myself too, you see, made exactly the same retort to [Musonius] Rufus when he chided me for not spotting the one thing omitted in a syllogism. I said:

It's not as if I've burned down the Capitol.
Slave (he said): the thing omitted here *is* the Capitol.   (1.7.30–2)

Evidently Musonius taught Epictetus how to use black humour and hyperbole to make a philosophical point. We can also gather from this passage that Musonius included logic in his curriculum. That is not evident from the digest of his lectures, but the Suda Lexicon describes him as 'Logician and Stoic'.

As Stoics, Musonius and Epictetus aligned themselves with the philosophy that elite citizens, or at least the few who had any time for it, found most in keeping with the traditional Roman virtues of rectitude in public and domestic life, material simplicity, and self-discipline. It was far from being their only option. Apart from Epicureanism, which was the philosophy most antithetical to Stoicism, Scepticism (alternatively called Pyrrhonism) was offering a lively challenge to both these schools. Aristotle's technical writings, after centuries of obscurity, were beginning to be closely studied. Academics, whose title registered their claim to be the heirs of Plato, were radically divided between a sceptical sect, who interpreted Plato's dialogues as authorizing suspension of judgement about everything, and those who took Plato to be voicing a systematic philosophy in these works. At the time of Epictetus, doctrinal Platonism was undergoing a revival that would eventually inspire the rarefied metaphysics and spirituality of Plotinus (that we call Neoplatonism); this development was coupled with an interest in number mysticism and magic, unhistorically linked to the name of Pythagoras (Neopythagoreanism).

Best known to the general public were Cynics, itinerant ascetics and preachers, whose official (though often sham) cult of austerity and opposition to conventional norms looked back to Diogenes and Socrates. Cynicism had been a powerful influence on the formation of Stoic philosophy. At the time of Epictetus it was enjoying a new vogue, and he treats it at its best as a calling that an unusually dedicated and qualified witness to Stoicism could adopt (3.22).

Besides all these philosophies, with their roots stretching back to Hellenistic and classical Greece, a potential student of Epictetus could encounter numerous teachers, intellectual movements and religions whose relation to established philosophies might be strong, eclectic, or non-existent. Two of the greatest scientists of antiquity, Galen and Ptolemy, would flourish a generation or so later; their copious writings are steeped in the philosophical tradition. This was an era, often called the Second Sophistic, when professional rhetoricians, such as Aelius Aristides, Favorinus, and Dio Chrysostom, all of them familiar with more than a smattering of philosophy, would lecture to mass audiences on political and cultural topics, cultivating a style that was studiedly classical. The houses of the highly educated would involve dinner parties where the entertainment included conversation by grammarians and other scholars, competing over their knowledge of recondite points of language and mythology. The religious scene was notably fluid. Traditional cults of the Graeco-Roman pantheon, including worship of the emperor, continued; but those attracted to a religion that promised salvation would turn to the worship of Isis and, with increasing momentum, to Christianity.

Locating Epictetus within this rapid sketch is relatively easy. So far as philosophy is concerned, he uses a number of terms that *we* associate chiefly with Aristotle, but he probably did not derive these directly from conning the Aristotelian corpus. At this date the language of philosophy had become too eclectic to warrant such an inference; Epictetus never names Aristotle, and he makes only one disparaging reference to Peripatetics (2.19.20). He was aware of moralizing verses (falsely) attributed to Pythagoras (3.10.2–3), but his discourses betray no inclination for the mystical and other-worldly tendencies of Neopythagoreans and some contemporary Platonists. Epictetus' religious sympathies and spirituality (a topic for Chapter 6) are broadly in line with traditional Stoicism, but they are also infused with a deep and ubiquitous affinity for the Socrates of Plato's dialogues. Along with Stoicism, Epictetus' philosophy is principally Socratic, with a lesser but still important affiliation to an idealized Cynic, Diogenes. The schools he explicitly attacks are Epicureanism and Scepticism, both Pyrrhonean and Academic. He shows no interest in technical science, and he strongly distances his philosophical project from the rhetorical and cultural embellishments offered by rhetoricians and grammarians.

As for salvation, Epictetus perhaps alludes without further comment to Christians in an intriguing passage that likens his students to being only 'nominally baptized' (2.9.21, p. 110 below), but, however one assesses his thought in relation to the New Testament, there is no reason to think that Christians or Christian texts have directly influenced him, though he could have encountered them while still a child at Hierapolis.[2]

A few words about this picture of Epictetus, as it begins to emerge. In contrast with some of his contemporaries, who have interests in dream interpretation, magic, incubation in temples, and other occult practices, his mentality is rationalistic and down to earth, though he consistently speaks of God (or Zeus) in tones that convey personal faith and experience as well as Stoic and Socratic piety. He believes, as leading philosophers before him had believed, that human beings are born with all that they need, in terms of basic capacities, to understand the world, and that impediments to living well can be corrected or at least ameliorated by a combination of the right doctrines and unremitting self-discipline.

Do these attitudes show Epictetus to have been conservative and unadventurous? That must be right, up to a point. Having encountered Stoicism through Musonius, studying and testing it in his own life, noticing its practice by others, and teaching it, he clearly found this philosophy not only theoretically sound but also validated by his own experience. He saw no reason to experiment with other options. One of my aims in this book, however, is to show that Epictetus used Stoicism selectively and creatively. That is partly due to his distinctively Socratic leanings, which have been insufficiently appreciated, but it also reflects his own interpretations of what it meant to be a Stoic philosopher and teacher.

---

[2] St Paul had missionaries in that city (*Col.* 4.13), and he spent time in Nicopolis (*Titus* 3.12).

1.4 STOICISM

What Stoicism signified by Epictetus' time can hardly be sum-marized in a few pages, but for the benefit of readers new to the subject something needs to be said about the history of the school and what it predominantly stood for. As a preliminary, it is essential to realize that Stoicism, like all other mainstream philosophies of classical antiquity, offered itself as a comprehen-sive outlook on the world rather than something narrowly tech-nical or academic in the modern sense. The choice of Stoicism over Epicureanism, its principal rival, was decisive not only for one's ethical values and priorities but also for one's understand-ing of the world's general structure, one's theology, and the importance to be attached to systematic reasoning and the study of language. Yet, however much these and other schools dis-agreed over their accounts of such things, they all shared the view that philosophy should provide its adepts with the founda-tion for the best possible human life—that is to say, a happiness that would be lasting and serene.

At Epictetus' date (and in fact, from long before) philosophy in general was taken to be a medicine for alleviating the errors and passions that stem from purely reactive and conventional attitudes. To put it another way, the choice of Stoicism over another philosophy depended not on its promise to deliver an admirable and thoroughly satisfying life (that project would not distinguish it from rival schools) but on its detailed specification of that life and on the appeal of its claims about the nature of the world and human beings.

Extending back from Epictetus by almost 400 years, the Stoic philosophy initiated by Zeno had been elaborated, interpreted, and modified in numerous ways. Modern historians have often distinguished three phases of Stoicism, Early, Middle, and Late, allocating Epictetus along with Seneca, Musonius, and Marcus Aurelius to the last of these. Their rationale for such categories was not simply chronological, but reflected the following assumptions about the main features of each phase.

Early Stoicism was the most creative stage in terms of hard-edged doctrine and debate, with its principal representatives, above all Chrysippus, establishing the system on a basis that would be treated as orthodox thereafter. Middle Stoicism included Panaetius and Posidonius, each of whom was too idiosyncratic and innovative to be seen as simply a continuator of the Early phase. Late Stoicism, by contrast, the phase of Stoics during the Roman Empire, showed an absence of significant innovation, a decline of interest in theory, and a focus on practical ethics at the expense of logic and enquiry into physical science.

This picture has its value as a broad generalization, but much of it is misleading and liable to distort an appreciation of the individuality and significance of the Roman Stoics, especially Epictetus. To correct it, we need to take account of at least four points.

First, differences in curricular emphasis and doctrinal formulation were characteristic of Stoic philosophers throughout the school's existence. It is true that Chrysippus' writings acquired canonical status, but this did not oblige the Late Stoics to become his clones or to give up thinking for themselves.

Secondly, treating philosophy as a guide to life was the dominant focus right from the start. It was for that that Zeno acquired his renown, and while he did not restrict his curriculum to ethics, one of his principal followers, Aristo, took that step.

Thirdly, leading Stoics tended to specialize in different fields—as, for instance, Posidonius' interests in geography and ethnography, and the work of Diogenes of Babylon on grammar and music.

Fourthly, logic was still so widely studied by Stoic philosophers at the time of Epictetus that he is constantly warning his students against treating it as an end in itself. As for technicalities of physics, which he scarcely explores in the preserved discourses, they engaged the interest of Seneca, who wrote about numerous physical phenomena in his *Natural Questions*.[3]

Epictetus does indeed concentrate his teaching on students' application of Stoic doctrines to their own lives; in this he seems

---

[3] Arrian wrote a work on comets, which, while it could signify an interest inspired by Epictetus, is more likely to have been stimulated independently. We have a detailed astronomical treatise by the Stoic Cleomedes, probably written in the later years of the second century AD; see Bowen and Todd (forthcoming).

to fit the model of so-called Late Stoicism. Yet this assessment of him also needs to be qualified in two large respects. First, as we shall see later, the surviving discourses do not exemplify all that he taught, and even they make it clear that his own pedagogy included logic. Secondly—and this is the most important point—his focus on applied ethics and his reticence about technicalities of physics, as distinct from general truths about nature, plainly reflect his own judgement of what Stoicism chiefly has to offer his students. He is not simply conforming to trends supposedly characteristic of Late Stoicism in general, but shaping the philosophy in the direction he finds in most urgent need of emphasis. He was not alone in this, as we can see from all that he shares with Seneca and Musonius. But we need to remember that the Stoicism we know best from the Roman period was preserved precisely because it was perceived to have great educational and ethical value. There were many Stoic philosophers at Epictetus' time who continued to write in a more detached and scholarly vein.[4]

My qualifications to the Early/Middle/Late categorization of Stoicism show that this school was never a closed shop, unaccommodating to innovation or the special interests of individual philosophers. Some of them, though not Epictetus, were primarily renowned for their technical writings, but from first to last Stoicism was a practice grounded in theory rather than simply a theory or method of enquiry.

As such—and notwithstanding the special interests of individual Stoics—what the school throughout its history primarily offered was a systematic plan of life that would, ideally, assure purposefulness, serenity, dignity, and social utility at every waking moment, irrespective of external circumstances. The Stoics' rationale for this bold project was founded on their understanding of nature in general (physical reality) and human nature in particular. They take all phenomena and living beings to be the

---

[4] An example of this is Hierocles' *Foundations of Ethics*, a work partially preserved on papyrus and therefore available to us purely thanks to chance discovery: see Long (1993a). Excerpts of another work by Hierocles (or conceivably from a part of the papyrus text that has not survived), which treat questions of practical ethics, are quoted extensively in a Byzantine anthology. This is transmitted, like most classical texts, through copies made by medieval monks.

observable effects of a cosmic order, constituted and implemented by a principle they called Zeus, God, reason, cause, mind, and fate. This principle, though divine, is not supernatural, but nature itself, as manifested in such different things as the movements of the heavens, the structure of minerals, and the vital properties of plants and animals. Everything that happens is ultimately an expression of this single principle, which by acting on 'matter' extends itself throughout the universe and makes it one gigantic organism.[5]

Hence Stoics take God/reason/fate to be present everywhere, but they do not take this fact to collapse the obviously vast differences between the kinds of things that make up the universe, or to reduce human beings to the level of cogs in a machine. As human beings, we share in the structure characteristic of minerals, the vegetative capacities belonging to plants, and the sentient and goal-directed mobility of animals in general. Yet, none of these things constitutes the nature distinctive of our species. That nature expresses itself in our minds, thanks to which we have the capacity to discover where human beings fit within the cosmic order and to organize our lives as a community of persons, cooperating in social objectives and respecting one another as rational participants in the scheme of things. This nature of ours equips us to become reflective, active, and confident contributors to every situation we encounter.

For this to happen, however, we are required to understand two corollaries to our position in the universe. First, everything that falls outside our own mentality and character is not our business but belongs to other parts of the cosmic plan. We have good reason to try to bring about certain outcomes, for ourselves and for others (health, material prosperity, family solidarity, and so forth), but our well-being does not depend on these eventualities; it depends solely on excellence of character (virtue), which

---

[5] In this summary, I am presenting a rounded view of Stoicism rather than its exact presentation by Epictetus. While he endorses much of what I have written, he has his own distinctive emphases and omissions. Thus, to anticipate Chapter 6 of this book, he is reticent about such details of Stoic cosmology as 'matter' and causal determinism or fate, and he prefers to speak of God in personalist rather than in pantheistic terms.

means consistently aiming to do what is best in the circumstances, under the dictates of optimal reasoning. The second corollary concerns our desires and emotions. We have good reason to desire anything that accords with our natures as rational animals and to take pleasure in such things, but desires and emotions pertaining to things outside our control are not compatible with our natures or with the cosmic plan.

Stoicism, then, views the world as a system that is both deterministic and providential. God, the omnipresent active principle, establishes and implements everything in a causal sequence that leaves no room for events to occur otherwise than the way they do, though it does leave room (here things get complicated) for us to be the agents of our own decisions and hence answerable, praiseworthy, or blameable for what we think and do.[6] Yet, because God is taken to be supremely rational and benevolent, the causal sequence is also and no less basically the fulfilment of divine providence. Hence no state of the world at any time could have been different from what it is, nor could it have been better planned than the way it is.

The deterministic thesis explains why Stoics find it irrational and pointless to wish that things might be otherwise than what they actually experience. But if that were all, Stoicism would be largely an attitude of mere realism, fatalism, or resignation. The crucial step is the combination of determinism with providence. If the situations in which we find ourselves are providentially determined, and if, further, we are equipped with minds that can understand this dual aspect of things, then we have reason not only to accept everything that happens as inevitable but also to regard whatever impinges on our individual selves as the allotment that is right for us and as the requisite opportunity for us to discover and play our human part in the cosmic plan. Hence committed Stoics will interpret circumstances that are conventionally regarded as misfortunes as challenges to be accepted and even welcomed because they give them the means of proving and showing their rationality and dignity as fully-fledged human beings.

---

[6] The complication concerns the compatibility of human responsibility with strict determinism. This subject is studied with great resourcefulness by Bobzien (1998). Where Epictetus stands on it is a question for later (pp. 162 and 221).

It is this last point that has regularly troubled critics of Stoicism who today, even more than in antiquity, are likely to find the philosophy's theology and unqualified faith in divine providence naive and unpalatable. Yet, it is a serious mistake, in my opinion, to interpret Stoicism, as some modern scholars have tried to do, in ways that tone down the cosmic dimension. For, whatever we may think of that, it was central to the Greek and Roman Stoics' outlook on the world and the mainstay of the confidence this outlook engendered. Epictetus speaks to this on numerous occasions, but, before I give an example from his own words, here is a sample of relevant passages from other Stoics.

First, the celebrated lines of Cleanthes, quoted by Epictetus (*Ench.* 53):

Lead me, Zeus, and you, Fate, wherever you have ordained for me. For I shall follow unflinching. But if I become bad and unwilling, I shall follow none the less.[7]

Next, two quotations from Chrysippus:

There is no other or more appropriate way of approaching the theory of good and bad things or the virtues or happiness than from universal nature and from the administration of the world . . . For the theory of good and bad things must be attached to these, since there is no other starting point or reference for them that is better, and physical speculation is to be adopted for no other purpose than for the differentiation of good and bad things.

(Plutarch, *On Stoic Self-Contradictions* 1035C–D)

Since universal nature reaches everywhere, it must be the case that however anything happens in the whole and in any of its parts it happens in accordance with universal nature and its reasons in unhindered sequence, because neither is there anything that could interfere with its government from outside, nor is there any way for any of the parts to enter any process or state except in accordance with universal nature.

(Plutarch, ibid. 1050C–D)

Now, an excerpt from Seneca (*On Providence* 5.6–8):

I am under no compulsion, I suffer nothing against my will. I am not God's slave but his follower, and the more so because I know that

---

[7] This was Epictetus' favourite Stoic citation; he quotes its first sentence four times in the discourses; see Ch. 6 n. 13.

everything proceeds from a law that is fixed and pronounced for all time. Fate guides us and it was settled at the first hour of birth what length of time remains for each. Cause is linked to cause, and a long sequence of things controls public and private affairs . . . Why do we complain? For this we were born. Let nature deal, as it wishes, with its own bodies. We should be cheerful and brave in relation to everything, reflecting that nothing belonging to us is perishing. What is a good man's role? To offer himself to fate. It is a great consolation to be moved along with the universe. Whatever it is that ordered us so to live and so to die, it binds the divine beings by the same necessity. An inevitable course conveys the human and the divine alike. It was the author and ruler of the world who wrote the decrees of fate, but he follows them himself.

Finally, Marcus Aurelius (v.8.2):

You must consider the doing and perfecting of what the universal nature decrees in the same light as your health, and welcome all that happens, even if it seems harsh, because it leads to the health of the universe, the welfare and well-being of Zeus. For he would not have allotted this to anyone if it were not beneficial to the whole.

Our modern languages are packed with expressions that, however superficially, reflect the popular diffusion of Stoicism as a response to severe challenges and adversity: Be a man; take what is coming to you; roll with the punches; what will be will be; show some guts; make the best of it; go down fighting; don't be a wimp; we had this coming to us; try to be philosophical; just my luck; go with the flow; don't make things worse; you'd better face up to it—and so forth. Such expressions, for all their familiarity and banality, have their uses, because every person sometimes confronts a situation for which the only alternative responses to this one are rage, despair, apathy, helplessness, or total collapse.[8] Yet, ancient Stoicism was not premised on its capacity to rationalize adversity *as distinct from* prosperity. While Stoics liked to invoke Socrates' equanimity at his trial and death as a supreme example of dignity and courage at the limit, they also insisted that outwardly favourable situations are just as demanding in

---

[8] Stoicism allowed suicide to be a positive or 'well-reasoned' response to circumstances and prospects that exclude the minimum provisions for continuing to live a 'natural' human life; see p. 203.

terms of the principles and care with which they should be handled.

This last point is a constant theme in Epictetus. Before concluding this chapter with an outline of his main ideas and originality, I append the full text of one short discourse (1.14).[9] This will serve better than any summary to show how he expresses and interprets the characteristically Stoic perspective on cosmic order (Epictetus prefers to call it God) and human nature.

6   *God's Oversight of Everyone*

When someone asked him how a person could be convinced that his every action is overseen by God, Epictetus said: Don't you think that the universe is a unified structure?

I do.

Well, don't you think that there is an interaction between things on earth and things in the heavens?

I do.

How else could things happen so regularly, by God's command as it were? When he tells plants to bloom, they bloom, when he tells them to bear fruit, they bear it, when he tells them to ripen, they ripen; and again when he tells them to drop their fruit, shed their leaves, contract into themselves, stay quiet and pause, they do these things? How else, at the waxing and waning of the moon and at the sun's approach and withdrawal, could we observe such changes and contrary mutations in the things on earth?

But if plants and our own bodies are so connected and interactive with the universe, does that not apply all the more to our minds? And if our minds are so connected and attached to God, as parts and offshoots of his being, does he not perceive their every movement as something belonging to him and sharing in his nature?

You, for your part, have the capacity to reflect on the divine government and each one of its features, and similarly on human affairs; and you have the capacity to be moved by countless things simultaneously, in your senses and your thinking, assenting to or rejecting some of them, and suspending judgement about others. In your mind you retain so many impressions from such a great range of things, and under their influence you find yourself having ideas corresponding to your initial impressions, and from countless things you secure a series of skills and memories.

---

[9] For a full commentary on this discourse, tracing its relation to the Stoic tradition and other sources, see Dobbin (1998).

Is God, then, not capable of overseeing everything and being present with everything and maintaining a certain distribution with everything? Yet the sun is capable of illuminating so large a part of the universe, and of leaving unlit only the part covered by the earth's shadow. Is he, then, who made the sun (which is a small part of himself in relation to the whole) and causes it to turn, is he not capable of perceiving everything? *I myself cannot follow all this at once.* But who tells you that your capacities are the equal of Zeus's? Yet, for all that, he has presented to each person each person's own divine spirit [*daimôn*], as a guardian, and committed the person's safekeeping to this trustee, who does not sleep and who cannot be misled. To what better and more caring guardian could he have entrusted us?

So when you close your doors and make it dark inside, remember never to say you are alone, because you are not; God is inside and your own divine spirit too. What need have they of light to see what you are doing? It is to this God too that you should swear allegiance, as soldiers do to Caesar. Now when they get their pay, they swear to put the safety of Caesar ahead of everything; so won't you, who have been given such great and numerous privileges, swear your oath, or if you have already done so, stick to it?

What, then, will you swear? Never to disobey, or press charges or complain about anything God has given you, or be reluctant in doing or suffering anything that is inevitable. Is this oath anything like that other one? There men swear to put no one ahead of Caesar. But here we swear to put ourselves ahead of everything else.

In this passage we see Epictetus giving his own *personalist* twist to Stoicism's standard conception of cosmic order and its implications for human beings' understanding of who they are and where they fit. Although he starts by justifying divine providence, the real focus of the discourse is less on this than on what it means to be endowed, as humans are, with the capacity to oversee themselves and to acknowledge their internal divinity (see Section 6.5), which is also the voice of objective reason and integrity, as their only authority.

Epictetus believed that our reasoning powers and moral sense are an 'offshoot' of the world's divine governor, whose cosmic order is a pattern for the harmony we should try to replicate in our thoughts and actions. But even if we reject that powerful though difficult idea, or treat it as no more than a metaphor, we are still left with a model of human agency that is characteristically Stoic: in other words, uncompromising self-respect and self-monitoring with a view to treating even adversity as the stimulus to live well rather than to be disappointed and frustrated.

1.5 FOUR UNIFYING CONCEPTS

Four principal concepts give Epictetus' philosophy its unity and coherence: freedom, judgement, volition, and integrity.

FREEDOM, underwritten by the theology we have just observed, has nothing to do with liberty in a social or political sense. The freedom that interests Epictetus is entirely psychological and attitudinal. It is freedom from being constrained or impeded by any external circumstance or emotional reaction. He diagnoses unhappiness as subservience to persons, happenings, values, and bodily conditions, all of which involve the individual subject in surrendering autonomy and becoming a victim to debilitating emotions. Happiness, by contrast, is unimpeded-ness, doing and experiencing only what you want to do and experience, serenity, absence of any sense that things might be better for you than you find them to be. This freedom, Epictetus proposes, is available to all human beings who are willing to understand certain facts about nature and their own identity and cultivate a corresponding character and outlook.

The basis for this ideal of freedom brings us to the second core concept, JUDGEMENT. Following his Stoic authorities, Epictetus regards all mental states, including emotions, as conditioned by judgements. In desiring or in being averse to something, a person, according to this view, has formed a judgement concerning what it is good to pursue or bad to experience; emotions are the outcome or concomitant of such judgements. On this model of mind, there is no such thing as a purely reactive emotion or at least a reaction that we cannot, on reflection, control. How we experience the world, and how we experience ourselves, depends through and through on the judgements we form, judgements about the structure of the world, the necessary conditions of human life, goodness, badness, and, above all, what is psychologically 'up to us'.

The crucial idea is that we do not experience the world without the mediation of our own assessments. Hence Epictetus constantly insists that what disturbs people is not an event as such—death or illness, for instance—but rather their judgement about this event, or the way they describe it and its bearing on themselves. By intruding evaluative judgements onto events, people make essentially neutral or indifferent circumstances bad or good. Thus, death as such is merely natural; its badness is a human overlay.

This rationalistic analysis of emotions and evaluations implies that they themselves, and the judgements on which they depend, are completely in our power, up to us, within the control of our will. Earlier Stoics had devoted considerable attention to the causal antecedents of mental states; as generally interpreted, they held that mental states fall within the scope of fate (universal determinism) but are 'not externally necessitated' because they depend on us—on our internal faculty of assent. Epictetus constantly affirms the complete freedom of assent from external necessitation, but he does not address the complex issue of how or whether this freedom is also compatible with fate. What he does, instead, is to draw a stark contrast between the mind's innate capacity for complete autonomy or self-government and the body's inevitable subjection to constraint.

This brings us to Epictetus' third core concept, VOLITION (my translation of his favourite term *prohairesis*, also translatable by 'will'; see Section 8.2), which is the most noteworthy feature of his entire philosophy. How it relates to the preceding Stoic tradition is a moot point, but not an issue that need concern us in this first chapter. The crucial idea is that volition is what persons are in terms of their mental faculties, consciousness, character, judgements, goals, and desires: volition is the self, what each of us is, as abstracted from the body. Epictetus has no interest in metaphysics, but his conception of human beings is dualistic, even though he probably accepted the standard Stoic position on the physicality of all existing things.

You and I are not our bodies, nor even do we own our bodies. We, our essential selves, *are* our volitions. In that domain, and only in that domain, we have the possibility of freedom. This freedom, though it is our inalienable nature, is typically jeopardized, because people identify themselves with their bodies and all manner of external things—other persons, commodities, political powers, and so forth. Real and lasting freedom is not available to humans in any of these domains; consequently, those who pursue them are constrained, thwarted, and emotionally enslaved as a result of the mistaken attachments they make. What is required of anyone who wants genuine freedom is to transfer all wants, values, and attachments away from externals and situate them within the scope of one's volition. *Prohairesis* or volition is the locus of all that truly matters to humans who have understood cosmic order and their own natures and capacities. Its perfection is the human good, and the goal of Epictetus' teaching.

Like earlier Stoics, he holds that goodness and badness in the strict sense pertain only to what accords or fails to accord with our essential human nature: that is to say, our nature as rational animals. A perfected volition, then, is good in this strict sense, and no other objective is comparably deserving. Consequently, everything that falls outside the individual's volition, including family, status, country, the condition of one's body, material prosperity—all of these are inessential to its perfection and the freedom or happiness that this perfection constitutes. Not only are these things inessential, but also attachment to them is a certain recipe for disappointment, anxiety, and unhappiness. We can understand, then, why Epictetus devotes the greater part of his work to underlining this point, giving advice or admonition on the necessity of practising detachment, not getting caught up in conventional ambitions and the emotional costs that these will bring.

What is harder to understand is how his insistence on limiting one's self to one's volition, and on securing it against contamination from dangerous attachments, can give him any kind of moral theory or social policy. Earlier Stoics had identified the perfection of the individual's mind (what they also called the rule of reason) with wisdom (*sophia*) and moral excellence (*aretê*), which included justice and other social virtues. They had proposed that all normal human beings are both self-interested and socially oriented in their innate motivations, and they had accommodated numerous conventional values (for instance, good health, wealth, reputation, and family solidarity), treating these as natural, reasonable, and preferable objectives in principle, albeit not strictly good or necessary to one's happiness.

Epictetus scarcely offers any explicit discussion of the Stoic distinction between these secondary 'natural' values and the unequivocal goodness of moral excellence. He is emphatic on the natural self-interestedness of human motivations, and he devotes much more explicit thought to care of the self than to what is incumbent on human beings as members of a society. Is he a Stoic in any obvious sense with respect to socially appropriate actions? How, if at all, does his focus on freedom and the perfection of volition relate to these?

The response to this question introduces the fourth core concept, INTEGRITY. I use this word to translate a cluster of terms Epictetus repeatedly uses that can be rendered by such words as shame, reverence, trustworthiness, conscience, decency. Integrity is as much a part of Epictetus' normative self as a good volition; in fact, it is not distinct from a good volition but the way that that mental disposition is disposed in relation to other persons. Integrity bridges the gap for Epictetus between egoism and altruism; or, better, it closes the gap. Volition, as one's self, is where one's interests lie. It determines what one calls 'I' and 'mine'. A good volition, because it values itself over everything else, includes integrity; it treats integrity as essential to its own interests. Integrity involves honouring all of one's ties to kin, social roles, and other acquired relationships.

Integrity is the concept in Epictetus that answers to moral sense. He is a moralist, not because he sets out from a position with regard to our duties to other persons, but because his bedrock principle of cultivating the self as a good volition entails uncompromising integrity (respect, cooperation, justice, and kindliness) with respect to every human being one encounters or is by family or circumstance related to.

The four ideas I have singled out here—freedom, judgement, volition, and integrity—are integral elements of Epictetus' philosophy both at the level of theory and for the training he hopes to impress on his students. We shall encounter them repeatedly, as this book proceeds, but not as abstractly as I have presented them for the purposes of this introduction. What many readers may find most interesting in Epictetus is the way he puts flesh on these ideas through his challenges to his students and his disconcerting shifts of context from a dinner-party or street encounter to an emperor's tyranny or a threat of mutilation. It is essential, in any case, that, before engaging further with his concepts and arguments, we take a close look at the literary and argumentative form of the discourses together with the educational setting in which they were delivered. These will be the topics of my next four chapters.

1.6 ORIGINALITY

One final introductory question. Was Epictetus an original thinker? If we take a philosopher's originality to consist in formulating fundamentally new theories or concepts or tools of analysis (as, for instance, Plato's theory of Forms or Aristotle's logic), the answer is no. Epictetus inherited the main lines of his thought from his Stoic predecessors, and he saw no need to diverge from what he took to be solidly grounded in fact and argument. In this respect he was a typical adherent of a philosophical school in later antiquity, living at a time when philosophers largely saw themselves as the continuators of long-established traditions. Most good philosophers, however, are not original in the manner of a Plato or Aristotle. Philosophical excellence probably has less to do with that kind of originality than with clarity of exposition, provocative and imaginative discourse, getting people to twist their minds in unfamiliar directions so that they rethink their beliefs and become open to what reason can offer them as alternative models of construing the world and their own lives. Epictetus' voice in all these respects is palpably his own.

But his originality does not end there. While we must acknowledge that too little Stoic literature has survived to warrant exact comparisons, much of Epictetus' philosophy appears to be fresh in formulation and distinctive in emphasis.

The Stoicism of Chrysippus had become notorious for its rigidity, paradoxicality, esoteric terminology, and fine (or in critics' eyes quibbling) distinctions. Among the many targets of criticism were the division of human beings into two absolute classes—perfectly rational, virtuous, knowing and happy sages, and unequivocally irrational, imperfect, ignorant, and miserable fools; the doctrine that transition from membership of the latter to the former class would be instantaneous and even unrecognized by the now suddenly perfect person; the Stoics' admission that none of themselves, and perhaps no actual person, not even Socrates, had been a sage; the claim that all good actions are equally good, all bad actions equally bad, and the absence of any purely neutral actions.

One is tempted to dismiss such histrionic statements as more to do with rhetoric than serious doctrine. Yet the early Stoic philosophers defended them as valid implications of the uncompromising rationality and consistency they took to be the essence of human goodness and happiness.

From the time of Chrysippus, if not earlier, the practice of Stoicism was treated as a way of trying to 'progress' towards this rational ideal. Strictly, 'progressives' were as much miserable fools as everyone else, but they might succeed in acquiring a mindset and character that would approximate to the wisdom of the elusive sage. Hence, to use one striking image, they would be like persons drowning just below the surface as distinct from remaining at the bottom of the sea. This image would be extremely chilling if Stoicism were a philosophy that measured success by outcomes. In fact, it placed the value of actions on a person's efforts and intentions to do everything possible to live well.

Epictetus was as much a proponent of uncompromising rationality as any of the early Stoics, but he generally eschews their most paradoxical formulations. We hear nothing in the discourses about the 'equality' of all faults or the ignorance and misery of everyone who has failed to achieve infallible knowledge. For Epictetus, Socrates was not an approximation to wisdom but the paradigm of a genuinely wise person. He rarely even refers to the ideal sage, and, when he does, he prefers the highly traditional expression *kalos kai agathos*, 'the excellent man', to the esoteric 'wise man' (*sophos* or *phronimos*; see the passages listed below, p. 37). Rather than constantly emphasizing long-term goals, he urges on his students the importance of what they can do to make progress *now*. Although his Stoicism is a counsel of perfection, neither he nor his students are destined to emulate the ideal sage:

7 It is impossible to be free from error. What is possible is to be constantly on the alert with a view to not erring; for we should be content if we avoid a few errors by never relaxing our attention to this objective.

(4.12.19)

Epictetus acknowledges that philosophy contains truths that outsiders find paradoxical (1.25.33), but he tacitly modifies the harshness and intransigence of his Stoic authorities. The ideal sage was supposedly pitiless and unforgiving, but Epictetus advocates gentleness and tolerance towards those who err.[10] We might call his Stoicism an ethics of the interval between wisdom and its contrary, a philosophy for persons who are fallible but completely committed to doing the best they can to live as free, thoughtful, self-respecting, and devoted family members and citizens.

The early Stoics had made elaborate classifications of 'virtues' and other 'values'. Epictetus takes no interest in such technicalities. He uses the standard word for virtue (*aretē*) sparingly, perhaps because it was too closely associated with the ideal sage. Instead, he favours words that signify the ethical qualities that his interpretation of Stoicism primarily seeks to promote, words that signify integrity, freedom, courage, sturdiness, and conscientiousness (see Section 8.4), all of which will have chimed well with the traditional Roman values of *virtus*, *pietas*, *dignitas*, and *fides*. At times he even treats such excellences as unacknowledged 'faculties' that every person already possesses (e.g. 1.6.28–9).

---

[10] See e.g. 1.18.3; 1.28.9; 2.22.36; 4.1.147; also Section 9.4 below. He devotes an entire discourse to chiding students (4.6) who resent being pitied by non-Stoics.

However we construe the central concept he calls *prohairesis* (that I generally translate by volition) and its intrinsic autonomy, this way of formulating the essence of each individual person gives his philosophy a distinctively 'existentialist' dimension because of the role it ascribes to individual responsibility, self-ownership, and self-determination. He was probably original in specifying the ethical project as 'making correct use of mental impressions'.[11] Finally, and most notably, Epictetus appropriates Plato's Socratic discourse and methodology to an extent that is quite without parallel.

FURTHER READING AND NOTES

Orientation

Summary introductions to the life, teaching, and milieu of Epictetus include Oldfather (1925–8: i, pp. vii–xxx); Souilhé (1948–65: i, pp. i–lxxi; Long (1982*a*: 985–96); White (1983: 1–10); Hershbell (1986); Gill (1995: pp. xvii–xxvii); and Dobbin (1998: pp. xi–xxiii). The most comprehensive treatment, outdated but still useful, is the French work by Colardeau (1903). In English the only books at all comparable to my own are Hijmans (1959) and Xenakis (1969). The first of these is a worthy but dull dissertation, while the second, though enthusiastic, tends to be chatty and superficial.

In her popularized version of the *Manual* Lebell (1995: p. xi) characterizes Epictetus' teaching as 'the West's answer to Buddhism's *Dhammapada* or Lao Tzu's *Tao Te Ching*'.

Biography

The evidence external to Epictetus' own words is collected in Schenkl (1916: pp. iii–xv), who discusses it in Latin in great detail, pp. xv–xxxiii; see also Souilhé (1948–65: i, pp. i–x). The most important testimonies are: Aulus Gellius, ii.18.10 (slavery), xv.11.5 (exile, Nicopolis); the Suda (Hierapolis, Epaphroditus, lameness from rheumatism (but see also Origen, *Contra Celsum* 1.7 and other Christian writers: lameness from

---

[11] On the basis of fr. 4, a text supposedly reporting a citation of Musonius Rufus by Epictetus, it is conceivable that the former had already made 'the use of impressions' a slogan. However, this text reads like a paraphrase of Epictetus 1.1.

beating)); Alcuin, *Ep.* 88 (Hadrian); Marcus Aurelius, *Meditations* 1.7 (expression of indebtedness); Lucian, *Demonax* 55 and Simplicius, *In Ench.* 272c (celibacy and subsequent child raising).

Other (near-contemporary) mentions of Epictetus include: Galen, *De optima doctrina* 1; Lucian, *Alexander* 2, *Demonax* 3, *Adversus indoctum* 13; Aulus Gellius 1.2.6, XVII.19.1–6, XIX.1.14–21; Philostratus, *Epp.* 65, 69. Epictetus was also the subject of celebratory verses; see Schenkl (1916: pp. vii–xi).

Autobiographical allusions in the *Discourses* include: 1.2.36; 1.9.10; 1.10.13; 1.16.20; 1.18.15; 1.30.6; 2.6.23; 2.24.13, 18; 3.20.19. For his consultation by others, see 1.9; 1.11; 1.13; 1.14; 1.15.

For Epictetus' familiarity with prominent persons and the imperial court, see Millar (1965, 1977). Starr (1949) argues that the ubiquitous figure of the tyrant in the discourses is modelled directly on Domitian.

Intellectual and Cultural Context

For various aspects, see Clarke (1971), Dill (1905), Bowersock (1969), Holford-Strevens (1988), Kaster (1988), Zanker (1995), and Griffin (1996). More technical studies in Griffin and Barnes (1989) and the volumes of *ANRW* II.36.1–3.

On Stoics and the principate, see Wirzsubski (1950), MacMullen (1966), Brunt (1975), and Griffin (1976, 1984).

On Stoicism and slavery in the Roman Empire, see Manning (1986). Hense (1905) edits the Greek text of Musonius Rufus, with introduction (in Latin). The surviving pieces are translated in Lutz (1947). On Euphrates, see Frede (1997).

On philosophy besides Stoicism, see Dillon (1996) for Platonism; Hankinson (1995) for the Sceptics; Moraux (1973–84) for Aristotelians; Branham and Goulet-Cazé (1996) for Cynics; and, for Epicureanism, Long (1986), LS, and Algra (1999).

Bonhöffer (1911) is the classic study of Epictetus' relation to the New Testament. He argues (correctly, I think) that, notwithstanding striking verbal parallels, there is no strong reason to think that the one has directly influenced the other.

Stoicism

For texts in the original and in translation, together with commentaries, on Stoicism in its Hellenistic phase, see LS. The bibliography in LS, vol. ii, is updated by Brunschwig and Pellegrin in their French translation of LS (Long and Sedley 2001: iii). See also the selection of translations in Inwood and Gerson (1997). Material on Panaetius is collected in Alesse (1994), and on Posidonius in Edelstein and Kidd (1972), with commentary and translation in Kidd (1988). Short introductions to Stoicism include Sandbach (1975), Long (1986), and Sharples (1996). For the most recent in-depth study, see Algra (1999), which contains a massive bibliography. On details of Stoic theory most pertinent to Epictetus, see Rist (1969, 1978), Long (1971b), Inwood (1985, 1996), Schofield and Striker (1986), Annas (1993), Long (1996a), Striker (1996b), Barnes (1997), and Ierodiakonou (1999). The Roman Stoics in general have been less thoroughly studied than their Hellenistic predecessors. Arnold (1911), though antiquated, is still worth consulting. For recent treatments see especially Foucault (1986), P. Hadot (1992) on Marcus Aurelius and Epictetus, articles in *ANRW* ii. 36.1–3, and also articles in Brunschwig and Nussbaum (1993), Laks and Schofield (1995), and Sorabji (1997b).

The most detailed treatment of Epictetus' Stoicism is the pair of books by Bonhöffer (1890, 1894), the second of which is translated by Stephens (1996a). These classic works are indispensable for close study of Epictetus' relation to the Stoic tradition, but they pay little attention to his pedagogical style and they tend to overemphasize his doctrinal orthodoxy.

The therapeutic goals and methods of Hellenistic philosophy are well studied by Nussbaum (1994). P. Hadot (1987) is a good introduction to Stoicism and other ancient schools as philosophies of life. My emphasis on cosmic order for understanding the foundations of Stoic ethics throughout its history is defended in Long (1971a) (with postscript in 1996a), and (1989); see also Striker (1991). Annas (1993) challenges it, as regards Chrysippus. She has been challenged in turn by Cooper (1995), to whom she responds in Annas (1995). I return to the issue in this book at the beginning of Chapter 7. Becker (1998) is a stimulating attempt by a modern moral philosopher to construct 'a New Stoicism' that dispenses with cosmic teleology.

For the continuing importance of logic in Roman Stoicism, see Barnes (1997).

Four Unifying Concepts, and Originality

These pages represent my own responses to Epictetus rather than even-handed attempts to digest accounts written by others; for which see especially Gill (1995: pp. xix–xxiii), Dobbin (1998: pp. xiv–xix), and P. Hadot (1992: 69–117). My comments on Epictetus' originality may be contrasted with the assessments in Bonhöffer (1890, 1894), and I find Epictetus much less focused on traditional Stoic virtue than Gill (1995: pp. xxi–xxii).

The Ideal Sage in Epictetus

In playing down this paradigm, Epictetus is in line with Panaetius rather than Chrysippus: see Long (1986: 213–15). Here I list the few passages where Epictetus alludes to the ideal sage in the early Stoic manner:

1.19.17–23: 'How could a person suddenly become wise [*phronimos*] when Caesar puts him in charge of his chamber pot?'

2.21.9: 'Am I myself acting like a wise man [*phronimos*]?'

3.22.37: 'Who are they [the Trojans]? Wise people or fools? If they are wise, why are you fighting them? If they are fools, why do you care?'

1.7.3/25–9: preconception of the 'good man' (*spoudaios*) as a person who is expert in logic.

2.22.3: '(Genuine) love is peculiar to the wise man [*phronimos*].'

3.6.5: 'The good man [*spoudaios*] is invincible.'

In the following passages Epictetus refers to the ideal of the 'excellent man' (*kalos kai agathos*): 1.7.2; 1.12.7; 2.10.5 (alluding to a Chrysippean doctrine); 2.11.25; 2.14.10; 3.2.1, 7; 3.3.1; 3.22.69, 87; 3.24.19, 50, 95, 110; 4.5.1; 4.8.24 (allusions to Socrates); 4.5.6.

In order to put these references in perspective, one should note that our record of Epictetus runs to some 450 pages of Greek text.

CHAPTER 2

The Discourses

Does a philosopher give invitations to a lecture? Isn't it
that, just as the sun attracts nutriment to itself, so he attracts
those who will be benefited? What physician issues invitations for someone to be cured by him?

(3.23.27)

2.1 EPICTETUS AND ARRIAN

Epictetus followed the examples of his teacher Musonius and his
ideal philosopher Socrates in writing nothing directly for publication. We owe our record of his philosophy and teaching
method to his student Arrian. Lucius Flavianus Arrianus
Xenophon, to give him his full name, was a typical pupil in his
background. He came from Nicomedia, a prosperous city on the
south-western coast of the Black Sea, where his father was
almost certainly a wealthy member of the local elite. Assuming
Arrian was about 18 when he joined Epictetus, his stay in the
school at Nicopolis occurred in the reign of Trajan during some
part of the years 105–13 when Epictetus was in his fifties or early
sixties.

Whether it was Arrian himself or his family that opted for his
studying under Epictetus is not known; either way, Epictetus
had clearly made a name for himself by this time and was attract-
ing well-to-do students from quite distant parts of the Roman

Empire. None of them had a more illustrious or more diverse career than Arrian. Under Hadrian he achieved the consulship, and as governor of Cappadocia he distinguished himself as a military leader. Outside his public life Arrian was a prolific writer. His extant works include a history of Alexander the Great (*Anabasis*), a history of India, military treatises, and an essay on hunting (*Cynegeticus*), and he also wrote on the history and geography of his home region Bithynia.

This is not a professional philosopher's bibliography, but it does recall a comparably versatile writer and man of the world from five centuries earlier—Xenophon of Athens. Most famous for his own *Anabasis*, charting the military expedition of the Persian prince Cyrus in Asia Minor and his own participation in it, Xenophon was a historian who also wrote on hunting and horsemanship. More directly relevant to our topic, he had associated as a young man with Socrates, and published a number of Socratic works, most notably four books of *Records* (*Memorabilia*). If Arrian wanted to present himself as the Roman Xenophon, a name that he bore (whether given or assumed), his own association with Epictetus must have struck him as an irresistible opportunity.

Arrian took it upon himself to edit or compile a large-scale collection of Epictetus' discourses. Four books of these survive out of an original eight. They are prefaced in the manuscripts by the following letter addressed to an otherwise unknown Lucius Gellius:

I have not composed the discourses (*logoi*) of Epictetus in the way one might 'compose' such works, nor have I published them myself; for I do not claim to have composed them at all. Rather, I tried to write down whatever I heard him say, in his own words as far as possible, to keep notes (*hypomnêmata*) of his thought and frankness for my own future use. So they are what you would expect one man to say to another spontaneously, and not compositions intended for posterity to read. Such being their character, they have somehow or other fallen without my knowledge or intention into the public domain. Yet it matters little to me if I shall be regarded as incapable of composition; and to Epictetus it doesn't matter in the slightest if anyone should despise his discourses, since in uttering them he was clearly aiming at nothing except to move the minds of his audience towards what is best.

So if these discourses achieve that much, they would have just the effect, I think, that a philosopher's discourse ought to have. But if not, those who read them should realize that when Epictetus spoke them the hearer could not fail to experience just what Epictetus intended him to feel. And if the discourses on their own do not achieve this, I may be to blame, or perhaps it is unavoidable.

What are we to make of this elaborate apology? It has sometimes been taken quite literally throughout, but Arrian's self-effacement cannot be accepted as simply as he professes. While the majority of the discourses are spoken by Epictetus in the first person, some are presented as dialogues between himself and a pupil or a visitor, with Arrian discreetly setting the scene, as for instance (1.15.1): 'When someone consulted him about how he could persuade his brother to stop resenting him, he said . . .'. There are also three pieces that look like sets of unworked up notes (3.6; 3.11; 3.14). In spite of their impression of spontaneity, the individual discourses and their ordering in the collection show some concern with literary organization. They also vary greatly in length from a simple moral message to an elaborate lecture on freedom (4.1) that is thirty times as long. None of this tallies well with the idea that Arrian has merely recorded what he heard with no intervention of his own. Given the precedent of Xenophon's Socratic *Records*, is it Arrian, rather than Epictetus, whom we read in these discourses?

So it has been argued by the Swiss scholar Theo Wirth (see p. 64), but such an interpretation is still less plausible than a purely factual reading of Arrian's prefatory letter. He had no reason to declare his purpose as he did unless it reflected his acknowledgement that the speaker in the discourses is the real Epictetus. He could have employed scribes to take down Epictetus' words in the shorthand that was in use at this time. More likely, perhaps, he made his own detailed notes, and used his memory to fill them out. No doubt he worked up the material into a more finished form. In some cases he may have relied on others' reports, or checked his own record with Epictetus himself. However Arrian actually compiled the discourses, there are numerous reasons, internal to the text, for taking the gist of his record to be completely authentic to Epictetus' own style and language. These include the distinctive vocabulary, repetition of key points throughout, a strikingly urgent and vivid voice quite distinct from Arrian's authorial persona in his other works, and a focus on Socrates that is far more reminiscent of Plato's dialogues than designedly evocative of Xenophon. Arrian clearly regarded Epictetus as the Socrates of his own day, and he could think of himself as the Roman Xenophon; but that does not prevent us from reading Epictetus himself as we read Arrian's record of his teaching.

There are also external reasons to confirm this point. By the time this collection of the discourses was in general circulation, Epictetus himself had achieved an eminence that would have immediately exposed any significant fabrication by Arrian. Within probably a few years of Epictetus' death the litterateur Aulus Gellius refers to 'books of Epictetus' discourses arranged by Arrian' (*Noctes Atticae* 1.2.6; cf. XIX.1.14–21), and Marcus Aurelius (1.7) thanks a friend for acquainting him with Epictetus' 'notes' (*hypomnêmata*), probably a reference to Arrian's edition. In later antiquity Epictetus' works are often referred to without mention of Arrian's name, which judging from his prefatory letter, he would have approved.

The principal point of interest about Arrian's relationship to Epictetus is the devotion it reveals in the pupil's attitude to his master. Even if Arrian's role in compiling the discourses were as restricted as he would have us believe, it would nevertheless have taken up a great deal of time and effort. Apart from the eight books of *Discourses*, Arrian excerpted from them in producing the celebrated *Encheiridion* or *Manual*, and, according to Simplicius, in the preface to his commentary on this work, Arrian also wrote 'on the life and death of' Epictetus. In the centuries after Plato and his contemporaries memorialized Socrates, there were many other students who wrote up their teachers' work; but Arrian, in the light of his later career, so different from Epictetus' studied obscurity, is one of the most remarkable. Because Epictetus' attitude to his students, as it emerges in his discourses, is more caustic than amiable, Arrian's devotion, which is unlikely to have been unique, is something important for ourselves as readers to keep in mind.

Before leaving Arrian, a few words about the title of his compilation. The Bodleian manuscript, which is our principal authority for the text, opens without a title. At the end of each book the scribe wrote *APPIANOY TΩN EΠIKTHTOY ΔIATPIBΩN*, followed by a numeral: 'The first [second etc.] book of Arrian's *Diatribai* of Epictetus'. Schenkl, the leading modern editor, supplies this title at the beginning. Simplicius, in the preface to his commentary on the *Manual*, refers to 'Arrian, who compiled Epictetus' *Diatribai*', and editors standardly supply this word, which literally means 'informal talks', as the work's title. Aulus Gellius, Arrian's contemporary, refers in Latin to Epictetus' *Dissertationes* and in Greek to his *Dialexeis*, words that also signify talks, conversations, or lectures. The Byzantine scholar Stobaeus mentions Epictetus' *Apomnêmoneumata* (records), which is almost certainly an alternative title for Arrian's collection. We also hear of Epictetus' *Scholai* (lectures), of his *Ethics*, and even of twelve books of Epictetus' *Homiliai* (lectures) by Arrian in addition to the eight books of *Discourses*.[1]

In view of all this variety, we can probably conclude that the compilation of which our surviving Epictetus constitutes one half entered circulation unadorned by any title bestowed on it by Arrian. This lends credence to his prefatory remarks on the work's dissemination without his permission. Had Arrian given it a title, to judge from his own words that would have been *Logoi* (discourses) or *Hypomnêmata* (notes). None of this matters intrinsically, because we are clearly dealing with more or less synonymous expressions, but it is important to undermine the ostensible authority of the title *Diatribai*. In reference to Epictetus, this word is generally translated 'discourses', and that by itself is fine. Yet it is also widely assumed that Epictetus' discourses are *diatribes*, a style or supposed style of sermonizing discourse particularly associated with the Cynics. This assumption, while not wholly mistaken, has been unfortunate: it has distracted attention from Epictetus' Socratic methodology, his analytical interests, and his audience. These are so distant from

---

[1] For full references to all these citations, see Schenkl (1916: pp. ii–xv, xxxiii–xxxv).

Cynic sermonizing that the term 'diatribe' is best withheld from Epictetus as a generic description of his teaching style.

2.2 SCOPE, FUNCTION, THEMES

Assuming, as we should, that Arrian has faithfully recorded the gist of his experience of listening to Epictetus, how should we as modern readers approach the discourses? They have a lot to tell us about his curriculum, his conception of his role as teacher, his hopes of his students, the training he expects them to pursue and in what ways he frequently finds them falling short. I discuss all this in Chapter 4. What concerns me now is a broader survey, for which we need to draw from material outside as well as inside the discourses. What should we bring to them that would have been self-evident to Epictetus' educated contemporaries as regards their literary form and purpose, their conformity to established practices, and, by contrast, their distinctive and special features?

As a preliminary response to these issues, we need to grasp two central facts. First, the discourses are not addressed to the world at large, as accounts of Epictetus generally lead one to believe. It is true that they deal accessibly with ethical and psychological issues pertinent to people of any time or place or background. That is obvious from the fact that his modern readership extends well beyond scholars of Graeco-Roman antiquity. If he taught in the open, as is probable, passers-by as well as his particular students could have heard him, and the discourses contain conversations between Epictetus and mature men, visitors attracted by his fame and locals desirous of consulting him (2.4; 2.14; 2.24; 3.4; 3.7; 3.9). Still, he is speaking primarily for and to his own group of students, a group comprised solely of males whose ages are likely to have ranged from about 18 to 25.

Often he addresses them collectively or individually as 'youths'. One potential student is there with his father (2.14.1); another is missing his mother and his comfortable bed (3.5.12). Others have problems with getting an allowance from their parents (3.17.7), or dealing with fathers who object to their studying philosophy (1.26.5–8). Difficult fathers and brothers are frequently mentioned.[2] The content of Epictetus' teaching is so grown-up, demanding, and tough that it comes as a shock to realize that some of his students were only teenagers or thereabouts.

The second central fact also bears on Epictetus' student audience. It is clear that the teaching they received from him was not confined to the kind of discourses Arrian chose to record. These were an informal supplement to a curriculum that included detailed study of classic Stoic texts, especially works composed by Chrysippus, written exercises in logic, and probably some Platonic dialogues.[3] Epictetus remarks on how, at dawn, he reminds himself of 'what author [or text] I need to read over' (1.10.8). He evidently set his students certain reading assignments, for them to present and interpret in class, as a basis for group discussion and his own commentary. Many discourses make reference to this formal training. Epictetus' students, taken generally, seem to be familiar with a good deal of philosophy, including the principal schools to whom Epictetus was vehemently opposed, Epicureans and Sceptics.

At what level Epictetus gave his class this training we can only surmise in broad outline, but it cannot have been quite elementary. Although the discourses mention rather than expound logical technicalities, they assume an understanding of the main terms, argument patterns, and paradoxes of Stoic logic.[4] One of his stock themes is berating students for regarding logical expertise as an end in itself and for confusing mastery of philosophical scholarship with understanding how to live well. We need not assume that Epictetus' students were solely dependent on him for their formal training. Some of them may have studied with other philosophers before joining his school, and all of them could have had access to philosophical literature.[5] The

---

[2] See 3.3.9; 3.17.8; 3.22.54; 4.1.43; 4.5.30.

[3] See e.g. 1.8; 1.10.10; 1.17; 2.1.33; 2.13.21; 2.19; 3.16.9–10; 3.21.6–8; 3.23.7, 20; 3.24.78–81; 4.6.12.

[4] See especially 1.7 (in full); 1.17; 1.8.1–3; 1.29.39–40, 51–2; 2.12.9–10; 2.19.1–4; 2.21.17.

[5] At Aegae, near to Nicopolis, Apollonius of Tyana (about AD 30) was able to find teachers of the four main philosophical systems—Platonic, Aristotelian, Stoic, and Epicurean—and also a Pythagorean teacher (Philostratus, *Life of Apollonius* 1.7).

important point is that the discourses presuppose more philosophical doctrine and technique than they typically exhibit.
This is not to say that a modern reader unversed in that background will fail to grasp Epictetus' leading ideas and their rationale. Much of his text is thoroughly approachable as it stands,
but it is often more complex than rapid reading may suggest.
There are also passages that suggest questions students have
raised outside the context of the discourses or that comment on
matters of doctrine or training in ways referring to his more formal teaching. For instance: 'When someone asked . . .' (1.2.30;
1.13.1; 1.15.1). 'Don't you remember . . .' (1.13.4). 'Shall we not
remember what we have learned from the philosophers . . .'
(3.24.9). Sometimes Epictetus corrects an anonymous student
for interpreting what he has previously said too literally or too
rigidly. Although most of his questions and rejoinders involve
only an imaginary interlocutor, some seem to reflect his actual
interactions with his students.

In order to grasp what the discourses are, we may take the following passage:

8 If virtue [*aretê*] has the manufacture of happiness and serenity and equanimity as its profession, progress towards virtue must be progress
towards each of these. For it is always the case that progress is an approach
towards the goal that anything's perfection brings us to . . . How is it, then,
that we agree on virtue's being this sort of thing, but seek progress and
display progress in other things? What is the product of virtue?
   Serenity.
Who, then, is making progress?
   Is it the person who has read many of Chrysippus' books?
But surely virtue is not knowledge of Chrysippus; for if so, it follows that
progress is simply getting knowledge of a lot of Chrysippus. That puts us
in the position of (*a*) agreeing that virtue produces one thing and (*b*)
asserting that the approach to virtue, progress, produces something else.
   This person (someone says) *can already read Chrysippus all by himself.*
Why, friend, you are really progressing, in heaven's name! What
progress!
   Why do you make fun of him?
And why do *you* divert him from awareness of his own weaknesses?
Aren't you willing to show him the product of virtue so he can learn
where to seek his progress? (1.4.3–10)

Here, as very frequently elsewhere, Epictetus chides his students for confusing means with ends and for aiming at technical proficiency rather than transformation of character and consciousness. He requires his students to study Chrysippus and to be able to interpret this Stoic authority, but the goal of this work and of their entire training with him is not mastery of Stoic scholarship but progress towards the goal of achieving virtue and real happiness. At the end of the discourse he praises Chrysippus for writing books that show how serenity is 'truly' grounded in the proper understanding of nature. In the main body of the text, however, his focus is not on this theory but on the mental disposition required of anyone who is sufficiently aware of his present inadequacies to be capable of making genuine progress towards that goal.[6] The introspection Epictetus calls for invokes his Socratic insistence (see p. 79) that awareness of one's confusion or ignorance is the fundamental precondition of any genuine progress.

He is not treating theory as dispensable. In the first words of this discourse he makes it also essential to progress that someone 'learn from the [Stoic] philosophers' about the relation between serenity and autonomy. On that favourite theme he says a great deal in other discourses as well as this one, but he leaves it to his students to have a prior grasp of virtue and the technical Stoic concept of 'progress'.

For our understanding of the general purpose, style, and scope of Arrian's record, this passage can be treated as characteristic. The discourses assume a fairly detailed understanding both of Stoicism and of philosophical issues that were alive at the time of their composition. Epictetus does not deliver the discourses in order to expound that tradition. Rather, he uses them for a combination of supplementary purposes. These can be broadly summed up under the following headings: theoretical, methodological, polemical, psychological, social, and educational.

Here is a selection of discourses arranged accordingly, with some modification to their transmitted titles.[7]

---

[6] 'Progress' (*prokopê*) is the Stoics' term for advancing towards the ideal excellence, characteristic of the perfected sage, but not exemplified in the actual world. Hence progress is Epictetus' aim for himself and his students. For early Stoic texts on progress, see LS 59I, 61ST.

[7] Arrian is probably responsible for those titles (see Dobbin 1998: 65).

Theoretical	*On what is up to us and what is not* 1.1
	On providence 1.6, 3.17
	On preconceptions 1.22
	On goodness 2.8
Methodological	*On the use of changing, hypothetical and similar arguments* 1.7
	What is the starting point of philosophy? 2.11
	On philosophical discussion 2.12
	What is the hallmark of error? 2.26
Polemical	*Against the Academic (Sceptics)* 1.5
	Against Epicurus 1.23
	Against Epicureans and Academics 2.20
Psychological	*On contentment* 1.12
	On tranquillity 2.2
	On despondency 3.13
	On freedom from fear 4.7
Social	*On love of family* 1.11
	How to discover a person's appropriate acts from his identifications 2.10
	That we should be cautious about social relationships 3.16
	On cleanliness 4.11
Vocational	*To those who are obdurate in sticking to their decisions* 2.15
	That we do not practise our doctrines about values 2.16
	To those who set out to become lecturers 3.21
	To those who rush to put on the appearance of a philosopher 4.8

These six headings would be radically misleading if they were taken to be mutually exclusive; almost every discourse includes features that are describable in all these ways. Epictetus is concerned throughout with elucidating, justifying, and internalizing Stoicism as *the* philosophy, with training his students, advising them on how to apply Stoic teaching in their own lives,

on what character they need to cultivate, on how they should deal
with the persons and situations they encounter from day to day;
he continually counsels and cajoles them to use the mental
resources they have at their disposal for tackling contingencies
that may be as trivial as a jealous brother or as serious as exile,
threat of execution, or loss of family.

Nevertheless, my headings reflect the fact that the discourses,
unlike Arrian's summary *Manual*, contain much more than potted doctrines and maxims. They are the best record we have of a
professional Stoic teacher's (or indeed any ancient professor's)
advisory sessions with his students, covering their life in and
outside the school, and ranging over consolidation and interpretation of Stoic theory, students' urgent needs to rethink their
intellectual and everyday priorities, exemplification of what
their training is designed to equip them for, and much more.

However, some of the discourses, especially those I classify as
psychological and social, would be immediately recognized by
educated contemporaries as belonging to a long-standing tradition of ethical advice, consolation, and exhortation that goes
back to the beginning of the Hellenistic epoch. Socrates, Plato,
Xenophon, and Aristotle belong to its prehistory, but its full
flowering starts with Epicurus, early Stoicism, and the Cynics. A
number of topics rapidly became standard, especially death,
exile, poverty, grief, anger, and old age. As this selection of topics shows, the tradition was particularly associated with correct-
ing conventional impediments to happiness. Lucretius, Cicero,
and Seneca included such themes in their published work. From
his Stoic teacher Musonius Rufus, Epictetus also heard disquisi-
tions of this kind. The tradition continues in the second century
AD with such contemporaries of Epictetus as Dio Chrysostom,
Favorinus, and Plutarch, and with such later figures as Maximus
of Tyre.

Not only the themes but also the styles of such discourses have
many generic features. They typically include anecdotes, examples, quotations, personification, imperatives, rapid sequences
of question and answer, and other rhetorical devices that would
be out of place in a purely expository treatise. In view of such
congruity of theme and style, some scholars have thought that

there existed not only a tradition of popular moral discourse but also a literary genre as its vehicle, a genre called 'diatribe', of which Epictetus' discourses are a prime example.

My main objection to this description of his work (to amplify what I have said above, p. 42) is threefold. First, as my sample of Epictetus' topics indicates, his educational programme ranges well beyond the stock repertoire of the so-called diatribes. In fact, none of the discourses is focused specifically on such standard themes as death or exile, although these furnish some of his material. The headings I have called psychological and social include a number of well-worn topics, but that does not hold for the other four.

Secondly, Epictetus was unlike many of the surviving authors of so-called diatribes in being a professional teacher. His discourses, as we have seen, are specifically designed for his own students. This explains my 'vocational' heading, which applies to that segment of his work in which he is concerned with their future careers, whether as philosopher teachers or in other fields.

Thirdly and most importantly, whatever topic he is addressing, Epictetus proceeds systematically; he frequently presents arguments, and, although he regularly uses examples, anecdotes, and other rhetorical devices, his main points are based upon concepts and procedures either that he explains and justifies within the context or that he can presume his audience to know because he has treated them fully elsewhere.

All three of these points are entirely compatible with the obvious fact that Epictetus' discourses have *some* affinity with the so-called diatribe tradition. It would be better, though, to redescribe that tradition, and to call it a practice, both oral and written, of ethical training to which professional teachers and didactic writers contributed in ways that were both generic and individual. While there is much common ground in the themes, the manner of their treatment varied greatly.

Contemporary figures such as Favorinus and Dio Chrysostom (often called sophists) were rhetoricians who held an audience because of their verbal pyrotechnics rather than through anything that was ethically creative or deeply thought out. Epictetus strongly distances himself from such displays, and he warns his

students against mistaking rhetorical for philosophical success.[8]
For his lecturing purposes, he often uses the vivid, brusque,
anecdotal style that was the Cynics' trademark (3.9.14); but in
his more ambitious discourses he combines this feature with
more rigorous elements of Socratic discourse and the Stoic tradition. Epictetus had no sympathy for the external trappings of
the Cynics, or at least for the kind of drop-out lifestyle by which
they were frequently characterized.[9] While there is virtually
nothing from the earlier Stoic tradition to compare with
Epictetus, the rhetorician Fronto, teacher of Marcus Aurelius,
applies to Chrysippus words that could describe Epictetus himself:

Wake up and hear what Chrysippus himself aims at. Is he content to
give information, expound the facts, make definitions and lay everything out? No. He expands on everything as far as possible, exaggerates,
anticipates objections, repeats himself, defers matters, retraces his
path, gives descriptions, makes divisions, introduces characters and
puts what he has to say in other people's mouths.

(*On Eloquence* 2.17)[10]

In the third part of this chapter, I shall review Epictetus'
didactic and argumentative style and consider how he positions
himself in regard to pre-existing models. But before that, I make
a few remarks about how the discourses relate to the strictly
philosophical, as distinct from the so-called diatribe, context of
Graeco-Roman philosophy.

If we treat perplexity as the proper condition of a genuine
philosopher's mentality, Epictetus scarcely qualifies. By the
time he delivered the material of the discourses he appears to
have had no doubts concerning the correctness of the Stoics'
theocentric cosmology, the rationality and benevolence of the
world's structure in relation to human beings, and the capacity of
human beings to organize their lives in ways that could be both
subjectively satisfying, whatever their circumstances, and objectively philanthropic. To be sure, he requires promising students

---

[8] See 3.21; 3.23; further discussion on p. 53.
[9] See 3.12.9; 4.8.34; also Epictetus' presentation of the Cynic as a rare and special
calling, 3.22, with further discussion below, p. 59.
[10] Aptly quoted by Dobbin (1998: p. xviii).

to be aware, at the outset, of their incapacity to deal with essentials (2.11.1; p. 79 below); his representation of his own philosophical identity is modest or even tacit (see Section 4.6). But, so far as the doctrines that inform his discourses are concerned, Epictetus speaks as someone totally committed to their truth and cogency.

Is this unusual within the general context of ancient philosophy? Certainly not. There were, of course, Sceptics who questioned whether human beings have any access to objective or ethical truths, and scholars will never cease from debating over what Plato's dialogues signify concerning the convictions of Socrates and of their author. But most philosophers from about 300 BC belonged to schools that looked back to their founders as absolute authorities for the doctrines and methodologies they themselves espoused. To be a philosopher in the Hellenistic and Roman world presupposed such school membership. This was quite compatible with independent emphases, research, and innovation, but within limits that defined one's identity as a Stoic, Epicurean, and so forth. Although ancient philosophy could comprise a much broader range of subject matter than philosophy does today, it was not a project of more or less free enquiry, unshaped by school affiliation.

What stopped the later philosophical tradition from degenerating into sectarianism was a pair of related features that are prominent in Epictetus. Committed Stoic though he is, he does not simply hand down a catechism. Where he has a doctrine to expound, as for instance the domain of autonomy or 'things that are up to us', he explains and justifies it (see Section 8.2). He expects his students to reason, and he reasons for them. Secondly, this dialectic, as we may call it, applies not only to his presentation of doctrines, but also to his criticism of Epicureans and Sceptics. He presents his teaching not in a vacuum but with his eye on rival schools. The need to rebut these schools and to do so through argument vivifies his Stoicism even though its essential content stretches back several centuries.

2.3 FORM AND CONTENT:
PROTREPTIC, *ELENCTIC*, DOCTRINAL

Form and content are too closely integrated in the discourses to be studied quite independently, but in order to appreciate this we need to start from Epictetus' own accounts of his didactic purpose and its distance from the fashionable lecturing that was so alluring to some of his students.

9 Does a philosopher give invitations to a lecture? Isn't it that, just as the sun attracts nutriment to itself, so he attracts those who will be benefited? What physician issues invitations for someone to be cured by him? (Though today I hear that the physicians at Rome are issuing invitations; in my day it was they who were called in!)
   I invite you to come and hear that you are in a bad way; that you are attending to everything except what you should be concerned about; that you are ignorant of what is good and bad; and that you are thoroughly unhappy and wretched.
A nice invitation! Yet, unless a philosopher's discourse instils this lesson, it's dead and the speaker too. [Musonius] Rufus used to say:
   If you have nothing better to do than praise me, I am speaking to no effect.
In fact he talked in such a way that as each of us sat there we thought that someone had informed on us; such was his grasp of our experiences and the vividness with which he set out each person's shortcomings.
                                                         (3.23.27–9)

This passage is an excellent illustration not only of Epictetus' teaching style and its rationale but also of what he expects from any promising student. It is his job, as a philosopher physician, to identify his students' mental and moral weaknesses, and to stimulate them to understand and practise the regime he prescribes. But it is also incumbent on them to be receptive and actively involved. He has no time for the kind of person who lacks the 'skill in listening' that a student needs in order to benefit from his teaching and who arouses no eagerness in himself (2.24.15).

   In his own way, obviously, Epictetus is a master rhetorician. He puts his own attitude in perspective by distinguishing between the need for 'a particular style, with variety and sharp articulation of key points', and merely 'staying there', or regarding eloquence as an end in itself rather than a necessary instrument of education (2.23.40–7). He asks an imaginary or perhaps a real student, who wants to be applauded as a lecturer:

10 When you are gasping for applause and counting your audience, are you wanting to be of benefit to people?
    Today I had a much bigger audience.
Yes, it *was* big.
    Five hundred, I think.
Nonsense. Make it a thousand.
    Dio [Chrysostom] never had such a large audience.
How could he?
    And they were really nifty at getting my points.
Beauty, sir, can move even a stone!

[And now, with heavy irony, to the rest of the class] Wow, listen to the words of a philosopher, the character of humanity's benefactor! Here's a person who has listened to reason, who has read [aloud] the Socratic literature in the genuinely Socratic way and not as something by Lysias and Isocrates[11] . . . *You* have been reading the Socratic literature as if it were an operatic libretto! (3.23.19–21)

The discourse from which this extract is taken is appropriately entitled 'To those who make a display of lecturing and discussing'. 'Display' is a marked term because it refers to the genre of *epideictic* oratory practised by rhetoricians whose mass audiences were acculturated to hearing hackneyed themes embellished by stylistic virtuosity. After denouncing its suitability for his students and himself, Epictetus anticipates and counters the objection that he has no interest in the style and rhetorical effectiveness of a philosopher's teaching. He endorses three styles, naming them *protreptic*, *elenctic*, and didactic [or doctrinal] (3.23.33). The scholarly literature has hardly noticed these terms; yet, unlike the *omnium gatherum* category 'diatribe', this triad can tell us a lot not only about how the discourses are constructed but also about how we as readers may best approach them.

[11] i.e. as if it were composed by two of the most famous Greek authors of rhetorical prose.

Protreptic and Elenctic: Socratic

The term *protreptic* can scarcely be translated by a single English word. It refers to a type of exhortative or admonitory discourse, either in monologue or in question-and-answer form, designed to make persons rethink their ethical beliefs and convert to a fundamental change of outlook and behaviour. Plato's *Apology* and *Euthydemus* exhibit Socrates engaging in both kinds of *protreptic*, and Socrates' historical association with such discourse is strongly suggested by the fact that works with this title are attributed to two of his immediate followers Antisthenes and Aristippus. From Aristotle onwards philosophers wrote *protreptics* as introductions and exhortations to the philosophical life advocated by their respective schools; and the genre was especially favoured by the early Stoics.

A few lines below **9** Epictetus gives the following description to the *protreptic* style (3.23.34–7):

11 It is the ability to show people, both individuals and groups, the inconsistency they are caught up in, and that they are focused on everything except what they want. For they want the sources of happiness, but they are looking for them in the wrong place. In order to achieve this, is it necessary for a thousand benches to be set down, the audience invited, and you wearing an elegant robe or cloak to ascend the podium and describe the death of Achilles?

> *For heaven's sake, stop doing all you can to discredit noble words and deeds. There is nothing more protreptic than when the speaker shows his audience that he needs them.*[12]

You tell me, then, which member of *your* audience agonized about himself or turned in on himself or said as he left:

> *The philosopher got a splendid hold on me. I mustn't act this way in future?*

Epictetus may give the impression that he is characterizing the *protreptic* style of any philosophy. In fact, he is describing his own practice in numerous discourses, which is not to say that he

---

[12] Unlike other commentators, I take this passage to be an imaginary retort to Epictetus by someone defending 'display' oratory and its need for a big audience that will inspire the orator to be *protreptic* by dwelling on examples of epic heroes.

had no precedent. We have noticed his acknowledgement of Musonius Rufus, but Epictetus' *protreptic* style is distinctive (so far as our knowledge of Stoic literature goes) because of the way he regularly combines it with the style that he calls *elenctic*.

This term also defies simple translation, for it combines the following connotations: interrogative, examinational, prosecutorial, and refutative. Epictetus' students would catch all this because they would immediately associate the *elenctic* style with the single philosopher whose special trademark it was— Socrates. Epictetus, moreover, makes sure that they do. In Plato's *Apology* (28e) Socrates speaks of his divine mission to practise philosophy by 'examining himself and others', and Epictetus alludes to this famous passage when he says (3.21.19) that Socrates was appointed by God to hold 'the *elenctic* position'.

Elenchus is Plato's name for Socrates' method of asking questions with a view to eliciting his interlocutors' opinions about a moral concept, examining their answers, and showing (typically) that they are radically confused and therefore do not know what they thought they knew. How the *elenchus* works in particular Platonic contexts is a complex question, which I will take up in the next chapter. What we should note, for our present understanding of Epictetus, are two features of the Socratic *elenchus* that no reader of Plato can miss: first, the objective of undermining the interlocutor's confidence in the correctness of his original opinion, and, secondly, as the means to this objective, getting the interlocutor's assent to a series of propositions that conflict with the opinion he originally advanced as his true belief.

Looking back to Epictetus' description of the *protreptic* style, we see that he has virtually characterized it in terms of the Socratic *elenchus*: showing people the inconsistencies or conflicts they are caught up in, and showing that they do not know what they thought they knew. The conflicts and the ignorance go together if (as the text assumes) people genuinely want happiness but are simultaneously motivated by false beliefs that are inconsistent with it. In the discourse 2.26 (which I fully reproduce later, p. 74) Epictetus is quite explicit about the tight linkage between both styles:

12 The person who can show each individual the conflict responsible for his error, and clearly make him see how he is not doing what he wants to do and is doing what he does not want to do—that is the person who combines expertise in argument, exhortation [*protreptikos*], and refutation [*elenktikos*]. (2.26.4)

A few lines after this Epictetus produces Socrates as the exemplary representative of all these skills.

As we have seen, Epictetus has Platonic authority for labelling Socrates *protreptic* as well as *elenctic*. The final sections of the *Gorgias*, probably Epictetus' favourite Platonic dialogue (see p. 70), are a Socratic homily on the risks people take who neglect their moral welfare; and a comparable passage is the long digression (so-called) in the *Theaetetus* (172d–177c), which witheringly contrasts the unwitting servitude of politicians and lawyers with the freedom and leisure of philosophers.

The Platonic Socrates, then, can be *protreptic* as well as *elenctic* in one and the same dialogue. But the latter is his dominant method. Also, Plato tends to separate the *protreptic* passages from Socrates' *elenctic* discussions rather than combining the two styles in one context. Perhaps acknowledging this practice, the Eleatic Stranger (who replaces Socrates as the principal speaker in Plato's late dialogue, *The Sophist*) draws a sharp distinction between education by 'admonition', which he characterizes as traditional and paternal, and the *elenctic* method. Treating the latter's practitioners as spiritual physicians, he says they favour it because 'they think that the soul will get no benefit from the lessons applied to it [i.e. by admonitory education] until a cross-examiner [*elenchôn tis*] has put the person being cross-examined to shame, by expelling the opinions impeding his lessons, and declares him purged and thinking he knows exactly what he knows' (*Sophist* 230c–d).

In the very discourse where Epictetus describes his three approved philosophical styles he harangues his students with the words: 'You men, the philosopher's school is a doctor's office; you shouldn't leave it in pleasure but in pain' (3.23.30). This startling expression for the therapeutic function of philosophy is his own, but in a context so redolent of Socrates we may be fairly confident that Epictetus has Plato's purgative *elenchus* in his mind. Epictetus, however, treats *protreptic* as no less medicinal than *elenctic*. Or, to put it another way, he regards Socrates not only as the master of both styles but also as a paradigm he himself can best try to imitate by blending both styles and treating them as mutually supportive.

Exactly how he does this we have yet to see. We also need to consider whether Epictetus' *elenctic* style has genuinely deep connections with Socratic methodology. In approaching that question, it will be necessary to say a lot more about the role that Socrates plays in Epictetus' discourses, and why Epictetus makes him more prominent than any other predecessor, including the Stoic Zeno and the Cynic Diogenes. But before that, the role Epictetus assigns to these two figures requires our attention because he gives Zeno the divinely appointed 'didactic and doctrinal chair', his third approved style; and in the same context (which is where he allocates the *elenctic* position to Socrates) he associates Diogenes with 'the kingly and reproving chair' (3.21.19).

Didactic and Doctrinal: Zeno

Zeno, in spite of his primary status, was not one of the Stoa's prolific authors. He is rarely quoted verbatim by any of our surviving sources, and at least one of Epictetus' citations of him is formulated in Epictetan language (1.20.15). By the Roman imperial period and probably for long before, Chrysippus had become the standard reference for Stoic doctrine, and it was probably from Chrysippus and later Stoic writers that Epictetus learned what he knew of Zeno's work.

There are two reasons why Epictetus assigns the 'didactic and doctrinal chair' to Zeno. First, all Stoics looked back to Zeno as their philosophy's founder. So it is natural for Epictetus to tie Zeno's name to the style appropriate to expounding Stoicism. Secondly, unlike Chrysippus or any other leading Stoic with the partial exception of Cleanthes, Zeno was hallowed as much for his exemplary character as for his doctrinal authority. Epictetus cites Chrysippus far more often than Zeno, but the Stoic philosophers whose lives he praises are Zeno and Cleanthes, sometimes coupling them with Socrates or the Cynic Diogenes (2.13.14; 3.23.32; 3.24.38; 3.26.23). His references to other Stoic philosophers, even including Chrysippus, acknowledge their scholarship but warn his students against identifying mere mastery of these works as the goal of their training (2.4.11; 2.17.40; 3.21.7).

Kingly and Reproving: Diogenes

Epictetus frequently cites Diogenes as the paradigm of what that training can ideally achieve, even awarding him, as we have just seen, the divinely appointed 'kingly and reproving chair'.[13] References to Diogenes in the discourses outnumber the allusions to any individual philosopher apart from Socrates. Their prominence may suggest that Epictetus presents himself as a Cynicizing Stoic or at least as a Stoic with strongly Cynic tendencies. Both descriptions are apt up to a point, but to put them in perspective we need to register several points.

Epictetus' concentration on Diogenes signifies the need for his students to focus on the primary and transformative message of Stoicism as distinct from its more scholastic developments: hence Diogenes' 'reproving' epithet. Zeno had allegedly been converted to philosophy by reading about Socrates and finding 'someone like him' in the person of Crates, a follower of the original Cynic Diogenes (DL VII.1–3); and Diogenes himself was believed to have been a second-hand follower of Socrates through the mediation of Antisthenes, a close associate of Socrates whom Epictetus names with great respect.[14] This is a tangled history. What matters about it, so far as Epictetus is concerned, is his entirely correct recognition that the principal influences on Zeno's Stoicism were Socratic and Cynic. In canonizing Socrates, Diogenes, and Zeno, Epictetus looks back to the founder of Stoicism and to the two great figures whom later Stoics regarded as the closest approximations to their ideal sage.

---

[13] For passages referring to Diogenes on his own, see 1.24.6; 3.2.11; 3.22.24, 57–60, 63; 4.1.30, 114, 152; 4.11.21.

[14] See 1.17.12; 3.22.63; 3.24.57; 4.6.20.

During the later part of the Hellenistic period, Cynicism seems to have more or less died out, probably because any philosophical value it was perceived to have had been absorbed into Stoicism. But it underwent a revival during the early Roman Empire, motivated perhaps by a belief that later Stoicism had lost touch with the simple and self-sufficient life advocated and practised by Zeno and his immediate followers. Cynics such as the Demetrius whom Seneca knew impressed their admirers by the rigorous indifference they displayed to all the ordinary comforts of life, offering themselves as examples of human capacity to master the vicissitudes of fortune and preaching that message in a style that was witty, caustic, and contemptuous of purely conventional values.[15]

While Epictetus cites Demetrius with approval (1.25.22), he is extremely critical of the tendency to identify the authentic spirit of Cynicism with its external accoutrements and insulting discourse. He says this to a would-be Cynic:

13 It is not what you think:

I wear a rough cloak now, and I shall have one then. I sleep on a hard surface now, and I shall do so then. I shall also get a bag and a stick, and I shall begin to go around begging from the people I meet and abusing them. And if I see someone removing superfluous hair, or with a fine hair style, or walking around in purple clothes, I shall rebuke him.

If you imagine the matter to be like this, keep away from it; don't go near it, it's not for you. (3.22.9–11)

This extract comes from the early part of a long discourse in which Epictetus characterizes Cynicism in the person of Diogenes as a life that demands quite exceptional qualities. He represents the ideal Cynic as sent by God to be an 'evangelist' for Stoicism. What differentiates him from the standard Stoic ideal is not his character or system of values—these are the same—but his being called to a nomadic life as 'citizen of the world', unattached to any particular community or to family life, in order to 'bear witness' to

---

[15] On Seneca's admiration for Demetrius, see his *Letter* 62.3. But Seneca, in contrast with Musonius and Epictetus, is critical of Cynic frankness (*parrhêsia*) (*Letter* 29.1), though he quotes two sayings of Diogenes approvingly (*Letters* 67.14, 91.19).

Stoic principles. Epictetus' Cynic ideal is a universal philan-
thropist, endowed not only with the physical and mental strength
that his calling demands, but also with 'natural charm and wit'.

By Epictetus' day (and in fact for long before) Diogenes had
become a quasi-mythical figure. Unlike the historical and philosophical record on Socrates, Diogenes was known only through
reputed sayings and by an anecdotal tradition that emphasized
such actual or supposed features of his life as exile from his native
Sinope, temporary enslavement, living easily on the street, and
an ability to challenge and attract such apparent models of success as Alexander the Great. Epictetus, embellishing the myth
of Diogenes, turns him into a Stoic icon and awards him the
'kingly and reproving' position.

Why kingly? Tradition associated Diogenes not only with
Alexander but also with the Great King of Persia, whose lack of
happiness he contrasted with his own state (3.22.60). When the
Stoics defined real kingship as the prerogative of the sage, they
were taking their lead from the Cynics for whom Diogenes represented the transference of rulership from command over others to command over oneself. It is the Cynic's self-mastery and
freedom that equips him, according to Epictetus, to 'supervise
the rest of us' (3.22.18).

Yet, in characterizing the ideal Cynic in this way, Epictetus is
also looking beyond Diogenes and back to Socrates. In illustration of how the Cynic should fulfil his admonitory role,
Epictetus says:

14 He should be prepared to mount the tragic stage and speak the words of
Socrates:
> *O people, where are you bound for? O miserable ones, what are you*
> *doing? You reel up and down, like the blind. You have left the real path*
> *and are going off on another one. You are looking for serenity and hap-*
> *piness in the wrong place, where it does not exist, and you do not believe*
> *when someone shows you. Why do you seek it in externals? It does not*
> *exist in the body.*   (3.22.26)

Epictetus draws on an explicitly *protreptic* passage from near
the beginning of Plato's *Cleitopho* (407a–b). There Cleitopho
addresses Socrates:

In my encounters with you, Socrates, I have often been amazed at your words. I find your speaking outstanding in comparison with other people, when rebuking persons, like a *deus ex machina*, you chant these words:

> *O people, where are you bound for? You act in ignorance of everything you should know, giving all your attention to securing wealth, and as far as your sons, your heirs, are concerned, you fail to find moral tutors so that they may learn how to use it justly.*

Epictetus has adapted Plato's text, but his closeness to the original is obvious. We should not, then, regard Diogenes' 'kingly and reproving' expertise as marking a fourth rhetorical style for the discourses, but see it rather as a variation of the *protreptic* style already associated with Socrates.

We are now in a position to draw some threads together concerning Epictetus' approved triad of styles (*protreptic*, *elenctic*, *doctrinal*), the philosophical 'chairs' he assigns to Diogenes, Socrates, and Zeno respectively, and the bearing of these styles and paradigms on his own teaching method.

The individual discourses are too diverse to fit a simple compositional formula, but, whether they are constructed as monologues or as conversations between Epictetus and someone else, they are consistently dialectical or dialogical. What I mean is that Arrian has transmitted the discourses in a form that uses 'I' or 'we' and 'you' (singular or plural) throughout. From beginning to end the theme of most discourses is developed through a rapid interchange of questions and answers, interspersed with imperatives, short expositions, anecdotes, examples, and quotations. By speaking in this way, Epictetus involves his audience continuously. His questions are ways of getting them to interrogate themselves, and his responses or illustrations are equally designed to shatter complacency and effect a transformation of consciousness.

We might say, then, that he interweaves the triad of styles in such a way that everything he says is an *elenctic* and *protreptic* formulation of Stoic doctrine: his words have a doctrinal content that challenges and corrects his students' beliefs and emotional attitudes (*elenctic*) and gives them advice and discipline on making progress as Stoics (*protreptic*). Although his style is too fluid for us to say this passage is simply doctrinal and that one *protreptic* or *elenctic*, he modulates his tone and procedures in ways that allow each one of these to make its distinctive contribution.

To illustrate, I select three passages from the programmatic first discourse. This text (entitled *On what is up to us and what is not*) begins quietly with an argument concerning the unique powers of our reasoning faculty.[16] The argument is in question-and-answer mode; we may label this passage doctrinal.

15 Speaking generally, you will find no art or faculty that can study itself, and therefore none that can approve or disapprove of itself. How far does grammar's studying capacity extend?
Only as far as discriminating literature.
And music's?
Only as far as discriminating song.
Does one of them study itself?
Certainly not.
Now if you are writing to a friend, grammar will tell you that you need particular letters; but it will not tell you whether or not you should write to your friend. The same holds in the case of music's relation to song. It will not say whether at this moment you should sing or play the lyre, or whether you should not do so. Which faculty, then, will do so?
The one that studies both itself and everything else.
And what is that?
The faculty of reason.
Yes; for this is the only faculty we have inherited that can perceive itself—what it is, what it is capable of, and how valuable it is—and also perceive all the rest. (1.1.1–4)

This quiet doctrinal opening prepares the ground for Epictetus to assert that the gods have given us unrestricted control over our reasoning faculty but not over anything else, not even our bodies. He then faces and answers the challenge that we would have been better off if the gods had also given us control over other things:

16 *Did they refuse us that?*
In my opinion, they would have entrusted us with those other things too, if they had been able to do so; but that was quite beyond their

---

[16] I reserve discussion of the psychology and theology of 1.1 to later pages; see especially Sections 6.4 and 8.3.

power. For since we are on earth, and bound to an earthy body and earthy associates, how was it possible for us not to be impeded by externals in relation to these things?

What does Zeus say?

Epictetus, if it had been possible, I would have made your little body and property free and unhindered. But in fact—take note of my words—this is not your own but only artfully moulded clay. Since I could not give you this, I have given you a portion of myself, this faculty of positive and negative impulse and of desire and aversion—the faculty, in short, of using mental impressions. By caring for this and by situating all that is yours therein, you will never be impeded, you will never be restricted, you will not groan or find fault or flatter anyone. Well, do you find this meagre?

Far from it.

Are you content with this?

Please God, I am. (1.1.8–13)

With the doctrine of the mind's unique and God-given autonomy now in place, Epictetus proceeds to explore its psychological and ethical implications in a staccato style that combines *protreptic* advice with *elenctic* questions and responses; the purpose of the latter is to undermine conventional beliefs that prospects of death and other extreme circumstances inevitably trigger emotional distress:

17 *What should we have ready at hand in [difficult] situations?*
Simply the knowledge of what is mine and what is not, and of what is possible for me and what is not.

I have to die.

Do I also have to die groaning?

I have to be fettered.

While moaning too?

I have to go into exile.

Does anyone prevent me from going with a smile, cheerful and serene?

Tell your secrets.

I refuse, because that is up to me.

Then I will fetter you.

What do you mean, fellow? Fetter *me*? You can fetter my leg, but not even Zeus can overcome my volition.

I will throw you into gaol.

No, my little body, rather.

I will behead you.
Well, when did I tell you that mine was the only neck that could not be severed?

These are what persons studying philosophy should practise, and write down each day, and train themselves in.   (1.1.21–5)

We can see from such analysis how a single discourse blends the three styles. Readers of this book can try their own hand at it. What they will find is that, while the *protreptic* style predominates, it is regularly anchored to doctrinal instruction, and so skilfully interlaced with *elenctic* questions and answers that we can regard Epictetus as positioning himself within three pedagogical traditions simultaneously—Stoic (doctrinal), Cynic (reproving/*protreptic*), and Socratic (combining *protreptic* and *elenctic*). It is in the *elenctic* respect, on which there is much more to say, that his style and methodology as a Stoic philosopher are most distinctive. For this reason, we need to take a closer look at his relation to Socrates.

FURTHER READING AND NOTES

Epictetus and Arrian

On Arrian both in general and in relation to Epictetus, see Brunt (1977) and Stadter (1980). On the question of Arrian's role in compiling the discourses, Wirth (1967) adopts the extreme view that they are essentially Arrian's compositions, modelled especially on Xenophon. Against this, see Long (1982a) and I. Hadot (1996). Dobbin (1998: p. xxii), suggests that Epictetus himself wrote the discourses 'as we have them'. This extreme reduction of Arrian's role is implausible. Epictetus hardly had any interest in presenting himself as an author as distinct from a purely oral teacher like Socrates. For discussion of the shorthand techniques Arrian may have used, see Boge (1973).

On Arrian's prefatory letter (p. 39 above), see P. Hadot (2000: 30–5), who refers to comments made by Galen on his practice of making notes, as distinct from fully-fledged books, for the use of his friends or students.

For Simplicius' commentary on the *Manual* compiled by Arrian, see I. Hadot (1996), who (pp. 156–7) defends the likelihood that Arrian, in work that does not survive, described Epictetus' life, just as Simplicius reports. For the influence of the *Manual* on early Christian literature, see Boter (1999).

On the MSS tradition and the editorial history of the discourses, see Schenkl (1916: pp. liv-cxv) and Souilhé (1948–65: i, pp. lxxii–lxxxvi). For the ancient evidence on Arrian's works on Epictetus and their titles, and on fragments cited by other authors, see Schenkl (1916: pp. xxxiii–liv), and Souilhé (1948–65: i, pp. xii–xix).

Descriptions of the discourses as 'diatribes' persist in Dobbin (1998: pp. xxii–xxiii), and I confess to having followed the fashion in Long (1982a: 995–6). Its shortcomings were already pointed out by Halbauer (1911), and the existence of the 'diatribe' as a peculiarly Cynic/Stoic literary form has been effectively demolished by Jocelyn (1982), followed by Douglas (1995), who should be consulted on the lecturing tradition miscalled 'diatribe'. See also the massive study by Fuentes Gonzalez (1998).

Scope, Function, Themes

Research on this important subject has not yet advanced far, mainly because of the misleading hold that 'diatribe' has exercised on scholars. For an excellent account of Epictetus' discourses in relation to higher education, see Clarke (1971). The best ancient texts to read as background are Plutarch's two essays: *On the Education of Children* and *On Listening to Lectures*. Plutarch was contemporary with Epictetus. Though highly critical of Chrysippean Stoicism, he echoes Epictetus very closely in his advice to students on how they should evaluate good teaching: they should not be impressed by a lecturer's impressive appearance or delivery, but ask whether they have been improved by what they have heard, had their minds cleansed, and been stimulated to cultivate excellence.

For the practice of philosophers to follow their formal lectures with a question-and-answer session, see Aulus Gellius 1.26.1–11. P. Hadot (1992) is good on some aspects of Epictetus' teaching, but focuses very narrowly on its function as 'spiritual exercise'. Epictetus' student audience is discussed by Hock (1991), who diagnoses Epictetus' results as a failure. That assessment completely overlooks Epictetus' hyperbole and irony.

Halbauer (1911) is one of the few scholars who has attempted to discover some rationale in the ordering of topics between the four surviving books of *Discourses*. Broadly speaking, the subjects of books 1–2 are more theoretical and methodological, while books 3–4 focus more on social and vocational themes. The first discourse of book 1 (excerpted on pp. 62–4) is plainly of cardinal importance. However, it is difficult to discern much system in Arrian's arrangement of most of the material, notwithstanding the attempt of De Lacy (1943) to argue that in book 1 Arrian 'has carefully planned a progressive exposition of ethical theory, collecting and organizing his material in terms of the principles of logic' (p. 113).

For the rhetoricians of the Second Sophistic, see Bowersock (1969), Jones (1978), and Gleason (1995). On the importance attached to allegiance to one's philosophical school, see Sedley (1989).

Form and Content: Protreptic, Elenctic, *Doctrinal*

Halbauer (1911: 46–7) is the only scholar who has previously connected Epictetus' three approved styles with the actual style of the discourses, but he does little more than state the point; see also Döring (1979: 70–1), who focuses only on the *elenctic* style. Bonhöffer (1890: 8 n. 1), follows his usual practice of playing down Epictetus' originality by attributing the three styles to the early Stoic tradition. There is no evidence at all to support this suggestion; and, apart from that, the entire interest of the material is what Epictetus himself does with it.

Slings (1999) should be consulted for a very detailed study of *protreptic* and its relation to the *elenchus*. On the evidence of Cicero, *Acad.* 1.16 (see Slings 1999: 86–7), Epictetus was not original in treating Socratic discourse as a combination of both styles.

For further bibliography on the Socratic *elenchus*, see p. 95. Documentation for my remarks about the relations between Cynics and Stoics may be found in Billerbeck (1996), Griffin (1996), and Long (1996b). For a special study of the Cynic Demetrius, see Billerbeck (1979). Billerbeck (1978) provides a detailed commentary on Epictetus' discourse 3.22, where he discusses the life of the ideal Cynic.

An earlier Stoic philosopher had described Cynicism as 'a short cut to virtue' (DL VIII.121). The reason for calling it a short cut was its exclusive focus on practice at the expense of the theory in logic, physics, and ethics that Stoic philosophers taught as the underpinning for their own art of living. Epictetus did not believe in short cuts, but his equivocal attitude towards the technicalities of orthodox Stoicism coheres with his image of the evangelistic Diogenes, too busy proselytizing to engage in scholarship.

CHAPTER 3

The Socratic Paradigm

The excellent person neither fights with anyone himself,
nor as far as he can, does he let anyone else do so. Of this, as
of everything else, the life of Socrates is available to us as a
paradigm, who not only himself avoided fighting everywhere, but did not let others fight either.

(4.5.1–2)

Whether we view the discourses from Arrian's perspective as
compiler or from Epictetus' perspective as teacher, they are most
conspicuously marked throughout by the figure of Socrates. No
other philosopher is named nearly as often. In the previous chapter we saw how Epictetus canonizes the Stoic Zeno and the Cynic
Diogenes as well as Socrates, but it is Socrates who primarily
authorizes everything Epictetus is trying to give his students in
terms of philosophical methodology, self-examination, and a life
model for them to imitate. This strikingly explicit coincidence
between Epictetus' objectives and Socrates makes the Stoicism
of the discourses particularly distinctive. In order to take the
measure of this point, we need to start from the role of Socrates
in the preceding Stoic tradition.

3.1 SOCRATES IN THE STOIC TRADITION

Stoic philosophers had drawn heavily on Plato's and Xenophon's Socrates—so much so that members of the school were happy to be called 'Socratics'. The details cover numerous doctrines in ethics, moral psychology, and theology, including the priority of the soul's good over everything else, the unity of the virtues, the identity of virtue with knowledge, and divine providence. The Stoics' hardest and most distinctive thesis was that genuine and complete happiness requires nothing except moral virtue. And on this above all they looked to Socrates, who had famously said at his trial: 'No harm can come to the good man in life or in death, and his circumstances are not ignored by the gods' (Plato, *Apology* 41d).

The Stoics had also treated Socrates' life as a virtual paradigm of Stoic wisdom's practical realization, and they were especially impressed by accounts of Socrates' fortitude, self-control, and imperviousness to physical and emotional stress. The exemplary Socrates—unflinching victim of a supremely unjust prosecution and sentence—became so popular with Roman moralists that Cicero and Seneca mention him in the same breath as such home-grown Roman saints as Regulus and Cato. When Epictetus aligns Stoic doctrines with Socrates or when he asks his students to reflect on Socrates' equanimity at his trial, imprisonment, and death, he is doing just what his Greek predecessors had done.

The great interest and distinctiveness of Epictetus' Socrates, or rather of Epictetus' dependence and reflection on Socrates, consist in the way the discourses appropriate and adapt Socratic dialectic; by which I mean the conversation Socrates practises in Plato's dialogues, including interpersonal discussion by question and answer, exposure of ignorance and inconsistency by means of the *elenchus*, and irony.[1] Too little Stoic literature has

---

[1] Zeno is the only Stoic who is attested to have written a work entitled *Elenchoi* (DL vii.4). His followers included in their dialectical curriculum 'knowledge of how to discourse correctly on arguments in question-and-answer form' (see Long 1996a: 87), as Epictetus himself acknowledges (1.7.3); but by the time the Stoa was founded, this specification had become too standard to allude specifically to Socratic

survived for me to claim that Epictetus was unique among his contemporaries in these respects, but I shall suggest reasons besides the silence of our sources for thinking this rather likely.[2] In adopting this interpretation, I do not mean that Epictetus regarded Socratic dialectic as more important than everything else in the Socratic record; his Socrates has a unity that helps us to understand why he made that figure the principal model of his own teaching method. But Epictetus' recourse to Socratic dialectic deserves our main attention in this chapter. Up to now it has been so neglected that modern studies of the discourses have lacked a crucial dimension.

Epictetus quotes or paraphrases or alludes to around 100 passages from sixteen of Plato's dialogues, nearly all of which are spoken there by Socrates. He was drawn to Plato not out of interest in Plato's speculative philosophy but because the Platonic dialogues were the richest source on Socrates' life, thought, and conversation. In the final text of the *Manual* (53), Arrian, no doubt reflecting Epictetus' priorities, concludes by giving Socrates the last say: first with a quotation of Socrates' words to Crito: 'If thus it [my execution] is pleasing to the gods, thus let it be' (Plato, *Crito* 43d), and then with an exact paraphrase of Plato's *Apology* (30c–d): 'Anytus and Meletus [Socrates' Athenian prosecutors] can kill me, but they cannot harm me.' Socrates' paradigmatic status is also summed up both in the *Manual* (51):

18 Socrates fulfilled himself by attending to nothing except reason in everything he encountered. And you, although you are not yet a Socrates, should live as someone who at least wants to be a Socrates.

and in the *Discourses*:

19 Now that Socrates is dead, the memory of what he did or said when alive is no less beneficial to people, or rather it is even more so. (4.1.169)

discussion. As for irony, it was officially excluded from the Stoic sage's character (*SVF* iii.630), whose dialectical virtues include 'irrefutability' (*anelenxia* (DL VII.47)).

[2] It has been suggested to me that Epictetus was probably influenced by his teacher Musonius. Maybe. But in the record of Musonius' discourses the allusions to Socrates are commonplace and do not in the least recall Socratic dialectic.

Epictetus concludes a discourse entitled *What is the Rule for Living?* with these words:

20   In the case of theory it is easy to examine and refute an ignorant person, but in the business of life no one submits to such testing and we hate the one who puts us through it. But Socrates used to say that an unexamined life is not worth living.   (1.26.17–18)

Here as elsewhere (3.12.15) Epictetus quotes one of the most memorable of Socrates' concluding sentences from the *Apology* (38a). His remarks about the hatred 'we' extend to anyone who makes us give an account of our lives comment on Socrates' explanation of his *elenctic* mission and the Athenian prosecution to which it brought him.

3.2 THE IMPRINT OF PLATO'S *GORGIAS*

In the preceding chapter we saw how Epictetus characterizes Socrates as the master of *elenctic* discourse. I now want to consider what this tells us about Epictetus' conception of Socrates' philosophical centrality, and what bearing the Socratic *elenchus* has on his own didactic practice. He draws, as we have just seen, on Plato's *Apology*, but the Platonic dialogue to which he attends most closely is the *Gorgias*. That is hardly an accident, for it is in this dialogue that Socrates makes his most explicit statements about the rationale of his dialectic in general and the *elenchus* in particular.

There can be little doubt that Epictetus knew the *Gorgias* more or less by heart, and he probably included it as one of the main readings for his formal curriculum. His liking for it was not due simply to its value as an exemplary exhibition of Socratic methodology. The *Gorgias* contains Plato's clearest and strongest statements of what many modern scholars take to be the core of Socratic ethics, more or less uninfluenced by Plato's own metaphysics and psychology. Here are some key examples, all of them echoed by Epictetus:

[A.] Nothing is worse than false beliefs about goodness and justice.
(458a; Epictetus 1.11.11)

[B.] It is worse to do wrong than to suffer wrong.

(474c ff.; Epictetus 4.1.122–3)

[C.] The paradigm wrongdoer, the tyrant, has the least power and freedom. (466b–e; Epictetus 4.1.51–3)

[D.] Every action is motivated by a desire for the good.

(468b; Epictetus 1.18.1–2; 3.3.2–4)

[E.] (as a corollary of D): No one does or wants what is bad, knowing or thinking that what he does or wants is bad [i.e. wrongdoing is involuntary]. (468d; Epictetus 2.26.1–2)

[F.] (as a further corollary of D): The wrongdoer does not do what he wants, but what (mistakenly) 'seems good to him'.

(468; Epictetus 4.1.3)

[G.] Untended diseases of the soul leave ineradicable imprints.

(525a; Epictetus 2.18.11)

The Stoic tradition had endorsed most if not all of these propositions, but Epictetus formulates them in ways that recall their original Socratic contexts in the *Gorgias*. Why would he do this? I propose two closely related reasons.

First, Socrates' three interlocutors in this dialogue *mutatis mutandis*, have great resonance and relevance for Epictetus' students: Gorgias, the celebrated professor of rhetoric, who (as presented by Plato) cares nothing for the ethical effects of his teaching on his audience; Polus, an over-eager discussant who cannot defend his conventionalist morality against Socratic challenges; and finally Callicles, the ambitious politician, whose 'might is right' conception of justice and extreme hedonism are pitted against Socrates' claims for the cultivation of a well-tempered soul. Epictetus' discourses include or allude to contemporary equivalents to Gorgias, Polus, and Callicles, each of whom is antithetical to the ideal he offers his students.

Secondly, Socrates in the *Gorgias* does not simply announce these startling propositions. He puts most of them forward within the context of his *elenctic* discussion with Polus. Shortly before Polus replaces Gorgias as Socrates' discussant, Socrates tells Gorgias:

What kind of man am I? One of those who would be pleased to be refuted [*elenchthentôn*] if I say something untrue, and pleased to refute if someone else does, yet not at all less pleased to be refuted than to refute.

For I think that being refuted is a greater good, in so far as it is a greater good for a man to get rid of the greatest badness himself than to rid someone else of it; for I think there is no badness for a man as great as a false belief about the things which our discussion is about now.

(458a = proposition A above)

In the course of his discussion with Polus, Socrates advances propositions C–F against Polus' attempts to defend the value of sheer rhetorical power untempered by moral knowledge. When Polus objects that Socrates' position is absurd, Socrates gives him a lesson in *elenctic* discussion, contrasting that with the kind of rhetoric practised in a court of law where defendants are often condemned on the basis of false witnesses. He acknowledges that Polus can adduce numerous witnesses who will attest to the falsehood of his own position, but he dismisses them as irrelevant to the kind of argument he and Polus are involved in: 'If I can't produce you, all alone by yourself, as a witness agreeing on the things I'm talking about, I think I have achieved nothing of any account in what our discussion is about. And I don't think you'll have achieved anything either unless I, all alone, bear witness for you, and you let all the others go' (472bc).

As the discussion proceeds, Socrates secures Polus' agreement to premisses that support his own position and conflict with Polus' initial support for sheer rhetorical power. Although Polus is scarcely convinced, he admits that Socrates' conclusions follow from the premisses that he himself has accepted (480e). Socrates' procedure in his final argument with Callicles is similar. At the outset he tells Callicles that, unless he can refute Socrates' thesis that doing injustice with impunity is the worst of evils—the thesis that Callicles vehemently opposes—Callicles will be 'discordant' with himself throughout his life (482b). This prediction anticipates the outcome of their argument; for, after eliciting a series of reluctant admissions from Callicles, Socrates tells him:

Those things that appeared true to us earlier in the previous arguments are held firm and bound down, so I say . . . by iron and adamantine arguments; so at least it appears thus far. And if you, or someone more vigorous than you, doesn't untie them, no one who says anything besides what I say now can be right. For my argument is always the same, that

I myself don't know how these things are, but no one I've ever met, just as now, is able to speak otherwise without being ridiculous.

(508e–509a)

The 'ridiculousness', Socrates explains, is conditional on the validity of his argument and the truth of its premisses. If these conditions are met, the inability of an opponent to refute his argument exposes such a person to the diagnosis of holding radically false beliefs about what is good for himself—beliefs, moreover, that actually conflict with his (and every person's) wish to flourish to the greatest extent possible.

Whether Socrates in Plato's *Gorgias* is entitled to claim these results need not concern us here. What we require is an outline of his *elenctic* strategy in order to compare it with Epictetus' procedural statements about the method. We may begin with passages that register his unmistakable allusions to Plato's dialogue.

Epictetus (almost certainly with Socratic irony) thanks a certain Lesbius for 'every day proving to me [*exelenchein*] that I know nothing' (3.20.19). On two occasions, when commending Socrates' *elenctic* methodology to his students, he cites Socrates' remark to Polus that the only witness he needs is his fellow disputant (2.12.5; 2.26.6). Most interestingly, he picks up Socrates' observation that his *elenctic* methodology benefits the questioner as well as the respondent, and turns the method into a metaphor about the way a philosopher should 'write' dialogues—not by literally inscribing different speakers but by examining himself, all alone:

21 Socrates didn't write? Who has written as much as he? But how? Because, since he couldn't always have someone to test [*elenchein*] his judgements or to be tested by him in turn, he made a habit of testing and examining himself, and was for ever trying out the use of some particular preconception. That is how a philosopher writes. But trifling phrases like 'he said' and 'I said' he leaves to others ... (2.1.32–3)[3]

---

[3] The text continues: 'either those who are blessed with leisure or those who are too stupid to calculate logical consequences.' With some hesitation, I suggest that the first group refers to the likes of Plato, who as a literal writer of dialogue understands the progression of the arguments he records, and the second group to people who merely parrot the form of Platonic dialogues. Epictetus may well be alluding to Socrates' definition of solitary thinking as 'writing in one's soul' (*Philebus* 39a). Special thanks to David Sedley for advice on this passage.

In a passage I have cited before (3.9.13; p. 12 above), Epictetus characterizes *elenctic* discussion as the essence of what it means to meet a philosopher, taking it, just like Socrates, to involve the participants' readiness to expose their beliefs to mutual scrutiny and susceptibility to refutation. He recognizes too the hostility that the practice frequently evokes (2.14.20; 3.1.19–23), and its lack of effectiveness in some instances (4.5.21).[4]

With this by way of introduction, we may now turn to passages that illustrate Epictetus' interpretation of the Socratic *elenchus* and his own practice of it.

3.3 THE SOCRATIC *ELENCHUS* IN THE DISCOURSES

Our best place to start is the discourse where Epictetus introduces Socrates as the paradigm for the *protreptic* and *elenctic* style. We are already familiar with an extract from this discourse (p. 56). Here is the entire piece (2.26):

22 (1) Every error involves a [mental] conflict. For since the erring person doesn't want to err but to be right, it's clear that he isn't doing what he wants. (2) For what does the thief want to achieve? His own interest. Therefore, if thieving is contrary to his interest, he is not doing what he wants.

(3) Further, every rational soul is naturally averse to conflict; but as long as someone is unaware of being involved in a conflict, there is nothing to prevent him from acting inconsistently. Yet, once he is aware, he is strongly constrained to abandon and shun the conflict, just as one who perceives that something is false is forcibly constrained to renounce the falsehood, though until it shows itself he assents to it as true.

(4) The person who can show an individual the conflict responsible for his error and clearly make him see how he is not doing what he wants to do and is doing what he does not want to do—that is the person who combines expertise in argument, exhortation [*protreptikos*], and refutation [*elenktikos*]. (5) For if a person can show this, the erring individual

---

[4] As a further allusion to the *Gorgias*, I note 4.1.128 where, in reminiscence of Socrates at *Gorgias* 506c, Epictetus formally reviews the premises to which his imaginary interlocutor has agreed.

will concede of his own accord; but as long as you fail to show it, don't be surprised if the other persists, because he is acting under the impression that he is right.

(6) That is why Socrates put his faith in this faculty and used to say: 'I make a habit of invoking no other witness to what I say; instead, I am always content with my interlocutor and call for his vote and summon him as a witness, and all on his own he is enough for me in place of everyone.' [Epictetus paraphrases *Gorgias* 474a.]

(7) That is because Socrates understood the motivations of a rational soul, and the way it inclines like a scale, whether you want it to or not. Show a conflict to a rational soul, and it will give it up. But if you don't point it out, blame yourself rather than the person who remains unpersuaded.

When Epictetus associates 'expertise in argument' (section 4) with the ability to expose a person's mental conflicts and reorient his volitions, we should not take him to be specifying a skill additional to *elenctic* and *protreptic*. These are rather the manifestation of Socrates' argumentative expertise. It is interesting, though, to note that the Greek I have translated by 'expertise in argument' (*deinos en logôi*) recalls the quality for which the rhetorician Gorgias was popularly renowned and that it is the purpose of Plato's so-named dialogue to transfer from Gorgias to Socrates. Our passage may appear naive in its presumption that no one is prepared to live with awareness of mental conflict. However, Epictetus acknowledges elsewhere (1.5, p. 105 below) that hardline sceptics are impervious to *elenctic* argumentation. For now, we should concentrate on how he implements the theory about exposure to mental conflict and the consequential reorientation of volition.

As we study Epictetus' conception of philosophy and its psychological foundations (Chapter 4), we shall see how he relies on a whole series of claims that are implicit in this passage. These include the need to start from awareness of one's own confusion about the application of moral concepts, the desire to resolve discrepant opinions about their application, and, above all, the assumption that human beings in general are lovers of truth and consistency and hostile to self-contradiction. He also relies on a further assumption that is not only fundamental to his entire outlook but crucial to our understanding of why he appropriated the Socratic *elenchus*. It may be stated as follows: human beings are innately equipped with the motivation to seek their own good, i.e. happiness, and to choose whatever means they think will promote that good. I will explain this assumption after we have observed his use of it in two *elenctic* passages.

First, a short but very telling instance:

23 *Can't people think that something is advantageous to themselves, and not choose it?*
They cannot.
What about the woman [Medea] who says: 'I understand the harmful things I intend to do, but passion rules my decisions'?[5]
The exact point is: she thinks that gratifying her passion and avenging herself on her husband are more advantageous than saving her children.
Yes; but she is deceived.
Show her clearly that she is deceived and she will not do it. But until you point this out to her, what can she follow except what appears to her [to be more advantageous]? (1.28.6–8)

Medea presents herself as *knowingly* doing what is harmful (killing her children) under the influence of passion, but Epictetus, like Socrates, denies that such an analysis of one's own motivations can ever be correct; he takes Medea, notwithstanding what she says, to be motivated by completely mistaken beliefs concerning where her own advantage lies. The passage says nothing explicitly about Medea's error being due to her suffering from conflicting beliefs, but that is the clear implication. We could represent Medea, as analysed by Epictetus, in the following imaginary conversation with him:

MEDEA. I want and therefore choose what is most advantageous to myself.
EPICTETUS. So does everyone.
MEDEA. Killing my children to spite Jason is what is most advantageous to me.

---

[5] Medea was one of the Stoics' favourite mythological paradigms for a noble nature gone wrong (see Gill 1983). Epictetus refers to her again at 2.17.19 and 4.13.14. The lines he cites above are from Euripides' *Medea* 1078–9.

EPICTETUS. That is a gross error. Nothing could be less advantageous to yourself than killing your children. Your anger is
causing you to be involved in the following conflict: wanting
what is most advantageous to yourself, and choosing what is
least advantageous to yourself.

Notice that Epictetus' diagnosis of Medea in **23** shares the lesson
of **22**: that persons suffering from conflicting beliefs will abandon
the conflict only when it is convincingly pointed out to them.
Both passages endorse the central Socratic proposition (proposition D above) that actions are always motivated by what the agent
(however mistakenly and self-deceptively) thinks will be good for
him or her. This intellectualist account of human motivation is,
of course, extremely controversial, but it was absolutely central to
Socratic ethics and completely endorsed by Epictetus. They were
equally adamant that what is truly advantageous for any person
must always coincide with what is morally right.

Next, I take a discourse (1.11) actually composed as a dialogue
between Epictetus and an unnamed government administrator
who has come to talk with him. In the course of conversation the
man tells Epictetus that he was recently made so distraught by an
illness affecting his young daughter that he could not bear to
remain at home until he got news of the child's recovery. The
point of the ensuing dialogue is to discover whether the father
was really motivated, as he professed to be, by love of his daughter. The text is too long to be cited in full, so I offer this translation of sections 5–15, flagging some of the most recognizable
Socratic features in brackets.

24 EPICTETUS. Do you think you acted correctly [*orthôs*]?
FATHER. I think I acted naturally [*physikôs*]. [*This is the belief to be examined.*]
EPICTETUS. Well, convince me that you acted naturally, and I will convince you that everything that occurs in accordance with nature
occurs correctly.
FATHER. This is the way all, or at least most, fathers feel.
EPICTETUS. I don't deny *that*; the question we are disputing is whether it
is correct. For by this reasoning we would have to say that tumours are
good for the body because they occur, and that erring is absolutely in

accordance with nature because nearly all of us, or at least most of us, err. Show me, then, how your behaviour is in accordance with nature. [*Pressure on the interlocutor to clarify his terms.*]

FATHER. I can't. Rather, you show me how it is not in accordance with nature and not correct. [*Confession of ignorance; inducement of aporia.*]

EPICTETUS. Well, if we were investigating light and dark, what criterion would we invoke to distinguish between them?

FATHER. Sight.

EPICTETUS. And if the question were about temperature or texture?

FATHER. Touch.

EPICTETUS. Accordingly, since our dispute is about things in accordance with nature and what occurs correctly or incorrectly, what criterion do you want us to adopt? [*Socratic style of analogical or inductive inference.*]

FATHER. I don't know. [*Further confession of ignorance, and aporia.*]

EPICTETUS. Ignorance about the criterion of colours and smells and flavours may not be very harmful; but do you think that someone ignorant of the criterion of things good and bad and in accordance with or contrary to nature is only slightly harmed?

FATHER. No, that is the greatest harm.

EPICTETUS. Tell me, is everyone's opinion concerning what is fine and proper correct? Does that apply to all the opinions that Jews and Syrians and Egyptians and Romans hold on the subject of food?

FATHER. How could that be possible?

EPICTETUS. Presumably it is absolutely necessary that if the Egyptians' opinions are correct, the others' are not, and if the Jews' are fine, the others' are not?

FATHER. Certainly.

EPICTETUS. Where ignorance exists, there also exists lack of learning and lack of training concerning essentials.

FATHER. I agree.

EPICTETUS. Now that you are aware of this, in future you will concentrate your mind on nothing else than learning the criterion of what accords with nature and using it in order to make judgements concerning particular cases.

Epictetus now gets the father to agree that love of one's family and good reasoning (*eulogiston*) are mutually consistent, with the implication that, if one of them is in accordance with nature and correct, the other must be so too. Pressed by Epictetus, the father accepts that abandoning his daughter was not a well-reasoned act. Could it, then, have been motivated, as he initially claimed, by love? Through a further induction, the father is led to agree that, if the child's mother and others responsible for the child's welfare had acted like himself, their behaviour would not have been loving. Thus, Epictetus concludes, the father, contrary to his initial belief, was motivated, not by an *excusably natural* love for his daughter, but by erroneous reasoning about the *properly natural* and correct thing to do. The father ran away, he concludes, because that was what mistakenly 'seemed good to him'.[6]

The Socratic features of this *elenchus* are too obvious to need full articulation. By the end, the father has been brought to agree (1) that his protestations of love for his daughter conflict with the standards of love he would apply to other people, and (2) that his initial appeal to the *naturalness* of his action, in the sense of its being what the majority of fathers would do, is incompatible with what he acknowledges to be *natural* in the sense of being the normative and properly rational behaviour. The point of the exercise is also thoroughly Socratic—not to blame or criticize the father but to show him how his judgement went astray, failing to fit the affection that he took to be his motive.

In order to understand the rationale behind Epictetus' Socratic mode of argumentation, we need to clarify his claim that, although (1) human beings are innately motivated to seek their own happiness and to prefer right to wrong, they typically (2) hold beliefs that conflict with the attainment of these objectives. Here is one of his clearest statements, taken from the beginning of the discourse entitled 'The starting point of philosophy' (2.11.1–8):

25 To make an authentic start on philosophy and to enter it at the front door, a person needs to be aware of his own weakness and incapacity concerning absolute essentials. For in regard to a right-angled triangle

---

[6] Throughout Epictetus' refutation, he is careful to describe the father's wrongly chosen act by the expression 'what seemed good to you' (*hoti edoxen soi*). Thus he explicitly registers Socrates' fundamental distinction in the *Gorgias* (see proposition F, p. 71) between doing what one thinks (perhaps mistakenly) will bring about one's good (the universal human desideratum) and doing what one 'wants' (getting that desideratum).

or a half-tone, we came into the world without any natural concept; it is through some expert instruction that we learn each of these, and consequently people who don't know them don't think that they do. But, on the other hand, who has entered the world without an innate concept [*emphytos ennoia*] of good and bad, fine and ugly, fitting and unfitting, and of happiness, propriety, and what is due and what one should and should not do?

For this reason, we all use these terms and try to adapt our preconceptions [about them] to particular instances, saying: 'He has done well, or as he should, or as he should not; he has been unfortunate, or fortunate; he is just, or unjust.' Which of us is sparing in using these terms? Which of us holds back his use of them until he learns to use them, like those who are ignorant of lines or sounds? The explanation is that we came into the world already instructed in this area to some extent by nature, and starting from this we have added on our own opinion.

By Zeus, you are right; I do know by nature, don't I, what is fine and ugly? Have I no conception of them?
You do.
Don't I apply the conception to particular instances?
You do.
Don't I apply it well?
That's where the whole question lies, and that's where opinion comes to be added. Because, starting from those concepts they agree on, people get into conflicts as a result of applying them to instances where the concepts don't fit.

If I had to choose only one excerpt from the discourses, to illustrate the essence of Epictetus' educational assumptions and methodology, it would be this one. His essential point is that everyone is *innately* equipped with a moral sense, or rather a shared stock of general concepts that furnish the basic capacity for making objective discriminations between good and bad, and so on. Because people naturally have this endowment, they tend to think, like his interlocutor here, that they *know* the specifics of goodness and happiness, or right and wrong, and can therefore make correct value judgements in particular cases. When Epictetus draws attention to the 'conflicts' that arise from misapplication of the natural concepts, he is referring not only to disagreements between persons but also to conflicts or contradictions that arise for the same reason within one person, like Medea.

How does Epictetus' theory about innate concepts of value relate to his use of the Socratic *elenchus*, and what does he mean by positing these concepts? I will approach these questions by taking the second first.

The innate concepts or 'preconceptions' (*prolêpseis*), as he often calls them, are explained as follows:

26 Preconceptions are common to all people, and one preconception does not conflict with another. For which of us does not take it that a good thing is advantageous and choiceworthy, and something to be sought and pursued in every circumstance? Which of us does not take it that justice is something honourable and fitting? When, then, does conflict occur? In the application of preconceptions to particular instances, as when someone says:

He acted in a fine way; he is courageous.

But someone else retorts:

No, he's crazy.   (1.22.1–2; cf. 4.1.44–5)

Here Epictetus makes two big claims concerning people's innate concepts of value: first, any two people have the same preconception about the same item; or, to put it logically, they agree about the connotation of a term such as 'good'. Secondly, people's stock of preconceptions form a mutually consistent set of evaluative concepts or meanings. We may recall his comment in the preceding passage about 'starting from those [agreed] concepts'.

These are obviously very bold claims. However, their boldness is tempered by a very important qualification. What gives preconceptions their universality and mutual consistency is their extremely general content: everyone, for instance, conceives 'good' things to be advantageous and choiceworthy, and 'bad' things to be harmful and undesirable, irrespective of what they actually take to be good or bad in particular instances.

More controversial, it may seem, is the claim that such universal and mutually consistent attitudes also pertain to the moral realm of justice, propriety, and so forth. Epictetus could reasonably respond that people in general do agree on the positive connotations of justice and on the negative connotations of injustice, taking these concepts or terms quite generally. Further, in claiming that these preconceptions are 'innate', his point is not that newborn infants are fully equipped with them but that our basic evaluative and moral propensities are hardwired and genetically programmed, as we would say today: they are not, in their general content, a cultural accretion.

He is emphatically not saying that preconceptions are sufficient criteria on their own to guide our judgements. We do not know what particular things are good simply by having the preconception of goodness as something profitable. All we know is an essential property of goodness. We need Stoic doctrine in order to learn that conventional goods such as health or wealth are not strictly good nor their opposites strictly bad because they are not unequivocally profitable or harmful respectively, or to learn that happiness does not consist in a succession of pleasurable sensations and an absence of painful ones. Our preconceptions need to be articulated by definitions far more precise than their 'innate' content involves; and we need unremitting training in order to make our conduct consonant with these refinements. The role of preconceptions is none the less fundamental and primary in Epictetus' philosophy.

If he is right, human beings all agree in wanting to flourish, to have their desires for happiness fulfilled, to possess what is really good and to avoid what is really harmful, and to favour justice over injustice. His task, as he sees it, is to show how people's particular value judgements are typically at odds with their ethical preconceptions, and thus people fail to achieve the happiness and correct behaviour they naturally want.

We can now identify a very exact role for the Socratic *elenchus* to play in Epictetus' educational agenda. The Socrates of the *Gorgias* does not talk about innate and universal preconceptions of happiness and so forth, but, if Gregory Vlastos (1983, 1994a) was broadly right in his brilliant analysis of the Socratic *elenchus*, Socrates' confidence in this mode of argument presumes that his interlocutors do have true beliefs that the *elenchus* can bring to light.

Vlastos asked why Socrates could claim, as he does in the *Gorgias*, that the outcome of his *elenctic* arguments was not simply a demonstration of the interlocutor's inconsistency but also an endorsement of Socrates' counter-proposal (for instance, that doing injustice is worse than suffering it). The answer, Vlastos proposed, requires a twofold assumption: first, that any set of entirely consistent beliefs must be true; secondly, and still more importantly, that whoever has a false moral belief will always have at the same time true moral beliefs entailing the negation of that false belief. Socrates finds that his own moral beliefs, because their consistency has been exhaustively tested, satisfy the first assumption; and in the *elenchus* he elicits from his interlocutor *latent* but true moral beliefs that are found to cohere with Socrates' own judgements.

I find Vlastos' interpretation of the Socratic *elenchus* quite persuasive. But even if it is rejected as regards the Platonic Socrates, it closely matches Epictetus' theory and practice. He too assumes that its qualified practitioner (ideally Socrates) has the consistently true moral beliefs that he can draw on to correct the erring person, and Epictetus' innate preconceptions play a role very similar to the role of latent but true moral beliefs in Vlastos' account of Socrates. Both philosophers are optimistic rationalists in the following sense: they assume, first, that human beings are naturally lovers of truth and consistency, and secondly, that they possess mental and moral resources that, when brought to light and properly articulated, can cause them to abandon their false and inconsistent moral beliefs.

However, the optimistic rationalism can be efficacious only when two further conditions are satisfied: the teacher or dialectician needs to approximate to Socrates' skills and insights, and his interlocutor must be susceptible to conversion instead of remaining an obdurate defender of his initial position. Before looking at Epictetus' representation of these two further conditions, I need to say something more about his appropriation of Socratic dialectic and its integration with his own methodology.

The criterial role and natural origin of preconceptions goes back to early Stoicism, but Epictetus was probably alone in making them equivalent to an *innate* moral sense. Platonism has previously been suggested as an influence on him, and that may be so in part; but Epictetus is not invoking Plato's fully-fledged theory that a learner *after* birth can *recollect* his prenatal

acquaintance with everlasting truths. As we have seen, the Plato
that interests Epictetus is the author of what we today call the
early Socratic dialogues.

I have already noted the importance Epictetus attaches to the
Socratic injunction on the worthlessness of living an 'unexamined life'. Both in Plato and in Epictetus *elenctic* discussion is a
methodology that gets its participants to examine their beliefs by
exposing unrecognized inconsistencies and involuntary ignorance. Plato's Socrates regularly asks his opinionated interlocutors to answer questions about 'what' some moral concept
(piety or courage, for instance) 'is', with a view to subjecting
their responses to *elenctic* examination.

Epictetus follows suit. He characterizes Socrates as a person
who said that 'the beginning of education' is the 'scrutiny of
terms' (1.17.12), and in hyperbolical but authentically Socratic
style he labels anyone who fails to know what basic values are as
'going around deaf and blind, thinking he is someone when he is
nothing' (2.24.19). More particularly, he connects the standard
Socratic question, 'What is *x*?', with his own diagnosis of the way
people typically err: by 'heedlessly applying their preconceptions to particular instances' (4.1.41; cf. **25**):

27 This . . . is the cause of everyone's miseries. We differ in our opinions.
One person thinks he is sick; no way, but he is not applying his preconceptions. Another thinks he is a pauper, another that he has a harsh
mother or father, and another that Caesar is not gracious to him. This is
one thing only—ignorance of how to apply preconceptions. For who
does not have a preconception of badness, that it is harmful, to be avoided, to be banished in every way? (4.1.42–3)

Epictetus repeats his point that preconceptions themselves do
not conflict with one another, and proceeds:

28 What, then, is this bad thing that is harmful and to be avoided? A person says he is not Caesar's friend.[7] He has gone off the right track,
missed the right application, he is ailing. He is seeking what has nothing

---

[7] On the semi-official status of being 'Caesar's friend', see Millar (1977: 110–22).
Epictetus satirizes the danger and 'enslavement' it might involve at 4.1.47–50, following **28**.

to do with the matter in hand. Because if he succeeds in being Caesar's friend, he has no less failed in his quest. For what is it that every person is seeking? To be serene, to be happy, to do everything as he wants, not to be impeded or constrained. So when someone becomes Caesar's friend, has he ceased to be impeded or constrained? Is he serene and flourishing? (4.1.45–6)

We are now in a position to see that Epictetus does not simply parrot the Socratic *elenchus* but adapts it to his own didactic purposes, assisted by his special concept of universal and correct preconceptions. He may, as we noted in his refutation of the would-be loving father, use interpersonal dialogue that exactly mimics the procedures and goals of Socratic dialectic, and he offers his students a lesson in how to practise that, as we shall see in Section 3.4. But his preferred procedure in his intimate dealings with students is to show them how to practise the *elenchus* on themselves by giving them such examples as the one above rather than engaging them directly in dialogue. In the same way, he urges them to interrogate their own impressions of particular things:

29 Just as Socrates used to say we should not live an unexamined life, so we should not accept an unexamined impression, but should say: 'Wait, let me see who you are and where you are coming from . . . Do you have your guarantee from nature, which every impression that is to be accepted should have?' (3.12.15)

Epictetus repeatedly expresses his cardinal rule of life in the formula: 'making correct use of impressions'.[8] That formula and the model of the mind to which it belongs are neither Socratic nor Platonic. I should also note that Epictetus does not imitate Socrates' use of the *elenchus* as an instrument for arriving at purely negative conclusions concerning the concept under investigation, as in such short Platonic dialogues as *Euthyphro*. However, the material I have discussed in this chapter proves that Epictetus had an acute understanding of the positive methodology and goals of the Socratic *elenchus*. His main departure from it was in

[8] e.g. 1.1.7; 1.3.4; 1.6.13; 1.7.33; 1.12.34; 1.20.15; see also p. 214 below.

training his students to engage in dialogue with their individual selves and to use this as their principal instrument of moral progress.

3.4 A LESSON IN THE USE AND ABUSE OF SOCRATIC DIALECTIC

Some of Epictetus' students had the ambition to become professional teachers of Stoicism. For their benefit he delivered a fascinating discourse on how to engage in discussion with a lay person (2.12). This provides a further perspective on his interpretation of the Socratic paradigm in general and the Socratic *elenchus* in particular. As often, the text is difficult to interpret in many of its details:

30   Our Stoic authorities have been quite precise in specifying the knowledge necessary for engaging in discussion; but we are quite untrained in our proper application of it. Give any of us a layman as our interlocutor, and we are at a loss in dealing with that person. Having stirred him a little . . . we are unable to handle him further, and either we abuse him or mock him, saying:

He's a layman; it's impossible to deal with him.

Yet, when a real guide finds someone going astray, he leads him to the right path instead of mocking or abusing him and going away. You yourself, then, should show him the truth, and you will see that he does follow; but as long as you don't show him, don't mock him, but rather be aware of your own incapacity.

How did Socrates act?

He made a habit of compelling his interlocutor to be his witness, and did not need another witness . . . [Epictetus refers to *Gorgias* 474a, p. 75 above] because he exposed the implications of that person's concepts (*ennoiai*) so clearly that whoever it was became aware of his inconsistency and gave it up . . .[9]

---

[9] Here Epictetus engages in a made-up example of Socratic dialogue, to illustrate how to expose a person's contradictory beliefs about 'malice' (*phthonos*). The text is too condensed to make the argument thoroughly clear. I conjecture that it should have the following structure.

The interlocutor starts by taking malice to be pleasure taken in someone else's misfortunes (cf. Plato, *Philebus* 48bc). Under challenge, he accepts that malice is a

Socrates did not say: 'Define malice for me', and then, when it had been defined, respond with the words: 'A bad definition—for the *definiens* [definition] is not extensionally equivalent to the *definiendum* [thing to be defined].'[10] Laymen find such technical jargon tiresome and difficult, but *we* can't give it up. Yet, we are quite unable to stir them when we do use terms that enable them, by focusing on their own impressions, to respond yes or no. Understandably, then, at least those of us who are cautious, recognize our inability and give up the matter. But when the impatient ones, who are more numerous, are involved in it, they get flustered and cause fluster, and finally walk away, after an exchange of abuse.

The first and chief thing about Socrates was that he never got worked up in a discussion, never uttered anything abusive or aggressive, but put up with others' abuse . . . What then? Well, nowadays the thing isn't very safe, especially in Rome. (2.12.1–17)

Epictetus explains that any current practitioner of Socratic dialectic 'had clearly better not do it in a corner'.[11] Rather:

31 He needs to approach a wealthy man of consular rank, as it might be, and ask him [such typical Socratic questions as]:

I say, can you tell me to whom you have entrusted your horses?
I can.
To some random person unacquainted with horsemanship?
Certainly not.
And to whom have you entrusted your gold or your silver or your clothes?
Again, not to just anyone.
Have you already thought of entrusting your own body to someone, to look after it?
Of course.
Presumably to somone experienced in physical training or medicine?
Yes.

painful emotion, contradicting his initial claim. He then agrees that it cannot be a pain aroused by others' misfortunes. So he is prompted to redefine malice as pain taken in someone else's good fortunes (cf. *SVF* i.434), a complete reversal of his starting-point.

[10] I draw on Barnes (1997: 29), for this skilful translation of Epictetus' logical jargon.

[11] See Plato, *Gorgias* 485d, where Callicles charges Socrates with 'twittering in a corner with three or four young men'.

Are these your chief possessions, or do you have something else super-
ior to all of them?
What sort of thing do you mean?
That which uses them, for heaven's sake, and judges and deliberates
each thing.
You mean the soul, I suppose?
Correct; that's just what I mean.
*For heaven's sake, I regard this as far superior to the rest of my posses-
sions.*
Can you say, then, in what way you have cared for your soul? For it's not
likely that as wise and politically prominent a man as you should care-
lessly and randomly let your chief possession be neglected and ruined?
Certainly not.
But have you yourself cared for it? Did you learn to do so from someone,
or did you discover that by yourself?
So now there's the danger that, first, he will say:
What business is it of yours, my fine fellow? Are you my master?
And then, if you persist in bothering him, he may raise his hand and box
your ears. There was a time when I myself was very keen on this activ-
ity, before I fell into my present situation.   (2.12.17–25)

What are we to make of this discourse? Is it a recommendation
to imitate Socrates or the reverse? Is the conclusion an honest
confession of Epictetus' own shortcomings as a discussant with a
lay person? How are we to interpret the praise of Socrates for his
effectiveness in using ordinary language, the remark that 'we'
cannot dispense with technical terms, and the injunction about
having to engage a prominent person out in the open?
　　The answer to all of these questions, I believe, requires us to
interpret the entire text as a lesson to the students in how to
apply, or rather how *not* to apply, the Socratic *elenchus* in the
everyday world of their own time.
　　As regards the statement, 'we' can't dispense with technical
terms, Jonathan Barnes has proposed that 'Epictetus is criticizing his fellow Stoics for their penchant for jargon: he is not beating his own breast; the first person plural indicates a polite
complicity rather than an honest confession'.[12] I am sure this is
right. But, if Epictetus is recommending his students to imitate

---

[12] Barnes (1997: 29).

Socrates' use of ordinary language, what does he expect them to make of his parody of Socratic questions in the conversation with the prominent Roman, the angry response it evokes, and his apparent admission of such an encounter's applicability to his youthful self at Rome?

Maybe Epictetus did have such a cautionary experience before his exile under Domitian's collective expulsion of philosophers in AD 95, but I take him in any case to be saying: Try to converse with your interlocutors on their own ground, and even in your use of Socratically leading questions, be careful not to proceed in a peremptory manner that will simply antagonize them. The advice to engage a big official is almost certainly ironical. That is to say, Epictetus is telling his students that they should not try to outdo Socrates or worry about Callicles' taunt of Socrates for preferring conversation with young men to engaging in politics (see n. 11 above). We should think of Epictetus as recommending his students to use discourse that is appropriate to their interlocutor's mindset and social status.

Readers of Plato are familiar with the way Socrates' dialectical style changes in relation to his discussants; the *Gorgias*, as it moves from Gorgias to Polus to Callicles, is a prime example. Similarly we find Epictetus varying his dialectic in relation to the age and background of the individuals he talks to. When he meets Maximus (3.7), an administrator and an Epicurean, he converses with him, as one philosopher to another, and does not avoid technicalities. In contrast, when a rhetorician on his way to Rome for a lawsuit consults him about his business (3.9), he informs the man at the beginning of their conversation that the kind of advice he is qualified to offer him cannot be provided in a brief encounter (see p. 12).

Here we observe Epictetus drawing on the Platonic idea of dialectic as a cooperative undertaking, wherein the questioner or philosopher no less than the respondent submits his judgements to examination. Viewed in the light of this passage, the mock questioning of the prominent Roman at the end of 31 was bound to fail because the conversation lacked the give and take and the mutual respect and encouragement of a properly Socratic encounter.

3.5 SELF-EXAMINATION AND
SELF-DISCOVERY

The material I have presented in this chapter reinforces my objections to calling the discourses diatribes or sermons. These labels treat Epictetus' pithy anecdotes, vivid and abrupt sentences, and hyperbole and exhortation as if they were the core and goal of his didactic style. While Epictetus constantly uses these rhetorical devices, his purpose in doing so is not simply to preach, but to get his students to see for themselves, first that they potentially have all the resources they need for a good and fulfilling life, and, secondly, that their own reasoning, self-scrutiny, and discipline are necessary to activate these resources.

Every discourse has this probative purpose. The proofs rarely have a strict logical form, but they contain at least implicit premisses and explicit conclusions. Their cogency is dialectical rather than formal. What I mean is that the discourses are addressed to individuals under the condition that they 'want' to live lives free from frustration and emotional disquiet. Epictetus does not think that his arguments can be effective in the abstract. He presupposes that he is addressing people who want to live free from error and distress. His proofs are conditional on these wants (see Section 4.3). They are not addressed to persons who choose to live, in his stark words, as 'slaves'.

By his time, Stoicism had become a highly scholastic system. Stoic philosophers were notorious for their interest in logical paradoxes, and their ethics and physics involved numerous fine distinctions with their own technical terminology. Epictetus does not object to these refinements, but he scarcely deals with them in the surviving discourses. The reason, as he constantly explains, is that such technicalities should be the province of very advanced students. His own chief concern is with what he calls 'the first topic' of philosophy—'desires and aversions'—which has as its goal to ensure that a person does not fail in his desires or have experiences he does not want (3.2.1, see Section 4.4). His focus on Socrates is a very strong sign of his determination to return Stoicism to its primary goal of radically reshaping people's values and goals.

Epictetus' warnings against confusing scholastic learning with genuine philosophical progress can give the impression that he disparages logical expertise or careful argument. Against this, it is only necessary to read 1.17. Here he justifies the criterial and critical functions of logic by appealing not only to the old Stoic authorities but also to Socrates, who insisted on beginning with 'the examination of words and asking what each means' (1.17.12). The logic that Epictetus regards as fundamental is any normal person's capacity to reflect on the grounds and consistency of his individual beliefs and desires and motivations. This explains why he himself avoids the technical terms of traditional Stoicism. He does not expound doctrines that are expressed in these ways. Instead, as he urges in the dialectical lesson of 2.12 (**30–1**), he tries to engage his audience by means of everyday terms such as desire, purpose, freedom, and happiness, with a minimal reference to esoteric theory.

His discourses are dialectical lessons—invitations to his audience to examine themselves by thinking about these everyday terms and comparing what they take them to mean with the proposals Epictetus offers himself. Thus, he takes it to be self-evident that people want their desires to be fulfilled. Yet, their actual desires are frequently frustrated and consequently cause them distress. The problem here, he suggests, is not in wanting a desire to be fulfilled; human beings naturally seek the fulfilment of their desires. Accordingly, the remedy for frustration is to focus one's desires exclusively within the area where success is assured.

How does Epictetus prove that there is any such area? In order to do this, he cannot simply appeal to people's untutored beliefs or preconceptions. However, he proceeds in ways that, instead of being merely dogmatic or prescriptive, require people to examine themselves and answer a set of questions. Here is a striking example (for the full context of the passage, see p. 209):

32 My friend, you have a volition (*prohairesis*) that is by nature unimpeded and unconstrained. I will prove it to you, first in the sphere of assent. Can anyone prevent you from assenting to a truth?
   No one can.

Can anyone compel you to accept a falsehood?
No one can.
Do you see that in this sphere you have a faculty of volition that is unimpeded, unconstrained, unhindered. Come now, is it different in the sphere of desire and impulse? What can overcome an impulse except another impulse? What can overcome a desire or an aversion except another desire or aversion?
Yet if someone threatens me with fear of death, he does constrain me.
What constrains you is not the threat but your decision that it is better to do something else rather than die. (1.17.21–5)

There is an implicit doctrine underlying the questions and responses that constitute Epictetus' proof. That doctrine, which he never tires of repeating, is the absolute autonomy, in principle, of volition or will (*prohairesis*). What Epictetus includes under this term is each person's individual self with the capacities of reason, desire, intention, and reflexive consciousness (see Section 8.1). Because he takes this autonomous faculty to be God's special gift to our species (1.1.12, p. 63 above), the doctrine is central not only to his ethics and logic, but also to his philosophy of nature.

Epictetus' distinctive focus on *prohairesis* has often been noted. Likewise, his lack of interest in the problems of fate and responsibility that had preoccupied Chrysippus. Yet, there is still a strong tendency to regard Epictetus as simply an orthodox Stoic. I prefer to view him as a more independent thinker and educator, Stoic in his general orientation but more Socratic than Stoic in some of his emphasis and methodology. His unequivocal faith in autonomous volition and in human beings' innate preconceptions of goodness and badness are quite distinctive and central to his philosophy. They also explain why his proofs and *protreptic* have so marked a Socratic imprint. Like the Socrates of Plato's early dialogues, Epictetus does not impose elaborate doctrines on his audience. Rather, he exhorts them to try to know themselves, to practise self-examination, and to discover a source of goodness that is purely internal, independent of outward contingencies, yet capable of generating both personal happiness and integrity.

Epictetus' greatness as a philosopher is his realization that the only ethical argument that can be suitable to human dignity is argument that persons are shown how to apply to themselves, doing so not because they are told their duty by an authority but because they are presented with reasons they are competent to examine, test, and, if they find them cogent, internalize. Notwithstanding his Stoic identity, Epictetus drew the inspiration for his *protreptic* and proof from Plato's Socrates.

3.6 THE ROMAN SOCRATES

There is much more to Epictetus' reflection of Socrates than I have treated in this chapter. Socrates' imprint is present on almost every page of the discourses; for, apart from appropriating and adapting Socratic methodology, Epictetus constantly mentions the exemplary moments of Socrates' behaviour at and after his trial. In addition, he likes to idealize and update Socrates, insisting, against the historical record, that he was a great family man (3.26.23) and even a model of cleanliness (4.11.19)! In the *Manual* we find Socrates cited for two of Epictetus' constant themes: judgements, not things, are what disturb people (*Ench.* 5); and the imperative never to relax attention to one's reason (*Ench.* 51).

In view of all this, it is curious that scholars in general have paid so little attention to the Socratic paradigm in Epictetus. One reason must be the authority exercised by the books of Adolf Bonhöffer (1890, 1894), where Epictetus is presented as simply a Stoic through and through with little attention given to the style and method of the discourses. Another reason is the fact that the discourses, for the most part, are very different from the Socratic conversations composed by Plato and Xenophon, which involve a cast of distinct and clearly drawn characters. A third reason, deeper than either of these, could be the perception that Epictetus cannot be authentically Socratic because he does not repeatedly declare his own ignorance or engage in apparently open-ended exploration of ethical questions.

Actually, however, Epictetus is consistently reticent and self-deprecating about his own competence and identity as a philosopher (see Section 4.6). We have noticed the modesty and puzzlement he expects from beginning students, and we have seen examples of his irony. Like Plato's Socrates, he professes no interest in speculation about the exact details of the physical world (see p. 149). Whether Plato's Socratic dialogues are as open-ended as some of them appear to be on the surface, and whether his Socrates is sincere or unqualified in his confessions of ignorance are matters of scholarly controversy. Even if we respond affirmatively to both questions, we must admit that Plato's Socrates, even in the so-called Socratic dialogues, strenuously argues for such doctrines as those I listed when outlining the *Gorgias*. Historically speaking, Epictetus' Socratic paradigm has a lot going for it.

He was obviously aware that Stoicism, however much it was prefigured by Socrates, was a subsequent development. Under his Stoic identity he presents himself as a pedagogue with a range of definite lessons to teach his students. Given his time and place, as a Graeco-Roman philosopher training Graeco-Roman youths, Epictetus had to adapt the Socratic paradigm to some extent. And so his Socrates, like himself, is a paternalist rather than a paederastic mentor, which would not have suited the society of his day. What we are left with, when all due qualifications are made, is the most creative appropriation of Socrates subsequent to the works of Plato and Xenophon.

FURTHER READING AND NOTES

Socrates in the Stoic Tradition

For the seminal influence of Socrates on Stoicism, see Long (1988), Sedley (1993), Van der Waerdt (1994), and Alesse (2000). The Stoic concept of dialectic is discussed by Long (1978) (last pages on Epictetus) with texts and commentary in LS 31. Socrates' enormous importance to Epictetus is not brought out in the classic works of Bonhöffer (1890, 1894), while Schweingruber (1943) offers little more than an incomplete catalogue of Epictetus' Socratic allusions. Studies that discuss Epictetus' treatment of Socrates comprehensively and with some appreciation of its bearing on his methodology include Döring

(1979) and Gourinat (forthcoming). Döring's monograph should also be consulted on the role of Socrates in the work of Seneca and Dio Chrysostom.

The Imprint of Plato's Gorgias

Jagu (1946) collects and discusses most of Epictetus' allusions to passages in Plato's dialogues. He takes little interest in Epictetus' remarks on Socratic dialectic, but he does show how Epictetus drew largely on Plato, especially the *Gorgias* (see his pp. 71–86), rather than Xenophon (p. 50) for his portrayal of Socrates. I take my translations of the *Gorgias* from Irwin (1979). On the *Gorgias* as prime source for Socratic ethics, see Vlastos 1991.

The Socratic elenchus in the Discourses

This is briefly treated by Döring (1979: 74–6). For full translation with commentary of Epictetus 1.11, see Dobbin (1998). Vlastos discusses the Socratic *elenchus* in Vlastos (1983 = Vlastos 1994a) and also in Vlastos (1991). For his debate with Kraut, see Kraut (1983) and Vlastos (1994a). In aligning Epictetus with Vlastos's treatment of the Socratic *elenchus*, I draw on Long (2000: 91–2). In Platonism after the time of Epictetus, the role I assign to 'innate preconceptions' in his adaptation of the Socratic *elenchus* is played by 'common notions' (*koinai ennoiai*). Olympiodorus, in his commentary on Plato's *Gorgias*, describes 'common notions' (from which all demonstrative proof should start) as including 'God-given' foundations for acting rightly (see Westerink 1970: 51). According to Olympiodorus, Socrates refutes Gorgias by showing that Gorgias' admission that an orator may do wrong is inconsistent with Gorgias' endorsement of the 'common notion' that an orator knows what is right (Westerink 1970: 63). Tarrant (2000: 116–17) finds that 'While Olympiodorus has actually anticipated many of Vlastos' claims about Socrates' arguments, in particular about the presence of true moral beliefs residing within questioner and interlocutor, he explains this with reference to one's awareness (conscious or unconscious) of common notions.'

As I indicated in Chapter 2 (p. 56), Epictetus takes properly Socratic discourse to combine *protreptic* and *elenctic*. I emphasize this point again, as a response to Kamtekar (1998: 154). Acknowledging Epictetus' dependence on Socrates, for his insistence on the need to remove conceit, she finds a 'marked departure from Socrates' in Epictetus' equal insistence on the need to remove diffidence (*apistia*). She cites 3.14.8–9 where Epictetus makes this point, and then adds:

'The *elenchus* removes conceit, and this is what Socrates does first.' In response, I remark that the transmitted text breaks off here, so we do not know whether Epictetus said what Socrates 'does second'. But since he never finds Socrates falling short in any way, it is a fair guess that he regarded the *protreptic* aspect of Socratic discourse as satisfying his point about diffidence.

Repici (1993) asks what role *elenchus* might have played in Stoic logical theory, but she does not consider its educational functions in Epictetus' methodology.

Impressions and Preconceptions

Material on the early Stoic concept of impressions (*phantasiai*) is collected and discussed in LS 39–40. For further discussion, see Inwood (1985) and Annas (1992). I have discussed Epictetus' concept of the 'correct use of impressions' in Long (1991).

The classic study of Stoic concepts (*ennoiai*) and preconceptions (*prolêpseis*) is Sandbach (1971), who indicates Epictetus' novelty in treating the latter as 'innate' ideas in the moral domain. Epictetus devotes an entire discourse (1.22) to preconceptions, well translated and discussed by Dobbin (1998), who makes the good suggestion (p. 188) that the originalities in Epictetus' treatment of them were motivated by the need to respond to Sceptical criticism; see also 2.11 and 2.17.

CHAPTER 4

Philosophy and Pedagogy

> Philosophizing is virtually this—enquiry into how it is possible to employ desire and aversion without hindrance.
>
> (3.14.10)

4.1 RATIONALITY, EMPIRICISM, EUDAIMONISM

Epictetus' conception of philosophy can be summed up as the Stoic 'art of life' (1.15.2), but in his general remarks on the subject he does not specify his Stoic affiliation as such. Instead, he offers thoughts about the nature and attractions of philosophy in ways that he can expect to interest those who may have been tempted by rival systems. Not only Stoicism but also expressions associated with other schools contribute to his remarks on the nature and aims of philosophy. He particularly aligns himself, as we have just seen, with Plato's Socrates. The breadth of his canvas serves two intimately related functions.

First, he presents philosophy as the requisite form of 'enquiry' for anyone who, having become dissatisfied with living on the basis of mere 'opinion', is prepared to investigate and try to establish exact criteria for an excellent and consistently satisfying life (2.11.23). Philosophy is what persons need in order to become properly themselves, to fulfil their natures, to achieve the happiness that is everyone's natural goal. It is the required route for anyone who wants 'to live well'. Epictetus can expect broad agreement to this general specification of philosophy across the competing schools of his day.

Secondly, however, he leaves his audience in no final doubt that there is only one philosophy worthy of the name, and that this philosophy is not a practice appealing to the mass of people (2.14.23–9). 'The philosophers' to whom he frequently refers by this general description are normally his Stoic authorities, with whom he characteristically associates Socrates and also the Cynic Diogenes.[1] Thus, while philosophy as such can be represented in terms that are not confined to Epictetus' allegiances, those who attend to him will rapidly learn to identify it solely and completely with the Socratic–Stoic tradition.

This approach to philosophy treats it as open in its psychological underpinnings or responses to human needs but closed in its doctrinal content. To a certain extent, Epictetus is following a familiar route here. From Aristotle onwards Greek philosophers had acknowledged their engagement in a common endeavour, while leaving no doubt about the superiority of their particular schools. They had mastered the art of defending their own positions by surveying and refuting the views of rival thinkers. Epictetus sometimes follows this practice, with the Epicureans or Sceptics as his particular targets.[2] Yet, he is quite distinctive, so far as our record goes, in his diagnosis of the general motivations to engage in philosophy irrespective of doctrinal affiliation. His stance here is his own, though it is influenced in thought and expression by Plato and Stoic rationalism:

33 To a rational animal the only unbearable thing is irrationality, but a reasonable thing is quite bearable. Flogging is not unbearable by nature.
    How so?
    Look how the Spartans take a whipping when they have learned that it is reasonable.
    But isn't it unbearable to be hanged?

---

[1] See 1.18.1; 1.26.3; 2.1.1; 2.1.22; 2.9.13; 2.10.5; 2.14.11; 2.17.2; 2.18.8; 3.13.11; 3.16.11; 3.21.6; 3.24.9.
[2] See 1.5; 1.23; 2.20.

Well, whenever someone has the feeling that it's reasonable, he goes off and hangs himself![3] In short, by paying attention we shall discover that nothing distresses our species as much as irrationality, and that, conversely, nothing appeals to it so much as reasonableness. (1.2.1–4)

(22) Every rational soul is naturally averse to conflict; but as long as someone is unaware of being involved in a conflict, there is nothing to prevent him from acting inconsistently. Yet, once he is aware, he is strongly constrained to abandon and shun the conflict, just as one who perceives that something is false is forcibly constrained to renounce the false-hood, though until it shows itself he assents to it as true.

(2.26.3; see p. 74 above for the full discourse)

34 What is the reason for our assenting to anything?
The fact that it appears to be the case.
Therefore, it is impossible to assent to what appears not to be the case.
Why?
Because it is the mind's nature to assent to truths, to dislike falsehoods, and to suspend judgement in relation to uncertainties.
What is the proof of this?
Experience at this moment, if you can, that it is night.
I can't.
Reject your experience that it is day.
I can't.
Have the experience that the stars are even in number, or that they are not.
I can't.
You can be sure, then, that whenever someone assents to a falsehood, he doesn't wish to do so; (for, as Plato says, every soul is unwillingly deprived of the truth) but the falsehood appeared to him to be true.

(1.28.1–5)[4]

These are but a sample of the numerous places where Epictetus voices his optimistic rationalism. What stands out here is his confidence that human beings have a profoundly natural

[3] A good example of Epictetus' black humour; he mockingly alludes to the Stoic doctrine that a well-reasoned suicide is justifiable. In the immediate sequel to this passage he shows that people differ widely in what they take to be reasonable or unreasonable; see p. 238.

[4] The Platonic text to which Epictetus primarily alludes is *Sophist* 228c; he cites it again at 2.22.36. For the Stoic epistemological and anti-sceptical tradition on which Epictetus draws in this passage, see Dobbin (1998: 219–20).

love of truth, as shown by their responsiveness to the availability or absence of evidence and by their resistance to self-contradiction and inconsistency.

The optimistic rationalism as such is quite general. As **34** shows, Epictetus is willing to illustrate it by appeal to standard examples of people's confidence in self-evident matters of fact. However, its principal application for him is based upon the equally general and analogous assumption that human beings have a profoundly natural set of preferences and motivations:

35 Just as it is every soul's nature to assent to truth, dissent from falsehood, and suspend judgement in relation to uncertainty, so it is its nature to be desirously motivated for the good, aversely motivated for the bad, and neutrally motivated for what is neither good nor bad . . . The moment the good appears it attracts the soul to itself, while the bad repels the soul from itself. A soul will never fail to approve a clear impression of good, any more than it will refuse Caesar's coinage. This is the source of every motivation for the human and the divine.   (3.3.2–4)

This passage is a further example of Epictetus' concern to court agreement in his advocacy of philosophy.[5] Goodness and badness, presented in these quite unspecific terms, stand for the beneficial and harmful dispensations that all human beings can be assumed to want, or respectively to avoid, for themselves. Epictetus could have made the same point, as he does elsewhere (see p. 191), by observing that every person is desirous of happiness and averse to its opposite. Let us call this point his eudaimonism. As an optimistic rationalist and eudaimonist, he associates himself with the general tradition of Greek philosophy.

Equally central to that tradition, however, was its lack of agreement on what rationalism could actually deliver and on what goodness and happiness in fact require. The love of truth in principle is quite compatible with actually being in error or with

[5] He does, though, express his point about human motivations by linking them to the standard Stoic division of values into the three categories—good, bad, and neutral or indifferent (neither good nor bad). He is not claiming that people in general are in agreement about what they allocate to each of these categories—for non-Stoics radically disagree with Stoics, who assign such things as wealth and poverty to the neutral category (see 4.1.136, p. 106 below)—but only that any human motivation naturally takes one of these three forms.

scepticism, and the desire for goodness and happiness may be ubiquitous but scarcely fulfilled owing to misconceptions or uncertainties about what these are and how or even whether they can be achieved. Epictetus was composing for an audience who were free to sit at the feet of Epicureans and Peripatetics, with their distinctive epistemologies, cosmologies, and ethics, and his potential students could also be tempted by the Sceptics' critique of all the doctrinaire schools, especially Stoicism. He needs to show why his own specification of philosophy requires unremitting dedication from those who are prepared to reflect on their natures as lovers of truth and aspirants to happiness.

He has many ways of encouraging and cajoling his audience, but I focus here on those that illustrate his efforts to base his approach to philosophy on well-established precedents. From Socrates onwards philosophy had been regularly characterized as the quest for knowledge. It was expected, ideally, to identify and solve problems, generating solutions that would constitute demonstrable understanding of basic truths concerning nature in general and human nature in particular. Acknowledging the inadequacy of mere opinion, being impelled by what one does not know to press forward with investigation—these Socratic presuppositions had been implicitly endorsed by representatives of all the schools. Epictetus draws powerfully on them, but his way of doing so has a strong contemporary relevance. Determined as he is to combat Scepticism, he borrows from its strategy of exploiting discrepant opinions, but he insists that philosophy does not stop there with the recommendation to suspend judgement about everything. Discrepant opinions should be regarded as the incentive to discover 'criteria of truth', which it is philosophy's task to review and confirm.

Epictetus' would-be philosopher needs to start from 'being aware of his own weakness and incapacity concerning absolute essentials' (2.11.1), or, with a direct allusion to Socrates, 'to throw away the conceit that he has knowledge' (2.17.1). The conceit is due to the fact that because everyone *naturally* has concepts of value—of good, bad, happiness, justice, and so forth—people use the corresponding terms as if they understood their correct application (see p. 80). They add this unjustified opinion to their innate 'preconceptions', overconfidently applying them to particular instances, and get into disputes with one another about the value of things. As long as the disputing parties have only their individual opinions to appeal to, they lack adequate criteria for adjudicating between them.

The disposition appropriate to philosophy emerges only when someone is thoroughly dissatisfied with making his own opinion the sole basis for value judgements, which are the 'essentials' mentioned above:

36 Observe the starting point of philosophy: awareness of human beings' conflict of opinions, investigation of the origin of the conflict, condemnation and distrust of mere opinion, investigation of the correctness of an opinion, and discovery of a certain standard, such as we have discovered in the case of the scale for weights, or the ruler for things straight and crooked. This is the starting point of philosophy:

Is everyone's opinion sound?
But how can conflicting opinions be sound?
Therefore not all opinions are sound.
Well, our opinions then?
Why ours rather than the Syrians' or the Egyptians'? Why mine rather than so and so's?
No reason.
Therefore the individual's opinion is insufficient with respect to truth. That is why for weights and measures we are not content with mere appearance but we have discovered a certain standard for each.
Is there here, then, no standard higher than opinion?
But how is it possible that the most essential items among human beings should be indeterminable and indiscoverable?
So there is a standard.
Why, then, do we not search for it and find it, and when we have found it use it unfailingly from then on, not even stretching a finger without it?
. . . What topic has arisen that we wish to investigate?
Pleasure.
Submit it to the standard; put it into the balance. Must the good be the sort of thing that merits confidence and trust?
It must.
Does something insecure merit confidence?
No.
Pleasure is not something secure, is it?
No.

Remove it, then, throw it out of the balance and drive it far away from the domain of good things . . . That is how things are judged and weighed when the standards are established. This is practising philosophy, scrutinizing and securing the standards.[6] But using them when they are known is the function of the excellent person.

(2.11.13–25; for the beginning of this discourse, see **25**, p. 79 above)

At the end of **36**, with his brief refutation of hedonism, Epictetus draws heavily on Stoic assumptions about the properties necessary to anything that is genuinely good. The interest of the text in our present context is not that technical point, but the light the passage sheds on Epictetus' readiness to introduce his philosophy without explicit appeals to doctrinal authority. Before his critique of hedonism, he expresses himself in a manner that could appeal to anyone who is troubled by uncertainty about the foundations of value judgements and by the disputes to which they give rise.

As the opening of this passage shows, Epictetus treats philosophy as an enterprise that is very specifically addressed to individual persons from whom it demands a frank recognition of their present needs and inadequacies. This is one of his constant gestures to the Socratic paradigm. Even when he does not mention or use the Socratic *elenchus* directly, he may allude to it, as when he describes 'the first and greatest function of philosophy' as 'testing impressions, discriminating between them, and deploying none that has not been tested' (1.20.7). The language of 'testing impressions' is Stoic, but the basic thought is also Socratic; for untested impressions are the mark of a mind that has not submitted itself to self-examination.

The 'criterial' role of philosophy has a still wider resonance. At this date, and for long before, facts in general and values in particular were taken to be such contentious matters that the only secure access to them would have to proceed by means of 'criteria of truth'. The rationale of this concept was the desire to establish unquestionable foundations for knowledge and for ethics, but, because the philosophical schools disagreed among

---

[6] For Socrates' concern with such standards, see Plato, *Euthyphro* 7c and *Protagoras* 356b–357a.

themselves concerning formulations of the criteria, they fed sceptical challenges concerning whether any such standards existed. Sometimes, Epictetus narrows the focus of the criterion to the specific materials of Stoic ethics—'learning and applying the criterion of what is in accordance with nature' (1.11.15)—but the lesson of **36** is largely compatible with his broad conception of philosophy.

4.2 REFUTATIONS OF SCEPTICISM

Epictetus' concern to situate Stoicism within this broad context is well illustrated in discourses that confront Sceptics directly. There had been long and technical disputes between Stoics and Sceptics over the Stoic doctrine that some of our perceptual experience is self-certifying and indubitable. Epictetus acknowledges that refined arguments on the issue are in order for experts who have no more pressing demands on their time, but he defends his confidence in the normal reliability of perceptual experience with sarcastic retorts that had been levelled against Academic scepticism from its beginning.[7]

37 I may not know how to adjudicate the question of whether perception is mediated through the whole body or only through a part of it; both views leave me troubled. But I do know with absolute certainty that you and I are not identical. How so? Whenever I want to swallow something, I never bring the morsel over there but here; whenever I want bread, I never get hold of the broom but I always go to the bread as my goal.

You Sceptics, who undermine the senses, do you act differently? Which one of of you, when he wants to go to a bath, goes to a mill?

(1.27.17–19)

The hardline Sceptic is charged with flagrant self-contradiction:

38 Even those who argue against things that are sound and self-evident are compelled to make use of them. As perhaps the best testimony of a self-evident proposition, one might take the fact that someone who argues

---

[7] See Plutarch, *Against Colotes* 1122E.

against it finds himself forced to make use of it. Thus, if someone should argue against the proposition that something universal is true, it is clear that he is obliged to make the contrary statement:

Nothing universal is true.

You slave, this is not true either. For what else is its meaning than: If something is universal, it is false? Or again, if someone comes up and says:

You should know that nothing is knowable but everything is uncertain.

Or someone else, who says:

Trust me and you will be helped: no person should be trusted.

Or another says:

Learn from me, my friend, that it is impossible to learn anything; I tell you this, and I will prove it to you if you like.   (2.20.1–5)

and with 'petrification of integrity':

39 Do you grasp the fact that you are awake?

No (he says); *for even in dreams I have the impression that I am awake.*

Do these impressions not differ at all?

No.

Am I still talking to this fellow? What fire or steel should I apply to him to make him aware that he is deadened? He is aware, but he pretends not to be; he is even worse than a corpse.

One man doesn't notice the conflict; he is in a bad way. Another fellow is conscious of it, but he isn't moved and he makes no progress; his state is still more wretched. His conscience and integrity have been amputated, and his rationality, though not amputated, has been brutalized.   (1.5.6–9)

This is strong language. It reflects two things: first, Epictetus' refusal to engage with the Sceptic on the Sceptic's own premises. Secondly, and more importantly, the optimistic rationality that we have already seen him emphasizing. He has calculated that, even if these familiar rejoinders do not impress hardline Sceptics, they will resonate well with anyone who has a smattering of other philosophies and with people in general. His contempt for the finer points of scepticism anticipates G. E. Moore's famous gesture of asking the sceptic whether he is uncertain that no elephant is lurking under a desk in the lecture room.

If the material presented just now were all that we had from Epictetus, we might take him to be a robust defender of common sense. In fact, if that characterization were wholly wrong, what I have called his broad conception of philosophy would be sheer pretence. He frequently requires his audience to attend to what is obvious or self-evident, as in texts already cited, to which we may add 4.1.136:

40 When do you ponder whether black things are white or heavy things light? Surely you completely accept appearances that are self-evident.

Epictetus was an empirical realist; but his chief purpose in adopting that position is not to contribute to the foundations of epistemology but to suggest, by analogy or even by inference, that the basic concepts of value and the principles of a good life can be exhibited to be no less certain or self-evident.

He makes this point in the words that follow his questions in **40**:

41 How is it, then, that you say you are now questioning whether indifferent things are to be avoided rather than things that are bad? In fact, these are not your judgements; you have the impression, rather, that these [imprisonment and death] are the greatest of bad things and that those [dishonourable and disloyal speech, betrayal of a friend, flattery of a despot] are not bad but things that do not concern us. For that is the habit you have acquired from the outset.   (4.1.136–8)

Epictetus imagines an interlocutor who, after learning to parrot the Stoic doctrine that things like imprisonment and death are indifferent rather than bad or harmful (see n. 5 above), is asked whether he will compromise his principles, to comply with a tyrant's demands, and says: 'Let me think about it.' If such a person had internalized the Stoic doctrine, Epictetus retorts, its truth and implications would be as obvious to him as self-evident matters of empirical fact: his interlocutor is no genuine Sceptic, who really intends to *think about it*. Rather, owing to bad habits, he is completely committed to the judgement that imprisonment and death, as distinct from unethical actions, exemplify the bad things he wants to avoid.

If everyone naturally desires happiness and is naturally equipped with the means of achieving it, why is philosophy necessary? Why doesn't nature deliver happiness along with all its other endowments? To these tough questions Greek philosophers in general had offered the same fundamental response. We could be happy and live good lives under two conditions: first, if we had the correct understanding of nature and the natural constituents of happiness; and, secondly, if we trained ourselves to abandon all false conceptions of a good life's requirements, basing our judgements and desires single-mindedly on the true or natural path to happiness.

Correct judgement together with the single-minded exertion to shape one's life accordingly is the standard recipe for a good life shared by Platonists, Aristotelians, Epicureans, Stoics, and even (with due qualifications) Sceptics. All the interest of the recipe and all the grounds for controversy lie in the specific requirements. No Greek philosopher states these more forthrightly and confidently than Epictetus. Yet, at the same time, none is more insistent on how testing they are. Throughout the discourses he combines encouragement to practise Stoicism with warnings against complacency and superficiality.

4.3 PREREQUISITES FOR WOULD-BE STOICS

We have already studied Epictetus' teaching method in the discourses and where he positions himself within the educational and intellectual tradition. Here I want to focus upon what he expects from prospective students, and on what those prerequisites tell us about his specific approach to philosophy. These are not simple issues, because, in excerpting his comments, it is always necessary to take account of their context. He may be addressing or referring to an actual or imaginary layman, a rival philosopher, beginning or mature students, or voicing thoughts that apply to anyone including himself. We also need to make constant allowance for his exaggeration, irony, and self-deprecation—all marks of his deliberate imitation of Socrates.

The first thing Epictetus asks of his students is that they satisfy the following conditions: (1) wanting to benefit from philosophy and (2) understanding what a commitment to philosophy entails. He characteristically puts such questions as these:

42 Tell me, you men (addressing his students), do you wish to live in error?
We do not.
That's right; no one is free who is in error. Do you wish to live in fear and distress and confusion?
Certainly not.
So, no one who is in fear, distress and confusion is free. (2.1.23–4)

This passage links Epictetus' optimistic rationalism—not wishing to live in error—to freedom and tranquillity, which he here treats as a single state of mind. The crucial move is the question, 'Do you wish?', or, as he will sometimes say, 'If you wish . . .'.[8] The unexpressed background to these expressions is the thesis that philosophy takes its starting point from two things: awareness of one's own ignorance about essentials and a readiness to make fundamental changes to one's current life. Epictetus is saying that to benefit from his teaching you must (*a*) confront your basic wants, (*b*) recognize the implications of not knowing how to fulfil them, and (*c*) acknowledge that, in order to fulfil them, you will have to make very demanding commitments and choices.

His frequent recourse to abrupt imperatives may give the impression that he is preaching to the world in general, exhorting everyone to come and be saved. That misses his method, or at least it fails to take account of what is required of anyone who genuinely wants to live free from error and emotional distress.

43 When some people have seen a philosopher and heard one speaking like Euphrates . . . they want to be philosophers themselves.
My friend, reflect first on what the thing is and next on your own nature and what you can carry. If you want to be a wrestler, look to your shoulders, thighs, and trunk. You see, people vary in their natural propensities. Do you think you can practise philosophy and act as you do now? Do you think you can eat and drink and get angry and

---

[8] Seneca is similarly insistent that moral progress is crucially dependent on 'wanting to become good'; see *Letters* 34.3, 71.36.

irritated in just the same way? You have to stay up at night, work hard, overcome certain desires, leave your family, be despised by a little slave, be jeered at by everyone, come off worst in everything, in office, rank, and court.

Review all this, and then come forward, if you make that decision—if you want to give up those things in exchange for serenity, freedom, and tranquillity. Otherwise, don't approach; don't be like a child, now a philosopher, next a tax-collector, then a rhetorician, then one of Caesar's bureaucrats. These things are not consistent. You have to be one person, either good or bad. You have either to work on your governing faculty or on externals, toil either over your inside or your outside. That is, you must take up the stance of a philosopher or of a layman. (3.15.8–13)

These stark choices and oppositions connect the condition of wanting to benefit from philosophy to the condition of understanding what a commitment to philosophy entails. The peremptory tone of the passage may seem to fit badly with the broader foundations of philosophy outlined in the first part of this chapter. There Epictetus was apparently interested in anyone's natural propensity to benefit from philosophy; here the insistence on choosing between the stance of philosopher or layman is a strong discouragement of the faint-hearted.

Epictetus says this kind of thing repeatedly, but his purpose in doing so is not to select a philosophical elite or to adopt a censorious attitude towards ordinary people. He acknowledges that he himself is no Socrates, and at the end of this chapter we shall observe his reluctance to apply the word 'philosopher' to himself and his students. The philosopher/layman contrast is a question not of choosing between professions, in the sense of careers, but of lifestyles. Or, to use another of his favourite images, it is a question of either remaining 'childlike' or wanting to be 'educated' in life (3.19.6).

There are, of course, professional 'philosophers', but in Epictetus' eyes these are worthy of the name only if they have already fulfilled what he calls 'the profession [*epangelia*] of being human'. He never tires of contrasting mere book learning and technical expertise with the much rarer and harder achievement of 'a mind in accordance with nature'.

44 Merely to fulfil the profession of being human is no ordinary thing.
What is a human being?
A rational, mortal creature.
From what, then, are we distinguished by rationality?
From wild beasts.
And from what else?
From sheep and the like.
Take care, then, never to act like wild beasts. Otherwise, you have
destroyed your humanity, you have not fulfilled your professon. Take
care, too, not to act like a sheep. Otherwise, your humanity is ruined in
this way too.
When do we act like sheep?
Whenever we act for the sake of the stomach or the genitals, whenever
we act in a random, dirty, or unconsidered way, to what level have we
sunk?
To sheep.
What have we ruined?
Rationality.
Whenever we act competitively, injuriously, angrily, and aggressively,
to what level have we sunk?
To wild beasts . . .
Through all of these the profession of being human is destroyed.

(2.9.1–7)

In the conclusion of this discourse, Epictetus chides his students
and himself with merely acting the part of philosophers, drawing
a fascinating comparison with vacillating or ambiguous Jews
(perhaps meaning Christians):

45 Whenever we see someone wavering [between creeds] we are in the
habit of saying:
He is not a Jew, but only an actor.
But whenever he takes up the condition of one who has been baptized
and has actually chosen, then he is a Jew in fact as well as name.
We too are only nominally baptized,[9] Jews in name but something
else in fact, not consistent with rationality, far from using the principles
we profess, yet priding ourselves on them, as if we knew them.

---

[9] Epictetus uses the word *parabaptistês*, which is not found elsewhere. At his date
it would be natural for him to call Christians Jews, but baptism was already used
prior to John the Baptist as a ritual for admitting gentiles to Judaism, so the allusion
to Christians is far from certain.

So, although we are not even able to fulfil the profession of being human, we take up the additional one of the philosopher—a huge burden. It's like a man incapable of lifting ten pounds wanting to lift the rock of Ajax. (2.9.20–2)

As the last three excerpts show, to satisfy the 'condition of wanting' to be a philosopher, you need not only aspiration and commitment, but also a ruthlessly accurate assessment of your qualifications and abilities.

What also emerges from these passages is an ambiguity I take to be deliberate in Epictetus' use of the terms 'philosopher' and 'philosophy'. As the 'art of life' for every lover of truth and aspirant to happiness, philosophy is not confined to 'professionals', or, to adopt the language of **44**, fulfilling one's function as a human being is itself an arduous 'profession', from which would-be 'philosophers' generally fall short. The goal of philosophy is to produce not career philosophers but 'excellent persons' (1.8.6). Along with the binary contrasts of philosopher and layman, Epictetus regularly insists that 'progress' towards the goal of philosophy can only be gradual, and will inevitably involve false starts:

46 We should not conduct our training through unnatural or out of the ordinary means; otherwise we who claim to practise philosophy will be no different from circus performers. For it is difficult also to walk on a tightrope, and not only difficult but dangerous. (3.12.1–2)

47 Consider which of the things you proposed initially you have mastered, and which you have not, and how it gives you pleasure to remember some of them and pain to remember others, and if possible recover the things you have let slip.

Those competing in the greatest contest should not fade out, but take the blows too. For our competition is not to do with wrestling or the pancration, where success or failure can make all the difference to a man's standing—and indeed make him [in his and the world's eyes] supremely fortunate or unfortunate—but over *real* good fortune and happiness.

What then?

Even if we fail here and now, no one stops us from competing again; we don't have to wait another four years for the next Olympics, but as soon as a man has picked himself up and renewed his grip on himself and shown the same enthusiasm he is allowed to compete. And if you give in again, you can compete again, and if once you win, you are like someone who never gave in. Only, don't let sheer habit make you give in readily and end up like a bad athlete going around beaten in the whole circuit like quails that run away.   (3.25.1–5)

When Epictetus speaks in this vein, he mitigates the philosopher/layman contrast. He includes himself and everyone else in the intermediate category of progressives or aspirants to the ideal happiness promised by philosophy.

   None the less, some of Epictetus' students had the ambition to become career philosophers, and all of them together with people in general require formal training if they are to make genuine progress in the art of life. For these reasons, Epictetus devotes much effort to distinguishing between the mentality necessary for philosophy to get under way and the technical expertise that can be a distraction and pretence, at least for people who have not mastered the basics.

4.4 THREE FIELDS OF STUDY

With a procedure that he may have invented, Epictetus distinguishes between three fields of study, characterizing them as 'necessary to the training of any prospectively excellent person' (3.2.1). Here is how he describes the first field:

48   It deals with desires and aversions, with the object of ensuring that a person does not fail in his desires or have experiences he does not want.

(3.2.1)

He amplifies as follows:

49   If you allow training to turn outward towards things that do not belong to volition (*prohairesis*), you will neither secure the attainment of your desire nor escape experiencing what you do not want . . .

Who is the trainee?
He is the person who abstains from desire, and who employs aversion only on the things that pertain to volition, practising especially on those that are hard to work at. (3.12.5–8)

And he characterizes the ideal beginning student as one who says:

50 I am willing to let everything else go. I am content if I shall be able to live unimpeded and undistressed, and to hold up my head to face things like a free man, and to look to heaven as the friend of God, fearing nothing that could happen. (2.17.29)

As these passages make clear, the first field of study is at the heart of Epictetus' Stoicism. It draws on the concepts of freedom and volition or will that are central to his account of where true happiness lies. We shall explore these ideas fully in Chapter 8. What I want to emphasize here is the way Epictetus' first and most essential field of study already presupposes his students' satisfaction of the prerequsites we have just noted.

He assumes (1) a quite general motivation to live free from frustration and anxiety; and he maintains (2) that this motivation can be effective only if one's wants and aversions are totally restricted to matters that pertain to one's volition, and are thus removed from external contingencies. Like every Greek philosopher from Socrates onwards, Epictetus takes it to be axiomatic that every person desires happiness. Yet, in characterizing trainees, as we have just seen, he specifies that they should provisionally abstain from 'desire' (*orexis*) altogether, and he makes the same recommendation repeatedly (3.9.22; 3.12.8; 3.13.21).

Is he telling his students that they should not make happiness and the virtues of which it consists their single-minded objective? That is out of the question. His point is rather that they should defer their natural desire for what is good until they are so secure in their understanding of goodness that they have detached any vestige of desirability from external things (see 3.12.4; 4.1.77). The 'promise' of desire is that it succeed, and it can succeed only if its scope is ruthlessly limited to a correct assessment of the mental and moral goods that fall within the domain of volition where we are capable of being fully autonomous (3.13.9; 4.1.83).

Understanding why this field of study is primary is the key to grasping Epictetus' ethics as a whole. Taken just by itself, the focus on living 'unimpeded and undistressed' does not appear to have any necessary link with social relationships, and even less with altruistic actions. It looks as if it could be a policy for a wholly self-absorbed life, keeping clear of anything that might jeopardize one's individual tranquillity. In a certain respect that impression is correct, but Epictetus' point (as we shall see more fully later) is that self-concern and tranquillity, so far from cutting people off from society, are the essential condition for acting well in every social role. Only those who have limited their desires and aversions to what they can actually 'will' and seek to implement, and who are wholly at peace with themselves, have the right kind of disposition to care effectively about other people as well.

The first field of study is 'most authoritative', because such passions as envy and jealousy (3.2.3) make us 'incapable of listening to reason', and they arise precisely when things happen that people do not want to happen. Training one's desires and aversions, the topic of the first field of study, is the prerequisite for emotional health and for all subsequent advances in philosophy.

Given this fundamental point, we can now appreciate why Epictetus devotes so large a part of his discourses to explaining the rationale for limiting desires and aversions to the domain of volition, and to practical advice on ways to achieve this. Numerous of his principal concerns (including what is up to us and what is not, the nature of goodness, the correct use of impressions, reviewing criteria) bear directly on his first field of study, but this care of the self is completely essential to the second and third fields as well.

Epictetus imagines the ideal student again, after mastering the first field, saying:

51 I do indeed want to be unmoved and undisturbed, but as a dutiful, philosophical and scrupulous person, I also want to know what is appropriate for me to do in relation to gods, parents, brothers, country, and strangers. (2.17.31)

This kind of person, Epictetus appends, is ready to advance to the second field of study:

52 dealing with positive and negative impulses, and, in a word, with what is appropriate [*kathêkon*], in order to act methodically, with good reason, and not carelessly . . . for I ought not to be unmoved [*apathês*] like a statue,[10] but I should maintain my natural and acquired relationships, as a dutiful man and as a son, brother, father, and citizen.

(3.2.2–4)

In making this field 'secondary' Epictetus clearly does not mean that his students should neglect their civic and social roles while they are working on the first field; nor does he mean that the intrinsic value of excellence in the first is superior to excellence in the second. I take his point to be, rather, that detailed study of how one should behave as a member of society introduces questions about one's particular identity and roles that go beyond the quite general ethics and psychology of the first field. I shall return to the second field in Chapter 9, in the context of Epictetus' treatment of the behaviour appropriate to a person's roles and character. For now, one further point of clarification may suffice.

We may broadly express the difference between these two fields by drawing distinctions between inner and outer, or oneself and other persons. The object of the first field, as we have seen, is liberating the self from false conceptions of goodness and badness and from the concomitant frustrations and passions. The focus of this field is designedly introverted. The second field looks outwards at our appropriate impulses in our relationships with others—not exclusively so, to be sure, because the Stoic domain of 'the appropriate' includes such self-regarding functions as care of one's health and property; but Epictetus, as we see above, does describe the field in a socially oriented way.

---

[10] 'Not . . . like a statue' is a very deliberate qualification of 'unmoved'. See p. 232.

These distinctions are broadly apt, but in making them we need to acknowledge that the lessons of the first field are crucial, in Epictetus' view, to successful mastery of the second. To repeat what I have already said, his ethics is premissed on the claim that we have to care first and foremost for our individual selves if we are to be properly equipped to do what is incumbent on us in our social roles. His educational principles, such as making correct use of our impressions, straddle both fields. What the second field indicates is that Epictetus' students require rigorous training in managing their day-to-day lives even after they have absorbed the truths about reconciling their desires and aversions with long-term freedom and tranquillity. Hence the subjects of such discourses as those on friendship and family affection.

Now the third and last field of study, which incorporates advanced logic:

53 The third field is the province of those who are already making progress; it deals with security in the area of the other two fields, to ensure that even in dreams or drunkenness or depression someone is not caught off guard by an unexamined impression.

That is beyond us (someone says).

Yet present-day philosophers, neglecting the first and second fields, concentrate on the third, studying changing, hypothetical, and questioning arguments, and paradoxes like the Liar.[11]

Yes (someone says); *when involved in these matters it's necessary to secure oneself against being deceived.*

Who must?

The truly excellent man.

Is this where *you* fall short? Have you really worked at the other fields? Are you proof against deception over cash? If you see a pretty girl, do you resist the impression? If your neighbour gets an inheritance, don't you feel the bite of envy? (3.2.5–9)

---

[11] This celebrated paradox can be formulated: 'If you say you are lying and you say so truly, are you lying or telling the truth?' (see LS 37H and Mignucci 1999). Epictetus refers to it disparagingly when he wants to focus his students' attention on the first field of study (2.17.34; 2.18.18; 2.21.17), but he finds the study of paradoxes quite appropriate for someone who has succeeded in 'conforming his mind to nature' (3.9.19–22).

When the ideal student, who has mastered the first two fields, declares his ambition to embark on the third, Epictetus applauds him: 'My friend, you are a god, you have great aspirations!' This hyperbole is explained by Epictetus' equivocal observations in **53**. The traditional goal of Stoicism had been the achievement of infallible understanding in every area of life, including debates with other philosophers (see 1.7.2–4). Hence the ideal sage was credited with a skill in logic so powerful that he would be immune from the slightest risk of error unless, as some Stoics proposed, he was subject to such contingencies as uncontrollable depression or (presumably unwitting) intoxication; and Epictetus in our extract jokingly exempts even these qualifications and dream deceptions from the security his ideal student can hope to achieve.

As the Stoic school evolved, logic became a major part of the curriculum. Although much of this work was highly technical, its official rationale was not logical theory for its own sake but mastery of all the reasoning requisite to perfect competence in every area of life. By Epictetus' time, however, the curriculum had become so strongly associated with logic that Stoic philosophers were notorious for their interest in handling such paradoxes as the Liar. Hence Epictetus' equivocal recommendation of the third field of study.

He has nothing against logic; he insists on its necessity (2.25), and he must have given his students sufficient instruction in the uses of logic for them to follow his allusions in the discourses to the forms and validity of arguments, proofs, sophisms, and the like. But he reserves concentration on advanced logic for those who have 'progressed' in the more immediately urgent fields. The reason for this precaution is the strong temptation for his students to think they are prematurely ready for this subject, or to substitute it for training in the first two fields.

How do Epictetus' three fields of study relate to the classic division of Stoic philosophy into the three parts—logic, ethics, and physics? The question has been much debated, but I think P. Hadot has given the correct answer (see p. 125 below). Epictetus' second and third fields obviously correspond to ethics and to logic. At first glance, the first field, dealing with

desires and aversions, looks simply like a preliminary to ethics,
or at any rate quite remote from physics or the study of nature.
The field is certainly remote from much of what Stoic physics
had traditionally included—the study of cosmology and the
basic principles of existing things. But Stoic physics was a very
broad subject. It included theology and the study of human
nature, with special emphasis on the soul and mental faculties.
A general grasp of these topics, as we shall see in later chapters,
is central to Epictetus' basic curriculum and to what he hopes to
teach his students concerning the rationale for how they man-
age their desires and aversions. So we should probably take the
first field to include such study of human and cosmic nature as
he deems necessary for beginning students to master.

4.5 EDUCATIONAL OBJECTIVES

Epictetus likes to characterize philosophy and education
(*paideia*) in terms that fit his dominant interests in the achievement of autonomy and of a volition that accords with nature.

54 The goal of the philosophers' principles is to enable us, whatever happens, to have our governing faculty [*hêgemonikon*]¹² in accordance with
   nature and to keep it so.   (3.9.11)

55 Being educated is precisely learning to will each thing just as it happens.
                                                                    (1.12.15)

56 Philosophy does not profess to provide a human being with anything
   external.   (1.15.2)

57 Philosophizing is virtually this—enquiry into how it is possible to apply
   desire and aversion without impediment.   (3.14.10)

58 Being educated is learning what is one's own and what is not.   (4.5.7)

All of these formulae are especially pertinent to Epictetus' first
field of study, 'desires and aversions'. In Chapters 6–9, we shall
see how they reflect his theology, anthropology, and psychology.

¹² 'Governing faculty' (*hêgemonikon*) is the standard Stoic expression for the
mind.

What is immediately obvious is how strongly such formulae have coloured the popular image of Stoicism in subsequent centuries and influenced the popular meaning of a 'philosophical' attitude to life. Epictetus has the authority of the Stoic tradition behind him, but his intense preoccupation with unimpeded volition, which will leave its mark on Marcus Aurelius, is quite distinctive.

As we have already seen, the would-be philosopher needs to satisfy certain prerequisites, including awareness of inability to live as he wants to, readiness to discover and internalize correct standards for making value judgements, and understanding what the commitment to living a properly rational life entails. Although Epictetus describes the human being as 'an animal that loves to theorize' (1.29.58), the 'theorizing' that he envisions as our natural goal (1.6.21) is not detached from action but involves the study of nature with a view to living accordingly. Hence he distinguishes between necessary and unnecessary principles, especially in contexts where his students need to be warned against absorption in advanced logic to the detriment of their training in the first field of study. Impersonating a despondent student, he says:

59 I don't exercise the necessary principles, the ones that launch a person on the way to becoming immune from distress, anxiety, passion, and impediment, and becoming free; and I don't engage in the practice appropriate to these. (4.6.16)

The necessary principles enable students to make correct value judgements:

60 What is being educated? Learning to apply the natural preconceptions to particular matters in accordance with nature; and further, to make the distinction that some things are up to us but others are not.
(1.22.9–10)[13]

Students who do not live accordingly 'discredit' philosophy's principles (3.26.13); they make them appear ineffectual, and that

---

[13] See discourse 1.1, excerpted on p. 62 above.

is especially the case when, having failed to master the first field of study, they try to undertake the third. A further distraction from the correct attitude to principles is wanting the mere appearance of a philosopher. The principles are not about the style of one's beard or hair:

61   But, as Zeno said, knowing the elements of discourse, what each of them is and how they fit together and all that follows from them.   (4.8.12)[14]

As this passage makes plain, Epictetus' position on principles is unequivocal with regard to his students' need to analyse their thoughts and the implications of their language. These aspects of logic are completely necessary to philosophical beginners.

Apart from describing philosophy in terms of his own doctrinal preoccupations, Epictetus constantly uses military, athletic, and therapeutic metaphors to illustrate how his students should approach their studies and regimen.[15] Each of these images underlines his message that the Stoicism he teaches is both the only way to acquire mental strength and health and a practice that requires unremitting commitment and seriousness. In the discourse where he refers to the God-given positions assigned to Socrates, Diogenes, and Zeno (see p. 57 above), he rebukes a real or imaginary student for showing off his skills in Stoic logic with the words:

62   You are trumpeting the Mysteries . . .You don't have the hierophant's proper clothes, or hair, or headband, or voice, or age. You are not ritually pure, as he is, but you have merely picked up the words themselves and utter them. Are the words in themselves sacred? One needs to approach these things with a certain attitude: the matter is of great magnitude, a solemn rite, not something ordinary or granted to just anyone.
      (3.21.16–17)

Epictetus borrows the language of religious ritual, not to suggest that Stoicism requires literal initiation but in order to emphasize

---

[14] This is unlikely to be an exact citation of Zeno. The founder of the school is often cited simply as the eponymous authority in doctrine.

[15] e.g. military: 3.24.31; 4.1.86; 4.5.25; athletic: 1.18.21; 1.24.2; 3.15.2; 3.10.7; therapeutic: 2.21.15; 3.21.20; 3.23.30.

that it is an all-or-nothing pursuit, a dedicated practice for every moment of one's life. Its doctrines, whether in logic or in any other field, are not for sampling or parading, but for converting those who will use them because they are committed to conversion. Like the philosopher of Plato's *Theaetetus* (173c–175e), who is too intent on studying timeless truths to be competent in the hurlyburly of politics and the lawcourts, so Epictetus tells his students that, if they are really in love with philosophy, they should be prepared to be ridiculed and to appear senseless in their dealings with external circumstances (*Ench.*13, 22). They are 'never to call themselves philosophers or talk in lay company about their principles but simply practise them' (*Ench.* 46). They should take Socrates as their model: he 'eluded the attention of most people, and they used to come to him asking to be introduced to philosophers' (4.8.22).

4.6 EPICTETUS ON HIMSELF AND HIS MISSION

Epictetus applies the public reticence he recommends to his students to himself. To an Epicurean visitor he describes himself as a 'layman' (3.7.1). To an effeminate youth, he remarks: 'It wasn't Epictetus who said these things—how could he?—but some kindly god speaking through him' (3.1.36). He is 'a lame old man' (1.16.20) with 'no natural talent' (1.2.35), and in the eyes of another philosopher 'the last thing I would want to become like' (3.8.7).

Why this reticence about the term 'philosopher' and the support for it by appeal to Socrates? Epictetus' discourses are packed with warnings against parading oneself, putting on finery to lecture, and so forth.[16] He praises Euphrates, his older contemporary, for disguising his philosophical identity, saying: 'What harm was there in having the philosopher that I was, recognized by what I did, rather than by the outward signs?' (4.8.20). Clearly, it befits a Stoic to disparage the value of mere

---

[16] See 3.12.16; 3.14.4; 3.23.

appearance (something morally 'indifferent') in order to emphasize what really matters—one's internal disposition and purpose.
It is equally clear from stock jokes about Cynics and philosophical hypocrites that any teacher as serious as Epictetus would
want to remove himself and his pupils from any suspicion of
falling into such categories. In addition, Epictetus knew what it
was to be banished from Rome. Was caution a factor in his reticence about the label 'philosopher'?

We can firmly dispel this suggestion. Epictetus gives no scope
to caution where it is a question of one's material safety (2.1 in
full), and in illustrating strength of character he even says that to
the command 'Shave off your beard, Epictetus', he would retort:
'If I am a philosopher, I will not do so' (1.2.29). Nor is the official Stoic indifference to external circumstances a sufficient
explanation. Zeno and the other early Stoics strongly professed
that doctrine, yet they are not known to have shown reluctance to
accept the title of philosopher. It is clear too that, notwithstanding his reticence, Epictetus knows he *is* a philosopher, and that
he is so regarded. When he tells his students that they should
regard the philosopher's school as a clinic (3.23.30) and that
genuine philosophers, unlike contemporary doctors at Rome,
don't advertise for patients (3.23.27), he is referring to himself.

To resolve this puzzle and to account for Epictetus' irony and
self-deprecation, we should distinguish, as the Greek does not,
between Philosopher with a capital letter and philosopher
uncapitalized. Epictetus disclaims being a Philosopher. He does
not want to be mistaken for a popular lecturer or sophist, for a
Favorinus or a Dio Chrysostom, who put on displays of erudi-
tion. He seeks, however humbly, to be the Socrates of the Second
Sophistic, a name given to the professional rhetoricians who
looked back to the sophists of fifth-century Athens.

We have already observed Epictetus' warnings to his students
against wanting to emulate the likes of Dio (see p. 53). The two
may have known one another if Dio was also a student of
Musonius, but their lives and styles went in very different directions, Dio the courtier and the modern equivalent of a media
personality, Epictetus shunning fame and teaching in provincial Nicopolis. Dio is pertinent not only because of being a

Philosopher, but also by the contrast between his and Epictetus' allusions to Socrates.

Unlike Epictetus, Dio is always talking about himself. Speaking at Athens on his return from exile, he parallels himself with Socrates (13.9–12). An oracular response has guided his life, as it did Socrates'. In his wanderings, though he has declined to be called a philosopher, people have consulted him about goodness and badness, and he addressed them with 'the trite old words' of a certain Socrates, preaching that Socratic education is indispensable for personal and civic well-being (13.14–15). Elsewhere he likens his own ignorance to that of Socrates, in contrast with the fifth-century sophists, draws attention to his unkempt appearance, and insists that he is no flatterer (33.14; cf. 54). In a lecture to the citizens of Prusa, he refers to charges against himself, by some ill-wishers (43.8–12): 'I am not surprised at my present troubles, since even the famous Socrates, whom I have often mentioned, did everything for the people during the tyranny of the Thirty', but was slandered and put to death.[17] Dio then goes so far as to describe the indictment against himself as 'larger and practically nobler', starting with his failure 'to honour the gods with sacrifices and hymns and annulling the ancestral festivals'.

I prefer not to quote more. Unlike Epictetus, Dio's recourse to Socrates is trite and self-serving. The more he professes his own ignorance, the less his words bear credence. Dio's fraudulent allusions to Socrates give us the measure both for assessing Epictetus' quite different uses of the Socratic paradigm, and also for his refusal to be a capitalized Philosopher.

Epictetus' preferred term for his relationship to his students is *paideutês*, 'trainer of the young'. Here is how he describes himself and his students:

63 So I am your trainer and you are being trained in my school. And my project is this—to make you unimpeded, unconstrained, unrestricted,

---

[17] Dio alludes to the Thirty Tyrants, who ruled Athens 404–403 BC after the city's final defeat by Sparta in the Peloponnesian War, and to Socrates' celebrated refusal to obey the Thirty's order to join a posse to arrest Leon of Salamis (Plato, *Apology* 33d); Epictetus refers to this episode too (4.1.160; 4.7.30).

free, contented, happy, looking to God in everything great and small. And you are here to learn and to practise this. Why then don't you finish the job if you have the right purpose and if I, besides the purpose, have the right qualifications?

What is missing?

When I see a craftsman who has available material, I expect the artefact.[18] The craftsman is here, and so too the material.

What are we lacking? Is the thing not teachable?

It is teachable.

Is it, then, not up to us?

It is the only thing in the world that is so. Wealth isn't up to us, nor is health or reputation or anything at all except the correct use of impressions. This alone is naturally unhindered and unimpeded.

So why don't you finish the work? Tell me the reason. For either it is due to me or to you or to the nature of the thing. The thing itself is possible and the only thing up to us. Therefore the failing is mine or yours or, more truly, it pertains to us both.

Do you want us to begin, here and now, to execute this project? Let's say goodbye to the past. Let's simply begin, and trust me, you will see.

(2.19.29–34)

This passage comes at the end of a discourse that begins with Epictetus' exposition of a famous logical crux. Here, as frequently elsewhere, his main purpose is to parallel second-hand mastery of a topic, whether in logic or some other field, with failure to exercise one's independent judgement in ethical practice. His point is not to belittle logic but to indicate the numerical gap he finds between those who parrot technical principles and those who try to fashion themselves accordingly. Shortly before **63**, he pleads to his students:

64 By the gods, I would love to see a Stoic. But you can't show me one fully formed. Well, show me at least one who is being formed, one who has tended that way. Gratify me. Don't begrudge an old man the sight of what I have never seen up to now.   (2.19.24)

As so often, the tone of the passage is complex—genial yet plaintive, appealing yet prescriptive, half-serious and half-tongue

---

[18] Seneca similarly presents himself in relation to his unofficial student Lucilius as a craftsman in relation to an artefact (*Letter* 34.2).

in cheek. Epictetus plays on the famous cliché about the Phoenix-like rarity of the Stoic sage, and when we remember his youthful audience we can imagine how they must have been simultaneously amused, impressed, and challenged. What is most striking is Epictetus' complicity and engagement with his students, pushing, cajoling, but in the final analysis sharing responsibility for their success or failure. His pedagogical stance shows that what really counts in his interpretation of the Stoic art of life is not achievement but the minute-by-minute aspiration to shape oneself, irrespective of one's natural gifts (1.2.35), into an excellent person (*kalos kai agathos*).

FURTHER READING AND NOTES

Rationality, Empiricism, Eudaimonism

For the Stoic background on rationality and empiricism, see LS, especially 39–41, 63, 68, and Frede (1999b). These studies also discuss the 'criterion of truth', on which see also Striker (1996a) and Hankinson (1995). Eudaimonism is discussed in great detail by Annas (1993), and see also Kraut (1979). On Stoic eudaimonism specifically, see p. 206 below. Dobbin (1998) should be consulted for further commentary on all the passages I have excerpted from book 1 of the discourses.

Refutations of Scepticism

Epictetus' argument in the first sentences of 38 (pp. 104–5) presupposes a technicality of Stoic logic. This is the formulation of universal propositions (e.g. 'No As are B') as indefinite conditionals ('If something is A, it is not B'); see LS i, 207 and the commentary on Epictetus 2.20.2–3 in Barnes (1997: 30–1).

We are asked to imagine a Sceptic who argues against the proposition SUT: 'Something Universal is True'. In that case, says Epictetus, the Sceptic is committed to affirming its negation = NUT: 'Nothing Universal is True'. That in turn is equivalent to affirming SUF: 'If something is Universal, it is False [not true]'. But NUT itself is a universal proposition and an instance of SU, and therefore false. Hence the Sceptic's claim that nothing universal is true is self-contradictory because if the proposition were true its universality would entail its falsity.

Three Fields of Study

For a detailed defence of the position I adopt concerning the relation of the three fields to physics, ethics, and logic, see P. Hadot (1992: 98–115), who aptly connects them (in this order) with Epictetus' three faculties of the soul: (*a*) desire, (*b*) impulse, (*c*) assent. Epictetus also refers to the three fields at 1.4.11, 3.12.13–14, and 4.10.13. At *Ench.* 52 he gives a rather different tripartite division, but I do not find this a reason for rejecting Hadot's interpretation. Epictetus' standard account of the three fields may be compared with Cicero, *De officiis* II.18, and Seneca, *Letter* 89.14. His classification is frequently invoked by Marcus Aurelius: see *Meditations* VII.54, VIII.7, IX.6. For Epictetus' remarks on logic, and how they relate to the later Stoic tradition, see Barnes (1997), and for the conception of the Stoic sage as an infallible dialectician, see Long (1978).

The Second Field: What is Appropriate (kathêkon)

For bibliography and further discussion, see p. 257.

There is a complication concerning Epictetus' formulation of this field that I do not discuss in the main body of the chapter. It is the fact that he describes the field (3.2.2) as 'dealing with positive and negative impulses' (*hormai* and *aphormai*) as distinct from desires (*orexeis*) and aversions (*ekkliseis*), the sphere of his first field. Inwood (1985: 115–26) should be consulted on this terminology and its deviation from early Stoic usage. His central point is that Epictetus applies the 'impulse' language to 'appropriate' actions in order to distinguish what it is reasonable to aim at in the external sphere, where the outcome is not 'up to us', from what we should 'desire'—namely, goodness of character—which is entirely achievable in principle. Epictetus, however, recommends beginners to abstain from *desire* because goodness of character is not yet within their powers, and to employ their positive and negative impulses 'only lightly and with reservation' (*Ench.* 2).

Inwood's interpretation of the terminology is correct. But it should not be taken to imply that Epictetus regards acting 'appropriately' as necessarily falling outside the sphere of goodness and 'desirability' . At 3.3.8, Epictetus says: 'If we situate the good in a correct volition [*prohairesis*], the preservation of social relationships [Epictetus' preferred reference to 'appropriate' actions] becomes a good' (i.e. something to be desired), which is orthodox Stoicism. At 3.12.13 he characterizes the second field, the one to do with appropriate actions, as aimed at generating 'obedience to reason' in one's exercise of positive or negative impulse (*hormê*/*aphormê*; cf. *eulogistôs* (3.2.2)); and, in saying that, he must mean that a well-reasoned impulse to perform appropriate acts or to refrain from inappropriate ones is good and therefore desirable.

I think that Epictetus places the field of desire first, not because it deals with the good *as distinct from* the appropriate, but because he reasons that people need rigorous training in their understanding of desire and desirables before they pass on to the study of how they should conduct their social relationships. We should note that, while Epictetus recommends trainees to abstain completely from desire (*orexis*), he also recommends them to exercise its negative correlate, aversion (*ekklisis*), on their specific weaknesses (for instance, inclination to pleasure or laziness (3.12.7–8)); and this proves that he regards trainees as competent to act on their judgements of what is bad.

Why does Epictetus treat aversion differently from desire? The answer, I suggest, is that trainees are more at risk of pursuing *good* objectives before they are ready to do so, than of falling short over exercising well-reasoned restraint. Thus, for instance, the mastery of Stoic logic is something good and desirable in principle, but it is not a suitable objective for students at the level of the first or second topics.

Epictetus on Himself and his Mission

Some of what I say in this section is taken from Long (2000: 93–5).

CHAPTER 5

Reading Epictetus

I think anyone would agree that whoever is going to listen to
the philosophers needs a considerable practice in listening.

(2.24.10)

On the surface Epictetus may seem thoroughly accessible. His
conversational idiom clamours for attention, and his rhetorical
devices—repetition, imperatives, homely examples, anecdotes,
and caustic injunctions—keep us engaged. Actually, however,
the discourses are often complex and sometimes obscure. When
they use dialogue, it can be difficult to assign the parts between
the authorial persona and the imaginary interlocutor. Epictetus
may alternate rapidly, as we have seen, between the *protreptic*,
elenctic, and doctrinal styles (p. 61). His more technical arguments can be far from straightforward. Above all, we need to be
constantly alert to his shifts of tone and to remember that the discourses in their delivered form would have been accompanied by
pauses, gestures, changes of facial expression, and vocal modula-
tion. All of these performative actions would have given his audience perspectives on his teaching that we can scarcely replicate,
though we may get some sense of them by dwelling on certain
expressions and by reading between the lines. We need also to
remember that Arrian's record, largely accurate though I take it
to be, probably involves more compression than Epictetus himself used.

Passages I have already selected will have given readers new to Epictetus some impression of his arresting manner. Now that we have studied the scope and style of the discourses, his Socratic paradigm, and his conception of philosophy and pedagogy, I offer in this chapter a close reading of two of the shorter pieces with a view to showing how his tone and method shift between various registers—professorial, peremptory, hyperbolical, ironical, satirical, amused, encouraging, and polemical.

Individual discourses differ in their deployment of these registers. Some are relatively dispassionate, others are intensely engaged. The purpose of this chapter is to present enough material to illustrate the rationale that underlies his characteristic ways of presenting Stoicism and training his students. Because the two pieces I have selected are thematically central, they also prepare the ground for the later chapters of this book.

A good many discourses, especially those I have labelled 'theoretical' and 'methodological' (see p. 47), begin in an abstract way that any professional philosopher might have adopted with his students. That applies to the opening of this example:

5.1 *ON HOW RATIONALITY IS CAPABLE OF STUDYING ITSELF* (I.20)

65 (1) Every craft or faculty has a special area as its field of study. (2) When the craft or faculty belongs to the same species as the object of study, it necessarily studies [*theôrein*] itself too. But when it is heterogeneous, it cannot study itself. (3) Thus, shoemaking works on leather, yet the craft itself is quite distinct from leather. Therefore it does not study itself. (4) To take another example, the art of grammar deals with written speech, but that does not make the art of grammar itself written speech, does it?

Certainly not.

Therefore it cannot study itself. (5) Why, then, has rationality [*logos*] been passed on to us by nature?

For the correct use of mental impressions [phantasiai].

So, what is rationality itself?

A structure [systêma] made up of various impressions.

Hence it naturally studies itself too.

Up to this point we might almost be reading Aristotle.[1] Epictetus states a general thesis (sections 1–2), which divides crafts and faculties into two types: self-studying and not self-studying.[2] The logic of his division is as follows: Let C = any craft or faculty, F = field, Hom = homogenenous field, Het = heterogenous field, SS = self-studying, and NSS = not self-studying. Presented formally, the train of thought is:

> If C, then F
> If F, then either Hom or Het
> If Het, then CNSS
> If Hom, then CSS

Epictetus next exemplifies the second type NSS (sections 3–4), and argues, from a description of rationality, that rationality belongs to the first type SS (section 5). Numerous passages of the discourses, in spite of their conversational and colloquial idiom, have a logical structure that lends itself to formal analysis. However, right at the outset this discourse is distinctively Epictetan in three respects.

First, there is the simplicity of the sentence structure, which interweaves statements with questions and answers.

Secondly, in section (5) Epictetus combines a standard Stoic account of rationality with his favourite slogan for prescribing a philosophically trained and excellent character—the capacity 'to make correct use of mental impressions', by which he refers to our thoughts and states of consciousness in general.[3] As we have already seen (p. 85), he likes to draw support for this formula by citing Socrates' insistence on self-scrutiny and living an examined life. Although he does not name Socrates here, he can expect his students to pick up the allusion, and other features of

---

[1] In section (2) Epictetus' word for 'of the same species' is *homoeidês*, a favourite Aristotelian term.

[2] His claim that some crafts are self-studying was controversial; see Dobbin (1998: 183).

[3] See p. 214, and for the description of rationality as 'a structure made up of certain impressions', see LS 53V = a passage of Galen citing Chrysippus' statement: 'reason is a collection of certain conceptions and preconceptions'. Note also LS 39F, where 'conceptions' are classified as 'a kind of impression'.

this little argument (for instance, the treatment of rationality as a craft and the use of the cobbling example) have a Socratic ring.

Thirdly, while the argument appears to establish a purely factual point—the reflexive aspect of rationality—Epictetus arrives at this inference by asking why we are rational animals. His answer implies that our capacity to reason reflexively is both fundamental to our human nature and also a capacity that our nature requires us to exercise *correctly*.

In the next movement of the discourse this ethical dimension comes to the fore:

66 (6) Further, what is the field that intelligence [*phronêsis*] has been passed on to us to study?
Things good, bad, and neither good nor bad.
What, then, is intelligence?
Something good.
And what is lack of intelligence?
Something bad.
(7) So you see, then, that intelligence necessarily studies both itself and its opposite. Therefore, the philosopher's greatest and primary function is to test and discriminate between mental impressions and to accept none of them that has not been tested.

Translators who render 'intelligence' (*phronêsis*) by 'wisdom' miss Epictetus' logic and the way his point here is connected with the previous argument. In strict Stoic theory, *phronêsis* is a name for the perfected wisdom of the ideal sage, but here Epictetus is using the word less strictly, for a species of rationality that could pertain to the likes of himself and his students.[4] He has already indicated (section 5) that rationality is something normative, whose nature it is to make correct use of itself. As rational beings, we find ourselves constantly having to make value judgements, so what he means by *phronêsis* is the application of rationality to the Stoics' spectrum of three types of value—good, bad, and 'indifferent' or neither good nor bad (see Ch. 4 n. 5): these constitute the field that it is the function of

---

[4] His only other use of *phronêsis* is at 3.13.19, a quite different context. Recall also (p. 33 above) that Epictetus is largely reticent about the old Stoic ideal of absolute and infallible wisdom.

intelligence to study. It follows, from the previous argument, that intelligence is homogeneous to its field of study, and thus reflexive and capable of studying itself.

Is Epictetus entitled, we may ask, simply to assert the goodness of intelligence, after nominating all types of value as its field? Should not intelligence itself, because of its homogeneity to its field, be good, bad, and neither good nor bad? He can take care of this challenge in two ways. First, in treating lack of intelligence as bad, he is not referring to the complete absence of reasoning, but rather to the misuse of this faculty. Reasoning, according to Stoicism, is constantly at work in every adult person's life, even though most people practise it imperfectly.[5] Further, having specified rationality as a craft (sections 1–5), he can expect his audience to let this concept carry through to section 6, and to understand the 'goodness' of intelligence as continuing the craft analogy. The crafts of grammar and shoe-making are concerned with *good* literature and with *good* leather, but their practitioners also need the expertise to judge bad and indifferent literature and leather.

This point resolves another difficulty some readers may find with section 6—namely, the connection between the generic badness that intelligence includes in its study and the specific badness of lacking intelligence. As non-Stoics, we think that all sorts of things besides lack of intelligence are bad. That, however, is not Stoic doctrine. Their thesis is that strictly nothing is good except good reasoning or moral knowledge and nothing is strictly bad except bad reasoning or moral ignorance. It is precisely this pair of opposites, or rather the virtuous and vicious character states and actions corresponding to them, that constitute respectively human excellence or imperfection. All other things—including bodily and external circumstances and all mental states or personality traits that have no essential bearing on our well-being—are 'neither good nor bad'.[6]

Once this background is understood, we are in a position to see the depth of Epictetus' point concerning the reflexivity and goodness of intelligence. In studying 'good, bad, and neither good nor bad', intelligence is studying how it differs in its goodness from

[5] For evidence and discussion, see Annas (1992) and Long (1999).
[6] See LS 58 and 60 for full details.

bad reasoning and how both of these differ from purely indifferent things; and because intelligence is not simply something good but *the* good, its practice and self-study are the very essence of goodness.

At section 7, Epictetus draws a conclusion that applies intelligence's sphere of operation and reflexivity—the study of values—to the mental impressions he had specified as rationality's material in section 5. Here again, a newcomer may have difficulty in following the train of thought, but his students have been given the requisite background in other discourses. By 'impressions' (*phantasiai*) Epictetus is referring not only to the evidence of our senses (as many of his translators have erroneously thought) but also to our awareness of anything at all.[7] Such awareness could include the appearance of a sexually alluring person, the recollection of a slave's careless behaviour, the thought of one's angry father, or the prospect of a legacy.

All of these examples involve states of affairs that Epictetus and any other Stoic would regard as intrinsically neither good nor bad. All of them, however, also involve thoughts that are open to strongly positive or negative evaluation and so capable of stimulating impulses to action. A non-Stoic might well judge the corresponding situations to be intrinsically good or bad, and respond to them with vehement emotion. A Stoic's proper attitude to them would be more complex. While treating the situations themselves as neither good nor bad, he would regard our thoughts and intentions in regard to them as falling unequivocally within the sphere of good and bad—that is to say, within the sphere of exercising reason well or badly.

We are now able to understand how Epictetus' conclusion concerning the philosopher's primary function of testing impressions is wholly coherent with his preceding findings about intelligence and values. Testing impressions is the way Epictetus recommends his students to manifest rationality and commitment to Stoicism. He is asking them to subject every situation and thought to their reflexive rationality and understanding of what is good or bad or merely neutral.

[7] See p. 214 and Long (1991).

67 (8) In the case of coinage, where we take it that our interest is involved, you are aware of how we have actually devised an art, and of all the ways an assayer uses to test coinage—sight, touch, smell, and finally hearing. (9) He throws the coin down, listens to the sound, and is not satisfied with a single ring but by attending to it frequently becomes a real musician![8] (10) Just so, in cases where we think it really matters not to make mistakes we pay a lot of attention to distinguishing things that might make us do that.

(11) But where our pathetic mind is concerned—our governing faculty—we yawn, go to sleep, and accept every impression that comes. This is because the damage does not hit us.

(12) So when you want to know how casually you deal with goodness and badness, and how seriously with things that are indifferent, compare your attitude to going blind with your attitude to being mentally in the dark; then you will realize that you are a long way from having the right feelings about goodness and badness.

After his abstract and compressed opening (**65–6**), Epictetus suddenly switches gears. His vivid example of the assayer serves both as an ironical paradigm for the way intelligence should test its materials, and as a serious paradigm for the way 'we' misapply that faculty: we are all equipped with an assayer's resources, as it were, but, instead of focusing them on the contents of our mind—the only location of genuine goodness and badness—we squander them on assessments of things like money that have no bearing on what is really good or bad for us.

Epictetus employs a characteristic complicity with his students in his use of 'we' here and an equally typical irony in his dubbing the assayer a master musician. Notice too his liking for images ('yawning and sleeping') that call his students' (and his own) attention to their neglect of what really matters. Then, he makes an equally characteristic switch from identification with his students to a professorial role (section 12), challenging them to recognize their philosophical shortcomings if, as he presumes, they are unable to assign to mental blindness the unqualified badness they mistakenly attribute to actually losing one's eyesight.

[8] As Dobbin (1998: 184), points out, the craft analogy with coinage was traditional.

68   (13) *But that requires a lot of preparation, effort and learning.*
So what? Do you expect that it's possible to master the greatest art briefly? (14) It's true that the principal doctrine of the philosophers *is* brief. If you want to know, read Zeno and you will see. (15) What time does it take to say:

> *The human goal is to follow the gods, and the substance of goodness is the proper use of impressions?*[9]

(16) Now say:

> *What, then, is God and what is an impression? What is the nature of an individual thing, and what is the nature of the universe?*

The answer gets long!

Here Epictetus makes another typically abrupt switch. He drops the earnest, though engaging, monologue of **67** and shifts into a rapidly conversational, tongue-in-cheek style. Imagining a student objecting to the time and effort required to internalize a properly Stoic sense of values (section 13), he responds with a tease about brevity and length. We could paraphrase like this. You only want a quick fix? Fine, it takes only a moment to state the principles of Stoicism.[10] Now, ask what those principles involve, and you have a corresponding analogy for the time and exertion they require from you.

69   (17) So, if Epicurus comes and says that goodness must be located in the flesh, that's again a lengthy issue. You need lectures on what the dominant principle in us is, that is to to say, what our substance and essence are. It's not likely that a snail's good consists in its shell, so is it likely that Epicurus is right about the good of a human being?

(18) You yourself, Epicurus, what do you have that is more authoritative? What do you have inside yourself that deliberates and reviews each thing, and which decides that the flesh itself is the principal part?

---

[9] Although Epictetus appears to be quoting Zeno here, the language he uses is his own.

[10] Cf. 2.9.15: 'Which of us cannot give a technical account of good and bad things: namely, that some existing things are good, others bad, and yet others indifferent? Good things are the virtues and whatever participates in the virtues; bad things are the opposites of these; and indifferent things are wealth, health and renown.' Epictetus is accurately stating, but also gently mocking, standard Stoic formulations (cf. **35**). His first sentence is a word-for-word citation of the Stoic doxography known to us from Stobaeus (2.57.19–20), and the rest of the passage is an entirely accurate paraphrase of Stobaeus' later account.

(19) Why, moreover, do you light your lamp and toil away for us and write so many books? Is it to ensure that we aren't ignorant of the truth? Who do you take *us* to be? What is our relation to *you*? Thus the discussion becomes lengthy.

Has anything prepared us for this abrupt transition to Epicurus? The most immediate connection to section 16 is effected by continuing the contrast between a brief philosophical slogan—now represented by one of Epicurus' most notorious expressions for his hedonism—and the lengthy time needed to explore and, in this case, refute it. However, an attentive listener will have noticed that, in turning to Epicurus at the end, Epictetus is reinforcing his earlier points about the goodness of intelligence and its centrality to the proper understanding of human nature and conduct. Epictetus charges Epicurus with refuting himself by living a life that, instead of concentrating on sensual and self-centred pleasure, confirms the value Epictetus assigns to intelligence and to exercising it philanthropically.[11]

The validity of this critique need not concern us here. What we should note is a further tease in this final part of the discourse. Is Epictetus quite serious when he insists that it takes a long time to respond to Epicurus? His rhetorical challenges are so pointedly phrased that we should take him to be employing heavy irony. In contrast with Stoicism, he is saying, Epicurus' philosophy is a soft option and its errors can be grasped as rapidly as they are stated.

5.2 *ON LAPSING FROM INTEGRITY* (4.9)

The discourse just examined is addressed to the students in general. Here now is one that purports to engage a single person who has lapsed from his former commitment to Stoicism. Unlike 1.20, this piece may seem to be doggedly *protreptic* as distinct from doctrinal; in fact it is a demonstration of Epictetus' ubiquitous message—that persons should look to their volition and judgements as the only criterion of living well or badly.

[11] For the details see Dobbin (1998: 185–6), and note that Epictetus mounts a lengthier attack on Epicurus, using the same self-refutation strategy, at 1.23.

70 (1) Whenever you see someone holding political power, set against it the fact that you yourself have no need of power. Whenever you see someone wealthy, observe what you have instead of that. (2) For if you have nothing in its place, you are in a miserable state; but if you have the absence of the need to have wealth, realize that you have something greater and much more valuable.

(3) One man has a beautiful wife, you have the absence of longing for a beautiful wife. Do you think these are little things? How much would these very people—the wealthy, the powerful, the ones who live with beautiful women—pay for the ability to look down on wealth and power and those very women whom they adore and get?

(4) Are you unaware of what a feverish person's thirst is like? It is quite different from a healthy person's. The latter drinks and he's over it; but the former after a moment's gratification is nauseous, turns the water into bile, vomits, has belly ache, and gets even thirstier than before. (5) It's just the same when wealth and power and sleeping with a beautiful woman are each combined with longing for these things. There is an increment of jealousy, fear of loss, foul talk, foul thoughts, ugly actions.

Epictetus begins this discourse, as often (e.g. 3.17; 4.3; 4.12), by inviting his audience to envision challenges that his philosophy is specifically designed to address. How do you avoid the unhappiness of missing out on some other person's seeming good fortune? His opening strategy, a repeated one (see 4.3), proposes that you make a comparative judgement, and his logic turns on the repeated use of the word 'have' (*echein*). Other people have things that you may not have—wealth, power, beautiful wives. With a bold extension of the normal concept of ownership, Epictetus contrasts these possessions with 'having' the absence of longing for them (sections 1–3).[12] Thus we are asked to take equanimity as a supremely desirable mental possession to be weighed against and judged greatly superior to these material possessions.

Next (sections 3–5), we are invited to put ourselves in the position of those who not only have such possessions but also *have* a passionate longing for them together with concomitant distress

[12] This is a good example of Epictetus' interest in what modern philosophers call 'second-order desires', i.e. wanting to want (or wanting not to want) something; see Inwood (2000) for an excellent treatment of second-order desires in Seneca.

and shameful consequences. Epictetus' point is not that there is
anything inherently bad about material possessions, holding
powerful offices, and so forth. Such things, taken by themselves,
are quite neutral in value. His point is that when *having* them is
combined with *longing for* them, the outcome is tantamount to an
incurable fever.

As section 4 shows, Epictetus can be as caustic as any ancient
satirist in his representation of the vanity of human wishes. His
focus on the 'ugliness' that unrestrained longing engenders prepares the way for a direct attack on this condition:

71   (6) *And what do I lose?* (says someone) .
My friend, you used to be a man with integrity [*aidêmôn*], and you no
longer are. Have you lost nothing? Instead of Chrysippus and Zeno you
read Aristides and Evenus.[13]

Have you lost nothing? Instead of Socrates and Diogenes you admire
the man who can corrupt and seduce the most women. (7) You want to
be handsome and you make yourself up to be, though you are not, and
you want to show off in glittering clothes to turn the women's eyes, and
if you get hold of some perfume, you think yourself in heaven.

(8) In the past you never gave these things a thought, but only where
you would find good conversation, an admirable man, a noble sentiment. So you used to sleep like a man, go out like a man, wearing a man's
clothes, talking in the words that suit a man. And now you tell me:
I have lost nothing.
(9) Is cash the only thing people can lose? Aren't integrity and decency
capable of being lost? Isn't the loss of these things a damage? (10)
Perhaps you no longer think so; but there was a time when you counted
this as the only damage and harm, when you were anxious that no one
should shake you out of these thoughts and actions.

Turning to a lapsed Stoic, whether actual or imaginary,
Epictetus exploits the language of profit and loss that he used in
the first part of this discourse in order to charge the person with
reneging on the values he used to endorse. In effect, the interlocutor has said: 'Why should I care about the bad moral consequences that you, Epictetus, associate with attachment to

---

[13] Aristides of Miletus (*c.* 100 BC) was the author of a notorious erotic novel. The
name Evenus may be a corruption for Eubius, whom Ovid, in a context where he
mentions Aristides, calls the author of an 'obscene tale' (*Tristia* II.416).

material possessions and the longing for a purely hedonistic life?'
Epictetus' retort is two-pronged. First, as elsewhere (3.24.5), he
associates hedonism with effeminacy, using 'manliness' as a
stand-in for the manners as well as the morals that befit a Stoic.
Secondly, instead of simply preaching at the person, he asks him
to reflect on his own change of outlook. To the interlocutor's
'Why should I care?', Epictetus responds: 'Well, once you did
care enormously.' In other words, Epictetus asks the person to
justify his change of mind, to himself. Since the whole point at
issue is personal integrity, that is a hard challenge for the lapsed
Stoic to refuse.

72 (11) Look, you have been shaken out [of your former disposition], but
by yourself, not by anyone else. Fight against yourself, claim yourself
for decency, integrity, and freedom.

   (12) If anyone had ever told you this about me—that someone was
forcing me to commit adultery, to wear clothes like yours, to put perfume on, wouldn't you have gone out and murdered the person for
abusing me in this way?

   (13) So aren't you willing now to help yourself? How much easier this
help is! You don't have to kill someone, or fetter him, or assault him, or
appear in court; all you have to do is to converse with yourself, who are
the best person to be persuaded and to whom no one is more persuasive
than yourself.

Here Epictetus shifts from the admonitory tone of **71** to a
more mentoring and genial voice. He offers the lapsed Stoic a
lesson in selfhood by drawing a vivid contrast between external
compulsion, which may require a third party's intervention,
and the self as a locus of internal dialogue and persuasion. The
recommendation to engage oneself in conversation is not simply
an injunction to pull oneself together. Rather, it reflects
Epictetus' tireless insistence that internal dialogue, self-
address, and self-examination are our essential resources for
monitoring experience and shaping one's life in accordance
with the normative principles of human nature (see 4.6.6).
Short of external compulsion, persons act on the basis of persuading themselves: the recusant Stoic has persuaded himself
out of his Stoic principles, and by the same token it is he, and

not Epictetus, who is best equipped to persuade himself back
into them.

But some advice can still be offered:

73 (14) To begin with, decide against what has been going on. Next, having done that, don't despair of yourself or be like the feeble people who,
once they have given in, completely give up on themselves and are
swept off, by the current as it were.
(15) Instead, learn from the sports trainers. The boy falls down.
Get up (he says); *wrestle again until you have made yourself strong.*
(16) That's the sort of attitude you should have. For you can be sure that
there is nothing more susceptible to influence than the human mind.
You need only will something, and it happens; the correction is made.
Conversely, you need only nod off, and things are ruined. For both ruin
and salvation have their source within you.

Is there more here than the threadbare maxim: if you don't first
succeed, keep on trying? Yes indeed. For the application of the
sports image stays within the previous diagnosis of the self.
Decision and volition are faculties whose exercise can have
immediately beneficial effects on our lives, but the mind's susceptibility is such that only constant vigilance can keep it focused
on the autonomy that generates self-respect and protects against
despair.

Epictetus is too hard-headed to suppose that these brief
remarks will suffice to return the recusant to the Stoic fold. He
concludes this short discourse as follows:

74   (17) *What good am I going to get after that?*
What are you looking for that is greater than this? You will pass from
being shameless to being a person with self-respect, from being a mess
to being in good shape, from lacking integrity to having it, from being
out of control to self-controlled. (18) If you are looking for anything
greater than this, stick to what you are doing now. Even a god won't be
able to save you.

Previously the interlocutor wanted to know what he was losing
by taking wealthy and powerful hedonists as his paradigms (section 6). Now he asks what he is going to get from dedicating himself to the priorities Epictetus recommends. Epictetus' ironical

response hardly requires analysis, but we should note that it maintains the emphasis of the whole discourse on internal reasoning and self-determination as the required instruments of moral education. As we have already seen (Section 4.3), Epictetus makes it a fundamental premiss of his teaching that the student should want to live the Stoic life. He can explain what that involves and why, in his view, nothing can compare with the value of trying to internalize Stoic principles. But if a person cannot see the point of that, he is beyond any help that Epictetus or philosophy can offer.

CHAPTER 6

Natures: Divine, Human, Animal

Whenever you are in company, whenever you take exercise, whenever you converse, don't you know that you are nourishing God, exercising God? You are carrying God around, you poor thing, and you don't know it. Do you think I am speaking of an external god made of gold or silver? You are carrying him around inside yourself, and you fail to realize that you defile him with unclean thoughts and foul actions.

(2.8.12–13)

6.1 THEOLOGICAL ORIENTATION

In the first half of this book our focus has been on Epictetus' didactic style and methodology. In the second half these matters will not drop out of sight, but we shall be chiefly concerned with the 'principal concepts' that I outlined in Chapter 1. There I presented a complete translation of the discourse 1.14 where Epictetus argues that everything we do is overseen by God, who is actually present in each person's mind. Readers may wish to review that text before proceeding further; for it registers the foundation of his entire outlook.[1]

---

[1] By contrast, Arrian's selection for the *Manual* is largely reticent on theology.

Like all Stoics, Epictetus sees himself as an interpreter of 'nature' (*physis*), but he does not discuss the world's microscopic structure nor does he give an account of time and space, as his early predecessors had done. The nature that interests him is exclusively animate, under which he includes not only human beings and other animals but first and foremost God. The only proper name that Epictetus mentions more frequently than Socrates is Zeus. Whether he speaks of Zeus or God or Nature or the gods, he is completely committed to the belief that the world is providentially organized by a divine power whose creative agency reaches its highest manifestation in human beings.

That was orthodox Stoicism, and much else that Epictetus attributes to divinity is quite traditional.[2] However, no theology is simply a matter of doctrine. Conceptions of the divine are indicated in numerous ways that go beyond such epithets as eternal, creative, providential, and beneficent, on all of which the Stoics were agreed. Awe, reverence, gratitude, joy, prayer, obedience—these are a sample of attitudes that a serious belief in a supreme divinity typically involves. Stoic philosophers, just like other believers, vary considerably over which of these attitudes they express and with what degree of emotional engagement.

When we review Epictetus from this perspective, his theology emerges as most distinctive in two respects: first, its serving as the explicit foundation for his moral psychology, and, secondly, its warmly and urgently personalist tone. More emphatically than any other Stoic in our record, Epictetus speaks of Zeus or God in terms that treat the world's divine principle as a person to whom one is actually present and who is equally present to oneself as an integral aspect of one's mind.

For modern readers, raised in the traditions of Christianity, Judaism, or Islam, the theology of Graeco-Roman philosophy is exceptionally difficult to grasp without falling victim to either over-assimilation or excessive differentiation. In the case of

---

[2] Like all Stoics, Epictetus regularly personifies Nature (*physis*) and attributes to it many of the same activities that he attributes to God or Zeus: see 1.6.20–2; 1.20.5; 2.11.6; 2.20.21; 4.1.51; 4.5.14; 4.11.17; fr. 14. Sometimes he employs both words together in a hendiadys, as at 1.29.19, 'the law of Nature and God'.

Epictetus the difficulty is extreme because he says so much that reads like, and sometimes has been read as, a direct echo of the New Testament.

He characterizes God as the 'caring father of human beings' (1.3.1; cf. 3.24.3), and he even treats adoption by the Roman emperor as conferring less status than his students enjoy as 'sons of Zeus' (1.3.2). He asks rhetorically, expecting an affirmative answer, whether God cares for individual persons (1.12.6). He tells his students to call on God to help them over difficulties (2.18.29) and to regard slaves as their siblings because they too are children of God (1.13.4). He is insistent that God and the nature of goodness or helpfulness coincide (2.8.1). In all things he and his students are to look to God as their benevolent creator and friend, to do God's will, to be thankful to God, and to please him (1.9.4; 4.1.98; 4.4.21; 4.12.11). God has given a portion of himself to each person, whose status is correspondingly exalted (1.3; 2.8.11). When Epictetus utters advice to a young man, he says that the voice really belongs to 'a kindly god talking through me' (3.1.36).

Epictetus speaks of the world's divine author with the commitment and even the fervour of such figures as St Paul or St Augustine. Nor is his tone significantly affected by the fact that besides speaking of God or Zeus he also speaks of gods in the plural. Monotheism in the strict Judaic, Christian, and Islamic sense was not a doctrinal issue in Stoicism. Because the Stoic divinity is everywhere, Stoic philosophers could accommodate gods in the plural. They even applied the divine names of Greek and Roman popular religion to the elements earth, air, fire, and water, and especially to the heavenly bodies. Strictly, though, these gods are only symbolical ways of referring to the world's most powerful constituents all of which owe their existence to the *single* 'active principle' named God in the singular or Zeus.

In his ubiquitous references to God or Zeus, Epictetus has in mind the creator of the world and all its natural contents. To that divine being, just like adherents of the great monotheistic religions, he ascribes wondrous providence, supreme goodness, and omniscience. Epictetus' divinity is the maker of the best of all possible worlds. Conformity to God and imitation of God are expressions that he uses in characterizing human excellence; for God is the paradigm of the virtues human beings are equipped to achieve.[3]

Epictetus' theological language betokens a personal belief and experience as deep and wholehearted as that of any Jew or Christian or Muslim. And there are further affinities to mention. As with these religions in at least their doctrinal strictness, Epictetus rejects the existence of any evil principle in the universe. Chrysippus in the early days of Stoicism had worried about how to reconcile providence with natural disasters and the suffering of the innocent, but Epictetus gives no attention to theodicy. There is nothing bad for which God is responsible because badness pertains exclusively to human deficiencies. The happiness God intends for all persons could be theirs if only they brought their minds and values into harmony with the 'laws' of their own and the world's natures.

One can scarcely avoid thinking about the great monotheistic religions when Epictetus refers to divine will, divine law, and obedience to God. Yet, however much his emotional involvement in these concepts may push us towards such assimilation, we need to step back and note a number of radical differences.

First, and most important, is the characteristically Stoic identification between God and *rational* perfection. There is no gap between an ideally wise Stoic and God because the human paragon, by virtue of being perfectly rational, is obedient to God and in conformity with the divine will and law. We have already noticed how Epictetus talks about 'the God within'. At times he seems to distinguish a human being's 'holy spirit' from God as such (p. 166), but we are never to think of the Stoic Zeus as transcendent in the Christian sense of the first person of the divine Trinity.

This is a second point of great difference from the other religions. For Epictetus, as for all Stoics, our minds are literally 'offshoots' of God, parts of God that God has assigned to be the mind or self of each person. As cosmic rationality, God also exists outside every individual's mind because he is the structuring

---

[3] See 1.12.7; 1.25.3–6; 2.14.12–13; also p. 171 below.

principle of the entire universe; and Epictetus, like other Stoics again, will sometimes use language that could suggest a god who is distinct from his creation. But this is not to be taken literally. The Stoic God *is* nature, extending through everything, and, while Epictetus, unlike the early Stoics, gives no attention to explaining how God can be physically present everywhere, he does not differ from his predecessors over God's identity with the *natural* order of things.

Because the Stoic God is immanent and identical with perfect rationality, Epictetus follows his tradition in taking the general character of God and his works to be fully accessible to human understanding. If we apply our minds properly to the study of our own and the world's nature, we are literally in touch with God. Physical nature, not a sacred text or revelation or inspired prophecy, is the Stoic's guide to the divine. The Stoic outlook on God is this-worldly in the sense that there is no supernatural domain for which we should be preparing ourselves in this life, no 'end of days' when lives will be judged. The life that we have now is what requires all of our attention; the only punishment for those who neglect the principles of Stoicism, Epictetus says, is to 'stay just as they are', emotionally disturbed and discontented (1.12.21–2; 3.11.1–3).

Yet, in another sense, the Stoic outlook on God can be viewed as an invitation to reject this-worldly values and become completely assimilated to divine rationality. Epictetus expresses this bold project by challenging his students to show him someone who 'is desirous of becoming a god instead of a man, and though he is in this little body, this corpse, has communion with Zeus as his purpose' (2.19.27).

Here we should note a further profound difference between Stoic and other theological attitudes. Because God's nature is perfect rationality, and this condition is at least theoretically available to human beings, it was Stoic doctrine that while God or Zeus was incomparably more powerful than any person could be, he was not necessarily superior in virtue and happiness to what a human being might in principle achieve. Epictetus never quite endorses this thought (which was worse than heresy to Christianity), but the assimilation to the divine that he advocates

(2.14.13) gives persons a potential status that virtually eliminates the qualitative difference between the ideal human and the divine. Far from being tainted by sin at birth, human beings are innately equipped by God to perfect themselves *by their own efforts*. There is no need, then, for a divine act of grace or redemption or sacrifice.

6.2 THEISM, PANTHEISM, AND PHYSICS

In his conception of divine providence, creativity, and rationality, Epictetus is completely in line with the general Stoic tradition. His distinctiveness, in what I have discussed so far, extends mainly to the enthusiasm with which he commends obedience to God and to the warmth he infuses in his expressions of God's concern for human beings.[4] No passage is more revealing of this outlook than one we encountered in Chapter 1 (p. 26): 'Remember never to say you are alone, because you are not; God is inside and your own divine spirit too' (1.14.13–14). Epictetus is as insistent as any Stoic on our need to accommodate ourselves resolutely to every external or God-given circumstance. But he premises that tough prescription on a literal association between the *person* of God and the individual self.

I emphasize this point because it helps to explain Epictetus' selective treatment of the theological tradition he had inherited. As originally propounded, Stoic theology was a complex amalgam of pantheism and theism, by which I mean that God was conceived as being both an omnipresent physical force embodied in fire or fiery breath (*pneuma*) and the world's governing mind or soul. Under the first description, God combines with 'matter' (the passive principle) to form the world, and indeed makes the world one with himself; in this pantheistic sense, the world is God. Pantheism has often been viewed as incompatible with a theistic or personalist conception of God, but the early Stoics were as committed to the latter as to the former. God's

---

[4] As far as our record goes. It is quite probable that Epictetus took himself to be reviving the religious strand of Stoicism pioneered by Cleanthes but less prominent in his successors.

mind, they claimed, has thoughts and impulses that differ in range and power rather than in kind from those available to human minds; and, as we have seen, they proposed that our own minds are integral parts or offshoots of God.

This combination of pantheism and theism raises enormous questions. God is the formative principle of stones, plants, and non-human as well as human animals. Not only that. The Stoic God is *embodied* in everything and is the cause of everything. Such pantheism makes it hard to understand how God can be present in an exemplary or specially refined way in the human mind. Moreover, if our minds are simply and directly 'parts' of God's mind, it is hard to understand how we as individuals are capable of thinking for ourselves and able to assume responsibility for our own lives. The early Stoics, especially Chrysippus, offered exceedingly complex answers to resolve these difficulties over pantheism and theism, and over the relation between cosmic and human nature, but in my judgement they left more problems than they resolved.

I think that Epictetus shared these worries. He countered them primarily by emphasizing theism over pantheism, or, more exactly, by asserting God's presence throughout nature as distinct from explaining it in physical terms or by identifying God with the world. Perhaps we should call Epictetus a 'panentheist' (one who believes in God's omnipresence, irrespective of its exact rationale); but, however we describe him, his conception of God will be most intelligible to modern readers if it is pictured as a universal mind.[5] Later in this chapter, we shall study a number of his theistic tendencies, but first we should note his reticence concerning the physical attributes and functions of God.

He has virtually nothing to say concerning the technicalities and complexities of early Stoic cosmology. He never refers explicitly to the passive principle 'matter', and when he mentions

---

[5] In Stoic doctrine God is 'embodied' in *pneuma*, literally 'breath', which becomes *spiritus*, 'spirit', in Latin. Thus the Stoics paved the way for the concept of a 'spiritual body'. My point in the main text is that Epictetus generally speaks as though God were purely mind.

'body' the connotations he attaches to the word are generally negative, as they are not in Stoicism officially. He says nothing about
God's physical identity as fire or fiery breath (*pneuma*) or 'vibrant
motion' (*tonikê kinêsis*). Just three times, in contexts concerning
the inevitability of human change and death, he refers to the
world's need for cyclical regeneration of its constituents (2.1.18;
3.24.10; 4.1.100–6), and once (again to make a moral point), he
opens a window on the notorious Stoic doctrine that our world
will end in a cosmic conflagration, during which Zeus com-
munes with himself over his re-creation of the next world-cycle
(3.13.4).

We may be tempted to explain Epictetus' selectivity as due
simply to a belief that what his students need is moral training
rather than esoteric physics. Or did he perhaps doubt his own
ability to deal with that subject, or treat it outside the context of
the discourses? There are much better explanations, which
accord with his preference for theism over pantheism. A fragment from a lost part of the discourses runs as follows (fr. 1):

75 Why (he says) should I care whether existing things are compounded
from atomic or incomposite elements, or from fire and earth? Isn't it
enough to learn the essence of good and bad and the measures of
desires and aversions and also of positive and negative impulses, to run
our lives using these as rules; and not to bother about those things that
are beyond us? Perhaps they cannot be known by the human mind,
and even if one were to suppose that they are perfectly knowable, what
is the advantage of such knowledge? Shouldn't we say that people
who make this *essential* to a philosopher's discourse are wasting their
time?
  So, is the Delphic precept, 'Know yourself', superfluous?
Certainly not.
  Then what does it mean?
If someone told a member of a chorus to know himself, wouldn't he
attend to the instruction by concentrating on his fellow singers and with
being in tune with them?
  Yes.
And so with a sailor or a soldier. Do you think that human beings have
been made to live alone or in a community?
  In a community.
By whom?

By Nature.
Is there no longer any need to busy oneself over Nature, what it is, how
it governs the world, and whether or not it is <knowable>?[6]

The main speaker of this dialogue is generally taken to be
Epictetus himself, and I am sure this is right.[7] However, I differ
from most translators in punctuating the last sentence as a
(rhetorical) question and not a statement, and with one editor I
supply the word 'knowable' at the very end. The train of
thought, I propose, goes like this.

Epictetus begins by contrasting the urgency and feasibility of
moral training, in words he uses to characterize his first two fields
of study (see Section 4.4), with esoteric physics. The exact truth
about the ultimate composition of matter may be beyond human
understanding, and even supposing otherwise we can question
the value or necessity of such knowledge to philosophy. But, as
human beings, we absolutely need to understand ourselves; that
is to say, to understand that it is our nature to be social beings.
Hence—and this is my interpretation of the crucial point—we
must not infer from the difficulty and even irrelevancy of doing
esoteric physics that we should dispense with the study of where
we fit within the system of Nature and of what we can learn about
Nature's government of the world.

Now, the justification for this interpretation. Throughout the
discourses Epictetus provides his students with detailed answers
to these very questions. Whether he speaks of Nature (as in
1.6.21 and 1.16.9), or of Zeus or God (as in 1.6.3 and 1.19.11),
Epictetus takes it to be completely certain that human beings are
equipped to understand how this cosmic principle excellently
governs the world and how, in particular, it has made human
beings not only social animals but also 'world citizens' (1.9.1;
1.19.13; 2.10.3; 3.24.11). It is unthinkable, then, that he should
end **75** by denying the need to study Nature, as most translations

    [6] I follow those editors who think that a word has dropped out here. It hardly
makes sense for Epictetus to be asking at this point whether nature exists.
    [7] A very different interpretation of the text is adopted by Barnes (1997: 25–7) who
proposes that its first part is spoken by a student, whom Epictetus then challenges to
take the opening questions seriously. I am not persuaded, on the evidence that Barnes
cites, that 'Epictetus was a devotee of the physical part of philosophy'.

render the text. Yet, as I have said, the surviving discourses are reticent concerning details of cosmology, and that reticence tallies with the dismissive comments at the beginning of the text. Are these last two points consistent? Perfectly so if, following his own practice in the discourses, we distinguish the study of Nature's providential management of the world from what I have called esoteric physics.

The importance of 75 is the explanation it gives for Epictetus' exclusive concentration on the former of these studies: he doubts not only the value of the latter but also its feasibility. In arriving at this judgement, he is likely to have been influenced by several considerations.

First, in the period after Chrysippus, Stoic philosophers disagreed with one another over many points of cosmology; and the absence of any consensus, together with the difficulty of integrating pantheism with theism, helps to explain why Stoic physics appears to have more or less atrophied after Posidonius. Given the exacting standards the Stoics expected scientific knowledge to satisfy, Epictetus' doubts about the possibility of settling questions concerning the world's elements were well grounded.

Secondly, because Epictetus was living through a period when philosophical scepticism was on the rise, he must have been aware of sceptical challenges to all competing physical theories. While he plainly thought that the general principles of theistic cosmology were demonstrable beyond any challenge, he would have good reason not to clutter his commitment to them by presenting his students with complex and unprovable ideas about the physical structure of the world and God's exact relation to matter. Theological arguments from nature's design, like those Epictetus endorsed, have long outlived ancient science, and have been endorsed by people who strongly disagree among themselves about the details of physics.

We should, then, absolve Epictetus from any taint of incompetence or narrowly moral vision. Excising what he took to be purely speculative physics, he focused on what he took to be essential and provable in the Stoic tradition on nature—God's unqualified providence and special concern for human beings.

Besides all this, there is a third explanation for Epictetus' procedure, hitherto quite unnoticed, which puts the deliberateness of his selectivity beyond question. The fragmentary text we have been studying, and indeed Epictetus' practice throughout the discourses, closely echo two famous passages of Xenophon's *Memorabilia*. In 1.1.11–16 Xenophon presents Socrates as someone who, in contrast to his scientific contemporaries, refrained from speculation about the world's elements, treating such enquiry as fruitless, fraught with disagreements, and irrelevant to achieving knowledge of the human condition and the norms of community life. However, Xenophon (4.3.2–18) also attributes to Socrates a concept of cosmic teleology and divine concern for human beings that fits Epictetus exactly. In Xenophon's second passage Socrates comments on the value to humans of the diurnal rotation, seasonal change, the earth's produce, the utility of domesticable animals, and, above all, the gift of rationality and language, taking all of this to be evidence of divine handiwork and providence. We can be certain that this was a favourite Stoic text and a mainstay of the Stoic appropriation of Socrates.

In view of this book's earlier chapters, readers will hardly be surprised to learn that on issues as large as theology and the appropriate study of nature Epictetus found himself in complete agreeement with Socrates. In numerous passages he explicitly attaches Socrates to his own treatment of theology (1.4.24; 1.9.1; 3.1.19; 3.7.36; 4.4.21). Thus we have further evidence of the course he weaves between traditional Stoicism and direct recourse to Socrates. Yet, here, as elsewhere, his alignment of himself with Socrates is not an instance of parroting. What Epictetus does with providence and divine teleology goes well beyond anything historically Socratic. Epictetus had his own reasons for being reticent on esoteric physics and pantheism, but he also knew that he had Socratic precedent for ignoring questions about the ultimate composition of matter.

6.3 THE COSMIC PERSPECTIVE

Although Epictetus is virtually silent on the physical details of cosmology, he drew closely on those parts of the early Stoic tradition that suited his dominant interest in the world's divine government and its implications for how human beings should dispose themselves. At one point he comes close to paraphrasing Cleanthes:

76 Education is precisely learning to will all individual things just as they happen. And how do they happen? In the way that he who ordains them has ordained. He has ordained that there be summer and winter, plenty and dearth, virtue and vice, and all such opposites on behalf of the harmony of the universe. And he has given us a body and bodily parts and property and fellow human beings. Remembering this dispensation, we should proceed to education not in order to change the conditions (for this is not granted to us nor would it be better) but in order that, with things about us as they are and as their nature is, we may keep our minds in harmony with what happens. (1.12.15–17)

Epictetus' context here is the freedom that we can achieve only by a proper apportionment of responsibility. Our responsibility as individual persons is solely over the area in which we are capable of being autonomous—the 'proper use of mental impressions' (1.12.34). Everything else is God's business; it concerns us only to the extent that we adapt ourselves to it by understanding its rationale within the world's inevitable and providential system.

Cleanthes (the one Stoic whom Epictetus ever quotes verbatim, see n. 14 below) had set the scene and tone for such thoughts in his celebrated *Hymn to Zeus*.[8] There he praises and prays to 'Omnipotent Zeus, prime mover of all nature'. Cleanthes addresses Zeus as both the rational agent of all natural processes (he mentions the earth's diurnal motion, the heavenly bodies, and terrestrial events) and as a father, who has given human beings a likeness to himself. He presents Zeus as creator of a human race that shares his capacity for intelligence and moral

---

[8] For translation of this text, see LS 54I.

understanding. Zeus stands to humanity and the world at large as the embodiment and enactment of 'natural law'. In Cleanthes' poem there is no explicit pantheism. Cleanthes credits natural law, also described as 'universal reason', with outer and inner aspects. Outwardly, it refers to the inevitable order of natural events—the sun's rising and setting, the particular structures of living beings, and so forth. All of these, we are asked to observe, display rationality and order, fitting together into a harmonious pattern. Inwardly, natural law or universal reason refers to the moral order, common to divine and human. In this moral sense, the community of law and reason is something that individual persons have the capacity to discover within themselves: in particular, they are equipped to understand that their natural good is premised upon intelligence and cooperation as distinct from self-seeking competition over fame or possessions, and sexual pleasure.

The only way the inevitable order of things could coincide with a universal moral law is for everything that happens to be right. Without qualification, such a thesis would be as repugnant as it is implausible (though Marcus Aurelius entertains it; see for instance *Meditations* II.17). What Cleanthes says is that Zeus determines everything that happens 'except what bad persons do in their folly'. Evil, then (anticipating St Augustine), is a purely human aberration, for which God is not responsible. Even evil, however, is ultimately harmonized with good, under divine direction; for Cleanthes writes: 'You [Zeus] know how to make things crooked straight.' There is a rationale for bad as well as for good because the coexistence of these opposites is a necessary feature of cosmic order.[9] In the divinely directed Stoic world everything *ultimately* fits together like the combination of concords and discords in a perfectly composed and conducted symphony.

Although Epictetus echoes this cosmic perspective, he prefers to focus his students' attention on their role and qualifications as the most privileged members of the divine orchestra. At the head

---

[9] Cleanthes' *Hymn*, like Epictetus 76, echoes Heraclitus' celebrated doctrine of the harmony of opposites. For Heraclitus' formative influence on Stoicism, see Long (1975/6). Epictetus calls him 'divine' (*Ench.* 15).

of this chapter I cited one of his most memorable sentences: 'You are carrying him [God] around inside yourself.' Here is what he says about persons as 'parts' of the universe or of God. First, a passage from the discourse already excerpted in **76**:

77　Do you not know how small a part you are in comparison with the universe? That is, as regards the body. But as regards rationality, you are not inferior to the gods nor smaller. For rationality's size is not assessed by its length or height, but by its judgements.　(1.12.26)

Next, setting a human life span in the cosmic perspective:

78　I am not eternal, but a human being, a part of the universe as an hour is part of a day. I must be present like the hour and be past like the hour.
　　(2.5.13)

Now, in a context that contrasts the effects of madness and rationality:

79　Is no one, by the agency of reason and proof, capable of learning that God has created everything in the world, and has made the world as a whole unimpeded and perfect but its parts instrumental to the whole? All other creatures have been excluded from the ability to understand the world's government; but the rational animal has capacities for reasoning out the following things—that he is a part and what sort of a part he is, and that it is good for the parts to yield to the whole. (4.7.6–7)

And lastly:

80　Are not the other creatures the gods' artefacts? They are, but they are not primary ones nor are they the gods' parts. But you are a primary one, you are a fragment of God. You have a part of him within yourself. Why, then, are you ignorant of your lineage? Why don't you know your source?　(2.8.10–11)

In these passages, which are as close as Epictetus ever comes to speaking of God pantheistically, he offers his own formulations of the part/whole relation by which Stoics characteristically expressed the relation of the human individual to the divine principle.[10] On the one hand, we are merely transient episodes in the everlasting life of the universe. On the other hand, in virtue of our minds, we are literally 'parts' of God or the cosmos (2.10.3). The first perspective invites us to diminish the import-ance we attach to our particular position in the world; but the second perspective elevates this position to divine status. By pre-senting both perspectives, Epictetus challenges his students to discover what makes the two perspectives mutually consistent. The answer is an attitude of indifference to our body and extern-al contingencies, on the one hand, and, on the other hand, an appraisal of rationality as the special feature of each human being's identity.

6.4 KINSHIP WITH GOD

Theist rather than pantheist, personalist rather than impersonal, ethical rather than physical—these are distinct tendencies in Epictetus' theological language and emphasis. I call them tend-encies because he was not a systematic theologian. He will cer-tainly have thought that he had Stoic authority for everything that he attributes to God, but as we look back at him from our own perspective it is essential that we give due weight to his own formulations rather than interpreting these as simply variations of a completely uniform tradition.

In this section of the chapter I identify three points that make his theological outlook particularly noteworthy: God's gift to human beings of the capacity for complete autonomy, 'the God within', and God's relation to the mind or soul as distinct from the body. All of these points are intimately connected, and for all three of them Epictetus interprets the Stoic tradition with his eye also on Plato or Plato's Socrates.

It will have been obvious to every reader that the primary goal of Epictetus' theology is the light it can shed on human self-understanding and moral orientation. He packs all this together in one of his most compressed and powerful discourses (1.3):

[10] At 1.14.10 Epictetus calls the sun a 'part' of God, but such explicit pantheism is not his normal way of speaking.

81 If a person could identify to the right extent with the following judgement—that we are all primary children of God and that God is the
father of both gods and human beings—I think that he would have no
low or abject opinion of himself. Now if Caesar should adopt you, no
one will stand your conceit; yet, aren't you going to be elated if you
know that you are a son of Zeus? Actually, we don't make this connection. Seeing that our birth involves the blending of these two things—
the body, on the one hand, that we share with animals, and, on the other
hand, rationality and intelligence, that we share with the gods—most of
us incline to this former relationship, wretched and dead though it is,
while only a few to the one that is divine and blessed. Since, then, every
person necessarily handles each thing on the basis of his opinion of it,
those few who think that they are born for integrity and security in their
use of impressions, have no low or abject opinion of themselves, whereas the majority think the opposite.

What am I? A wretched little person; [and] my pathetic little flesh.
Yes, it is wretched, but you have something better than wretched little
flesh. Why, then, do you let that go and cling to the flesh? Because of this
latter kinship, some of us who incline that way become like wolves, lacking integrity, treacherous and harmful; others become like lions, fierce,
bestial and untamed; but most of us become foxes, the utter wretches
among animals. For what is a slanderous and ill-natured person but a
fox or something still more wretched and abject? See to it, then, and
watch out that you don't turn into one of these wretches.

The argument of this discourse relies on a scale of nature that
treats God and non-human animals as a pair of simple extremes,
and presents human beings as complex intermediates. By virtue
of our bodies, we are akin to the other animals, but by virtue of
our minds, we are akin to God. Elsewhere, Epictetus defines the
human being as 'a mortal animal that has the capacity to use
impressions rationally' (3.1.25); it is this second differentia that
elevates us above the rest of the animals. Epictetus does not
regard human mortality as a bad thing; he takes it to be simply a
fact about the way we are constituted. However, he frequently
denigrates our 'bodily' aspect, often calling the body a corpse or
mud or earth, and using the diminutives 'little flesh' or 'little
body'.

There is no clear precedent for this denigration of the body in
our surviving evidence for early Stoicism. That tradition, to be

sure, drew an absolute distinction between the 'good' of the soul and the 'indifference' of the body, but it did not attach negativity to the body as such. According to Stoic metaphysics, every existing thing, including God and the soul, is corporeal. But Epictetus is as reticent on this basic doctrine as he is about God's physical relation to the world.

Should we, then, infer that he takes the human mind, the 'divine' part of our nature, to be incorporeal, as Plato did? The answer to that question is certainly no, because he twice, though without emphasis, refers to 'breath' (*pneuma*) as the mind's substance (2.23.3; 3.3.22). Rather, we should take his sharp contrast between the body and the mind to be Platonic in an ethical rather than a metaphysical sense. Just as he takes no interest in the exact composition of the world's elements, so he virtually ignores the mind's physical structure. What he wants to emphasize is a duality in our human constitution that gives us the option of deciding whether we shall be godlike (by identifying with our minds) or merely animal (by identifying with our bodies).

Although this distinction between the body and the mind does not import Plato's doctrine of the soul's strict incorporeality and immortality, it strongly recalls numerous Platonic passages where Socrates voices just the same kind of dualism. The chief lesson of Plato's *Phaedo* is the philosopher's need to shun the body, whose hold on a soul that identifies with it will involve just the kind of unethical conduct that Epictetus specifies in **81**. Epictetus' recollection of the *Phaedo* is certain because he draws on the dialogue in order to make a point that not only aligns him with Socrates but also corrects students who had overinterpreted the implications of his own negative assessment of the body.

Socrates in the *Phaedo* had characterized the body as the soul's 'prison' or 'fetter', and Epictetus picks up this expression in a passage that closely recalls **81**:

82 I think that as the older man I should not sit here working out how to stop you from being abject or from having mean and low discussions about yourselves. Rather, if there are any young men among you who have learnt of their kinship to the gods and that *we are attached to these chains*—the body and its property and everything that we need for their sake in order to keep our lives going—I should stop them from wanting to discard these things as merely troublesome and useless burdens and to depart to their kindred.   (1.9.10–11)

In **81** Epictetus recommends his students to elevate their assessment of themselves by identifying exclusively with their minds or kinship to God. In **82** he indicates that while he agrees with Socrates in regarding the body as an encumbrance, he also agrees with him that the nuisance of having a body is not a reason for loathing it or for opting for suicide. In Plato's *Phaedo* (62c) Socrates had virtually prohibited suicide, saying that one's own life should not be ended 'until God enforces this in some way, as he does with me now' (referring to the hemlock he must drink that day). Stoics had traditionally permitted suicide as a 'rational exit' *in extremis*, and though Epictetus accepts this doctrine he also echoes Socrates' theological caveat (see p. 204): it would be wrong to choose to die simply to escape from one's material circumstances. The proper attitude to one's body, he proposes, is to treat it as completely unimportant (1.9.17).

That might seem a recipe for extreme asceticism, but Epictetus does not advocate neglect of the body and still less is he in favour of its mortification. For the requirements of a particular context, he likes to speak exaggeratedly; hence the 'complete unimportance' of the body is relative to the duality of the human constitution.[11] To actualize our divine kinship, we need to treat our minds as the exclusive locus of our human identity. That project requires us to regard our bodies as merely instrumental to our lives and as distinct from our essential selves, but these are not reasons for our neglecting the body. His advice to an effeminate young man devoted to cosmetics runs:

83 How, then, should you treat your little body? According to its nature. These things are in another's [i.e. God's] charge. Trust them to him.

---

[11] In the context of divine providence, Epictetus is quite prepared to express gratitude for our bodily instruments (1.16.15; 2.23.5), but his calling the body a 'corpse' has left its explicit mark on Marcus Aurelius, IV.41.

What then? Should I leave my body unclean?
Of course not. But keep yourself clean in relation to who you are by
nature, clean as a man if you are a man, as a woman if you are a woman,
a child if you are a child.   (3.1.43–4)

With a nice touch of hyperbole, Epictetus assures his students
that even if Socrates bathed infrequently, his body gleamed and
was erotically attractive (4.11.19).

By minimizing the importance of the body, Epictetus keeps
his focus on the mind as the essential bearer of human identity.
We may recall his statements from the first discourse of book 1
(see p. 62).

There he tells his students four things: first, that rationality is
a reflexive and quite general faculty of judgement; secondly, that
this faculty, which enables us to make correct use of our mental
impressions, is our most precious endowment; thirdly, that God
has given us complete autonomy over this faculty; and, fourthly,
that God, had he been able to do so, would have extended such
autonomy to our bodies. He then imagines an address from Zeus,
which is so striking that it bears repeating in full:

(16) Epictetus, if it had been possible, I would have made your little body
and property free and unhindered. But in fact—take note of my
words—this is not your own but only artfully moulded clay. Since I
could not give you this, I have given you a portion of myself, this faculty of positive and negative impulse and of desire and aversion—the
faculty, in short, of using mental impressions. By caring for this and
by situating all that is yours therein, you will never be impeded, you
will never be restricted, you will not groan or find fault or flatter anyone.

(1.1.10–12)

Epictetus names this faculty *prohairesis*, which I translate by
'volition' (see Section 8.2). In drawing moral implications from
the divine dispensation, he continues:

(17) *What should we have ready at hand in [difficult] situations?*
Simply the knowledge of what is mine and what is not, and of what is
possible for me and what is not.

I have to die.
Do I also have to die groaning?
I have to be fettered.
While moaning too?
I have to go into exile.
Does anyone prevent me from going with a smile, cheerful and serene?
Tell your secrets.
I refuse, because that is up to me.
Then I will fetter you.
What do you mean, fellow? Fetter *me*? You can fetter my leg, but not even Zeus can overcome my volition.   (1.1. 21–3)

This stark contrast between my alienable leg (the body) and my inalienable self (my mind/rationality/will) is Epictetus' most striking expression for what he takes the properly Stoic attitude to be. Did Zeno, Cleanthes, and Chrysippus agree with him?

Too little of their work survives for us to give a categorical answer, but my own view is that Epictetus emphasizes the mind's capacity for autonomy to a degree that is without clear parallel in the preceding Stoic tradition.[12] He does so, we should note, by a combination of steps: the contrast between body and mind, the identification of the mind with the individual person or self, and the allocation to the mind of an absolutely invincible capacity for self-determination. In addition, he signifies the incomparable value of this capacity by making it the best thing in the world, 'a portion of God'. He tells us elsewhere that God made human beings with a view to their happiness (3.24.2, p. 191 below). That providential thesis underlies the present passage, as is especially clear when he makes Zeus remark that he has done the best he could for human beings, and that, had it been possible, he would have given us invulnerable bodies as well.

This last point is particularly striking. In early Stoic cosmology 'matter' is 'substance devoid of quality'—a principle so plastic that the divine 'cause' can mould it in whatever ways it wishes. In creating the world, God imposes properties on the elements that inevitably limit the complex bodies formed out of them; so one might read the regrets concerning the human body

---

[12] I don't mean that he invented the doctrine; for the 'wise man' as 'unimpeded', see Cicero, *De finibus* III.75.

that Epictetus attributes to God as simply a rhetorical expression of this fact. But, even if we take that view, we are still left with a conception of God that oversteps traditional Stoicism not only because it treats the human body as an obstacle to divine omnipotence but also because it acknowledges that bodily constraints have limited divine beneficence.[13] The effect of Epictetus' distinctive theology is to defend divine providence against the evidence of our bodily and external vulnerability, and to emphasize its remarkable gift of our mental autonomy.

What this autonomy signifies is a question for discussion in Chapter 8. There is, though, one point that needs to be anticipated in our present context. The Stoic divinity was traditionally identified with fate, and in physical terms with the causal nexus of 'pneumatic' motions that determines everything. Early Stoics, especially Chrysippus, went to great lengths to show how divine fate was compatible with human agency and responsibility, but they were equally adamant that nothing, including the mind's decisions and choices, is free from determination by antecedent causes.

Epictetus is as reticent about the workings of fate as he is about the physical nature of God.[14] What he says about the completely unimpeded mind might suggest that he has abandoned the Stoic doctrine of universal determinism, but he never engages with the issue of how autonomy is compatible with fate. His doctrine of the mind's freedom from constraint leaves that question entirely open. Instead, he asks us to accept, as an article of faith, that nothing external to a person's mind, including even God in his role as the ultimate agent of the world's events, *can exercise compulsion on* one's desires, choices, or decisions.

I turn now to 'the God within', as described in the text at the head of this chapter.

---

[13] Here we may see the diffused influence on Epictetus of the Platonic idea that divine creativity is limited by material necessity; see Dobbin (1998: 70–1).

[14] Aside from his repeated citations of Cleanthes' verse, 'Lead me, Zeus, and you, Fate' (2.23.42; 3.22.95; 4.1.131; 4.4.34), Epictetus refers to fate only twice in the discourses—once in what reads more like a piece of mythology than sober doctrine (1.12.25), and the other time with a citation from Chrysippus concerning how he would act if he *knew* that it was foreordained that he would now be sick (2.6.9–10). See further, Section 8.3.

6.5 THE INTERNAL DIVINITY

Right from the beginning, Stoic philosophers had treated the affinity between God and human beings as a 'partnership', with the human soul taken to be an 'offshoot' of the divine mind. A text that I take to report Chrysippus' thought and language prefigures Epictetus' formulation of this relationship:

> Our own natures are parts of the nature of the universe. Therefore, living in agreement with nature is the goal of life, that is, in accordance with the nature of oneself and that of the universe, engaging in no activity that the universal law is wont to forbid, which is the right reason pervading everything and identical to Zeus, who directs the organization of reality. And when the principle of every action is concordance between each person's divine spirit (*daimôn*) and the will of the director of the universe, precisely this is the virtue of the happy human being and his good flow of life.   (DL VII.87–8)

In this memorable passage Chrysippus echoes Cleanthes' *Hymn to Zeus* (see p. 153) by identifying God with the universal author and law of nature, and by treating 'us' as its or his 'parts'. He also goes beyond Cleanthes' poetic words when he describes happiness and virtue not only as obedience to divine law and right reason but also as a concordant relationship between 'each person's divine spirit' and the will of God in God's capacity as administrator of the world.

We are clearly intended to take these two descriptions as a hendiadys: the concordant relationship is the requisite obedience and rightful reasoning, and these latter are the concordant relationship. More difficult to determine are the connotations of 'each person's divine spirit' (*daimôn*). The word *daimôn* can be equivalent to god in the fullest sense, but in Greek generally it is more frequently applied to a demigod, something intermediate between the human and the fully divine. In addition, *daimôn* often signifies a person's fate or fortune, as in the words *eudaimôn* meaning happy and *kakodaimôn* meaning unhappy.

What Chrysippus' text leaves quite unclear is the exact relationship between 'each person' and the person's *daimôn*. It does not help to translate *daimôn* by 'guardian spirit', as is sometimes done, because the same question recurs: Is the *daimôn* internal to the person, or something like a guardian angel? My own guess is that Chrysippus had no interest in guardian angels; what he means by 'each person's *daimôn*' is each person's share of divine reason. Not only is this a relatively straightforward Stoic concept; it also fits the context that allows a person's *daimôn* or view of its own fate to fail to be in accord with God's will.

If this is right, Chrysippus' *daimôn* is little more than an elevated name for each person's governing or rational faculty. It is up to individual persons to make their own *daimôn* accord with God: they will be virtuous and flourish if they do this, and not otherwise. From the fact that we are endowed with a 'divine' faculty of reason, it does not simply follow that its dictates in us, that is to say our own reasoning to ourselves, will be good.

But the later Stoic, Posidonius, went this further step; for he characterized emotional disturbance as 'failing to follow completely the *daimôn* in oneself, which is akin . . . to the one that governs the world' (Edelstein and Kidd 1972: f. 187). For Posidonius, one's internal *daimôn* is the voice of *good* reasoning.

We know where Posidonius took this idea from: Plato's *Timaeus*. There Plato had said: 'We should think of our soul's most authoritative part as what God has given to each person as his *daimôn* . . . and we would speak most correctly by describing it as raising us from earth to our kinship in heaven' (90a). As Plato continues, he contrasts the purely 'mortal' life of those who focus upon their appetites and ambitions with the happiness and virtual immortality of those who are devoted to philosophy and 'always cultivate the divine element in themselves'. Plato's *daimôn* or divine element is the faculty of reason, which, according to his tripartite psychology, has to vie for supremacy in the soul with the two lower parts, appetite and ambition. Posidonius largely endorsed this Platonic model of the soul; it allowed him to explain deviations from good reasoning as due to the bad influence of the soul's other parts.

For Plato and Posidonius, the dictates of reason are good in themselves; or at least, they are so when that faculty is allowed to speak with its own voice, untramelled by the soul's other parts. This was not Chrysippus' psychological model. He held that the human soul is unitary and rational through and through. What

Plato and Posidonius explained as the result of conflict between reason and passion or as the dominance of passion over reason, Chrysippus interpreted as faulty reasoning, reasoning that has gone wrong, fluctuation of judgement, miscalculation of values. To put this difference another way, whereas Plato and Posidonius can speak of reason *simpliciter* as the guide to living well, Chrysippus needs to specify that the reasoning be *correct*.

Where does Epictetus stand on all this? Unquestionably, he sides with Chrysippus over the through-and-through rationality of the human soul. This explains why he consistently attributes all error and wrongdoing to mistaken judgements as distinct from acting under the influence of an irrational part of the soul. At the same time, his emphasis on the duality of body and mind and many of his images for this duality (earthy/divine etc.) recall Plato. We need to take a close look at how Epictetus describes the 'God within'.

Here are the relevant passages:

84 Does anyone tell you that you have a faculty equal to that of Zeus? None the less, he has presented to each person each person's *daimôn*, as a guardian, and committed his safekeeping to this trustee, who does not sleep and cannot be misled . . . Remember never to say that you are alone, because you are not. God is within and your own *daimôn* is within. (1.14.11–14)

Here Epictetus speaks as if the *daimôn* were an alter ego or at least a superego. But now, in a context where he stresses the complete autonomy of the person over moral as distinct from external values:

85 I do have one being whom I must please, to whom I must subordinate myself and be obedient—God, and after him myself. God has entrusted me to myself and he has subordinated my volition to me alone, giving me standards for its correct use. (4.12.11–12)

Finally, from the text excerpted at the head of this chapter and part of its sequel:

86 You are carrying God around, you poor thing, and you don't know it. Do you think I am speaking of an external god made of gold or silver?

You are carrying him around inside yourself, and you fail to realize that you defile him with unclean thoughts and foul actions . . . God has committed yourself to you and he says: 'I had no one more trustworthy than you; keep this person for me in the way that is his nature, reverent, trustworthy, upright, undismayed, unimpassioned, undisturbed'.

(2.8.12–13, 23)

In his comments on the presence of a divine guardian within the person, Epictetus is at one with Seneca and Marcus Aurelius (see p. 177). Where he perhaps differs from them is in the strict coincidence he postulates between the 'God within' or *daimôn* and the normative self. Epictetus' *daimôn* is his and every person's normative self, the voice of correct reason that is available to everyone because it is, at the same time, reason as such and fully equivalent to God. Although Epictetus sometimes speaks as if the presence or availability of this voice pluralizes the person, or makes the person distinct from his *daimôn*, we should regard that language as metaphor or, better, as a way of articulating the idea that in listening to and obeying one's normative self one is at the same time in accordance with the divinity who administers the world.

Epictetus stays close to the thoughts that I cited from Chrysippus, but with three differences. First, Epictetus' *daimôn* is quite certainly, as Chrysippus' is not, the ideally rational or normative self; in this Epictetus verges closely on the Platonic conception adopted by Posidonius. Secondly, by so clearly positioning God within the person, Epictetus gives an extremely powerful emotional charge to the doctrine that, by virtue of our minds in their proper functioning, we are not only parts of God but acting with God, or as God would have us act. Third, Epictetus' language has a fervent commitment that is absent from the sober Chrysippus.

Epictetus' *daimôn* concept clearly has much in common with what we call conscience. Which prompts me to bring Socrates back into the discussion.

Plato's dialogues have left a clear mark on Epictetus' expression of his theology and the norms of human nature, but he does not flirt, as Seneca for instance does, with Plato's other-worldly metaphysics and eschatology. What he chiefly draws from Plato is the support of Plato's Socrates for his own outlook on such issues as obedience to God, assimilation to God (2.14.13), identification with the soul as distinct from the body, and the confluence of all of these with moral autonomy and integrity. By this selective appropriation of Plato Epictetus contrives to remain broadly in line with the Stoic tradition while at the same time underwriting his own theistic tendencies.

Socrates had been notorious for relying on his *daimonion* or 'divine sign', which he took to be an infallible monitory voice. Epictetus refers to this (3.1.19) when he says that Socrates stuck to his military duty 'under the god's command' (Plato, *Apology* 28e), and we can hardly doubt that in extending the *daimôn* to every person, he also had this Socratic 'conscience' in mind.[15] I have already commented on the way Epictetus appropriates the metaphors of Plato's *Phaedo* in order to warn his students against becoming 'burdened' and 'dragged down' by their bodies, and I argued that he takes the proper relation of the body to the soul to be purely instrumental. That is exactly the way Simplicius in his commentary on the *Manual* (pp. 195–7) interprets Epictetus; for he goes out of his way to associate this instrumental interpretation with Socrates' famous proof to Alcibiades that human beings are neither bodies nor composites of body and soul but pure souls that 'make use of' bodies (Plato, *Alcibiades* I. 127e–130c).

As for the mind's normative autonomy and excellence, there are numerous passages in Plato that are so close to Epictetus' terminology that his reminiscence of them is highly probable. One of his favourite terms is 'unimpeded' (*akôlutos*); the adverbial form of this word first occurs in Socrates' etymology of 'virtue' where it is contrasted with the 'impededness' of 'vice' (Plato, *Cratylus* 415c). Epictetus repeatedly endorses the words of

---

[15] There is a similar Socratic resonance when Epictetus tells a would-be Cynic to consult his *daimonion* (3.22.53). Twice Epictetus cites Socrates' comments in prison to Crito (43d): 'If it [my death] please the gods, so be it' (1.4.24; 4.4.21). By Epictetus' date, there was great interest in demonology, a fact reflected in Plutarch's work on Socrates' *daimonion* (*De genio Socratis*). However, in striking contrast to Plutarch and late Platonists in general, Epictetus shows no sympathy for the idea that Socrates experienced a divine voice that existed independently of his own mind.

Plato, *Laws* IX. 875c, where it is stated that 'it is not right for the mind to be subordinate to anything or subservient but it should be completely in charge if it is to be authentic and genuinely in possession of its natural freedom'. And he will certainly have remembered Socrates' saying in the *Apology* 38e: 'I did not think at that time that I should do anything servile on account of my trial, nor do I now regret the defence I have made, but I would much rather choose to die with this defence than to live with making a different one.'

6.6 METAPHORS OF GOD AND HUMAN STATUS

At the beginning of this chapter I emphasized the fact that Epictetus' theology cannot be adequately reduced to a set of doctrinal statements. His religious outlook is as evident in how he speaks of God as in what he attributes to God by way of formal properties. We might say that Epictetus combines natural theology with theological poetics. By using numerous metaphors drawn from social and political life, he offers his students an understanding of how human beings should see themselves in relation to God.

We have already noticed his use of the family relationship—God as *loving* father of his human children, but, because 'father', in Greek and Roman culture, carried a strongly authoritative charge, Epictetus can slide immediately from 'good king' to 'literally father' (1.6.40). Within the Roman Empire, which it was easy for people to equate with the civilized world, the Emperor combined the office of ruler with generalissimo. Epictetus often contrasts the actual Caesar with Zeus (1.9.7; 1.14.15–17; 1.29.61), but he also invokes the imperial office in a series of images for God's management of the world. He pictures someone whose judgements are out of line with that government as a military rebel (3.24.21). By contrast, a dutiful world citizen should treat his life as serving in God's army (3.24.31), 'doing what he is commanded to do, or if possible divining the General's wishes' (3.24.34). Epictetus develops this metaphor:

87 You have been given a rank in an imperial city, not in some lowly place, and you are a senator not for the year but for life. Don't you realize that such a person must be little engaged at home but mostly away, in or under command, or serving some office, or on campaign, or sitting as a judge? (3.24.36)

Such images remind us that many of Epictetus' students were destined for careers in the imperial service. That life could be exacting, but Epictetus' point is that service to God is exponentially more so. The students will also have been familiar with strenuous physical training, and Epictetus is fond of picturing God as a tough athletic coach:

88 It is difficult circumstances that show real men. So, when a difficulty occurs, remember that God, like a trainer, has matched you with a rough youngster.
Why (someone says)?
So you can become an Olympic victor. But that doesn't happen without sweat. In my opinion, no one has got a finer difficulty than you have got, if you are willing to use it as an athlete uses his young assailant.
(1.24.1–2)

In the same vein, Epictetus describes life as 'a contest for good fortune and happiness', which, in spite of failures, we can keep re-entering (3.25.3–4). Hence challenging circumstances are to be seen not merely as compatible with divine providence but as God-given opportunities for us to overcome and thereby display the mental and moral strength that constitutes human happiness. In another image, God's gift of autonomy is represented as 'emancipating' people from slavery (4.7.17).

Roman citizens were expected to play as well as to work. Epictetus likens life itself to an ongoing holiday, in order to picture the way we should regard our mortality and limited lives:

89 God has no need of a fault-finding spectator. He needs those, rather, who join in the festival and the dance, to applaud the gathering, and celebrate it with hymns of praise. He will not be sorry to see the sluggish and the faint-hearted omitted from the festival. For when they were there they didn't behave like people on holiday and they did not fulfil their proper place; they moaned and criticized the divinity and fortune and the company, insensitive to the dispensations and to their own capacities, which they had received for the opposite purpose—high-mindedness, nobility, courage, and the very freedom that we are presently seeking.   (4.1.108–9; see also 3.5.10)

With language of this kind Epictetus emphasizes his personalist conception of God. In approaching the conclusion to this chapter, I want to ask how this bears on his interpretation of the Stoic tradition and on his more theoretical expressions of the good life.

At Epictetus' date, 'seeking to become like God' was taken to be the cornerstone of Plato's philosophy. Plato uses the expression in more than one context, but most famously in the homily in the *Theaetetus* (176a–b), where Socrates expounds the philosopher's contemplation of eternal values and disengagement from mundane life. That disengagement is described as 'likening oneself to God as far as possible', and this in turn is explained as 'becoming just and pure, with understanding'.

Epictetus did not advocate Plato's mode of disengagement and abstract contemplation, but he appropriated the expression 'seeking to become like God'. After telling a visitor from Rome that the first lesson of philosophy is learning that there is a providential and omniscient God, he says:

90   Next, it is necessary to learn what the gods are like; for, however they are found to be, one who intends to please and obey them must try to become like them as far as possible. If the divinity is trustworthy, one too must be trustworthy. If the divinity is free, one too must be free, and so also in the case of beneficence and high-mindedness. And so in everything one says and does one must act as an imitator of God.

(2.14.12–13)

The early Stoics, especially Cleanthes, had anticipated Epictetus in regarding God as the exemplar of *all* the virtues that constitute human excellence, but when God is conceived pantheistically, as physically present in all beings, it is hard to understand what properties he could have that constitute the paradigm of a virtuous *human* character—trustworthy, high-minded, and so forth. Even Cleanthes, who says that we humans are endowed with a 'copy' (*mimêma*) of God, expresses our requisite relation to the divine in terms of obedience rather than assimilation and imitation. Epictetus appears to be the only Stoic who includes the exact Platonic expression in his theological repertory.

An early Stoic, committed to a combination of literal pantheism and theism, would no doubt say that God's virtue is the perfection of divine reason: God manifests this in the way he organizes the whole of nature and in the share of rationality that he extends to each human mind. What God does for the entire world, we are designed to do for ourselves; the perfection of a human being's rationality should be regarded as a microcosm of the order and harmony enacted throughout the cosmos.

That is a heady thought. Yet even if it succeeds in giving people a sense of their intrinsic relation to nature in general and to a superhuman intelligence, it offers no clearly applicable paradigm for morality and responsible social life. There seems to be an unbridgeable gap between the harmony of nature, as manifested in the world's regularities, and the harmony of human conduct.

Epictetus, like all Stoics, invokes the world's regularities as a sign of divine providence, but his preferred expressions for God, as we have seen, are personalist. Is he more successful than his predecessors in showing how God can be both the author of all nature and at the same time the paradigm of human virtues? At least he aims to put the human relevance of God's excellence beyond doubt. To support this proposal, I draw on some passages we have already studied in this chapter.

Epictetus constantly emphasizes God's gift to human beings of a capacity for self-determination that is supremely beneficial and impervious to any external impediment. Nothing, not even God himself, can prevent persons from reposing their happiness on the correctness of their judgements and on their personal integrity. In stating this, Epictetus goes out of his way to personalize God, making Zeus say that it is the best thing he *could* do for human beings, that the gift is 'a portion of' Zeus, and that Zeus was unable, as he would have wished, to make the human body similarly 'free and unhindered' (see p. 160).

Here, it seems to me, we see Epictetus offering his students his own distinctive answer to the question of how the Stoic deity can serve as a paradigm for human virtues. Zeus is not omnipotent in what he can do with bodily matter, but that limitation has no bearing on his altruism. He wishes nothing but good for human beings, and that is demonstrated by his giving them the potentiality to share his own rational excellences. To put this another way, Zeus's virtue is manifested in his doing the best he reasonably can with the materials at his disposal, and doing so with the best of intentions. He instantiates not only beneficence but also integrity and reliability within external constraints.

Under this conception of Zeus, Epictetus makes God a paradigm of virtue in a sense that is humanly applicable. Just as God has done the best he can with the materials at his disposal, so individual persons can be invited to take this divine model as an authority and guide for their own lives. We are not capable of autonomy over our bodies and external circumstances, but we have been given the mental and moral resources to make the best possible use of these materials; by doing so, we shall exercise the very same virtues that God exercises in fashioning us:

91   Study the capacities you have, and after studying them say:
      Zeus, bring whatever circumstance you like; for I have the equipment and resources, given to me by you, to make a cosmos of myself [*kosmêsai*] by means of everything that happens.   (1.6.37)

I translate the word *kosmêsai* (literally embellish, adorn, or decorate) 'make a cosmos of' myself because Epictetus' context here is how human beings should study and internalize God's providential government. Like his Stoic predecessors, he treats the ideal human life as a microcosm of the divine cosmos, but his conception of the latter is decidedly warmer and more personalist.

6.7 RATIONAL AND NON-RATIONAL ANIMALS

This chapter would be incomplete if it left the impression that Epictetus, in his theological statements, set human beings completely apart from other animals. He does, as we have seen

(p. 157), bifurcate human nature into mind and body, and consign those who identify with their bodies to the status of beasts. But his references to non-human animals can be neutral and even complimentary, depending on the needs of particular contexts.[16] Lions and birds furnish models of freedom and autonomy:

92 Consider how we apply the concept of freedom in the case of animals.
People rear tame lions in cages and feed them and some even take them around with them. Yet who will call such a lion free? Isn't it true that the more softly the lion lives, the more slavishly he lives? And what lion, if he acquired consciousness and reason, would wish to be one of those lions?
Or consider the birds over there and what, when they are caught and brought up in cages, they are ready to suffer in their attempts to escape. Some of them starve to death rather than endure such a life, while those that survive barely do so and pine away, and escape if ever they find any opening. Such is their desire for natural freedom and to be independent [*autonoma*] and unrestrained. (4.1.24–8)

Epictetus supports the Stoic doctrines that human beings start their lives with the same self-preservative impulses as other animals, and that rationality, the property that defines our species, takes many years to develop. Comparative zoology is one of his characteristic ways of showing where human beings stand in relation to God:

93 You will find many things in us alone, of which the rational animal had particular need, but also many things that we share with the non-rational animals.
Do they too attend to what happens?
By no means. 'Using' and 'attending to' are different from one another. God had need of the animals' making use of impressions, but of our attending to their use. For this reason, it is sufficient for them to eat and drink and rest and procreate and do everything else that each kind of animal does. For us, on the other hand, to whom God has also given the power of attending to things, these animal activities are no longer sufficient, but unless we act appropriately and regularly and in agreement

---

[16] I have benefited from reading an as yet unpublished paper by W. O. Stephens: 'The use of animal examples for moral pedagogy in the Imperial Stoa'.

with our individual nature and constitution, we shall no longer attain our own end.

Beings that have different constitutions also have different functions and ends. So for one whose constitution is only for use, the use of that constitution is quite sufficient. But one who has also the faculty of attending to the use will never attain his end unless propriety is added to the use.

Very well. God constituted each of the other animals, either to be eaten, or to serve in farming, or to produce cheese, or for some other use; what need with regard to these functions would be served by a capacity to attend to impressions and to distinguish between them?

But God introduced the human being to be a student of himself and his works, and not merely a student but also an interpreter of these things. Therefore it is wrong for a human being to begin and end where the non-rational animals do; he should rather begin where they do and end where nature has ended in our case. Nature ended at studying and attending to things and a way of life in harmony with nature.

See to it, then, that you do not die without having studied these things. (1.6.12–22)

The central idea in this characteristically anthropocentric text is the teleology of nature. Nature in general is the world's systematic structure, as constituted by God. Nature in particular comprises the constitutions of living creatures, making them capable of performing the functions specific to their identities. These functions, then, identify the 'ends' or fulfilments of each type of creature's nature. To live 'in accordance with nature' is to play one's specific part within the structure of the cosmic plan.

This cosmic teleology was central to Stoicism from the beginning. What chiefly distinguishes it from its obvious Aristotelian antecedents is the treatment of nature as the indwelling mind and purpose of God, whom Aristotle detached from the physical world. Doctrinally, our passage sticks closely to the mainstream Stoic tradition, but Epictetus seizes the opportunity to present this in a way that suits his urgent tone and his personalist representations of God.

No other Stoic seems to attribute 'needs' to God.[17] Etymologically, the words translated by 'need' (*chreia*) and by 'use'

---

[17] Epictetus speaks of God's 'need' of the world as it is at 1.29.29, and of what he needs from human beings at 1.6.13; 1.29.29; 4.1.108.

(*chrêsis*) are identical, but Epictetus distinguishes them in order to make the point that a creature's conformity to, or proper use of, its nature is a *service* to God. He tells his students to regard the human contribution to that service as 'studying and interpreting' God and his works. This is what it is to be a *rational* animal. We are equipped with the capacities to take a synoptic view (1.6.1–2) of divine providence, and that special human capacity enables us 'to attend to our mental impressions', as distinct from merely reacting to them, as other animals do.

What Epictetus means by 'attend to' (*parakolouthein*) combines the notions of understanding, being aware of, and reflecting on. He identifies 'proper' human conduct with 'attending to' impressions. We have frequently encountered his favourite slogan for a good life: 'using impressions correctly'. Here he relates that practice to our God-given nature. What primarily distinguishes us from other animals is our capacity to reflect on everything we experience and to interpret it as contributors to God's providential government.

Our next task, then, is to study how Epictetus moves from theology to ethics, with a view to seeing what it means for persons to use or misuse their natural and God-given resources.

FURTHER READING AND NOTES

Theological Orientation

For a wide-ranging introduction to the Greek philosophers' contributions to natural theology, see Gerson (1990). Book two of Cicero's *De natura deorum* is the most accessible source for early Stoic theological arguments and attributes; however, Cicero's detached tone may understate the religious attitudes of the philosophers he summarizes. For a selection of other texts with commentary on early Stoic theology, see LS 54, and for the role of God in early Stoic cosmology, LS 44–7 and 55. Mansfeld in Algra (1999) gives a good conspectus of this topic, discussing it alongside Epicureanism. Dragona-Monachou (1976) deals thoroughly with Stoic arguments for divine existence and providence, including a chapter devoted to Epictetus. On 'the God within', see Rist (1969: ch. 14). On God as 'father of human beings' and the importance of this concept for Epictetus' ethics, see Inwood (1996: 258–61).

Theism, Pantheism, and Physics

The works of Bonhöffer (1890, 1894) are especially valuable, both for the range of material they cover and for the author's assessments of Epictetus' religious beliefs and the bearing of his theology on his ethics. Bonhöffer (1911) is an exhaustive study of Epictetus' relation to the New Testament, showing that, in spite of numerous verbal affinities, there are no decisive grounds for positing any direct influence of one on the other. The position I adopt on Epictetus' preference for theistic as distinct from pantheistic language is broadly shared by Bonhöffer (1894: 81), but I think he is mistaken in treating it as 'simply' due to Epictetus' 'practical' orientation and disinclination for metaphysics. Bonhöffer ignores the Socratic factor and other points I have adduced. Here, as elsewhere, he is much too inclined to reduce Epictetus to a supposedly early Stoic orthodoxy; see the criticism by Jagu (1946: 120–2).

I do not maintain that Epictetus has *formally* abandoned pantheism in favour of a strict theism. He does not address that issue directly. If, however, we confront him with it, asking what he believes about God and how he wants his students to think of God, the answer of the *Discourses* seems to be the 'personalist' conception that I have emphasized. In this, Epictetus differs strikingly from Marcus Aurelius, who rarely writes of God in this way but constantly personifies 'Nature' or 'the world' or 'the universe', seeing himself as 'a part of the whole', rather than as a 'part of God'. For an acute comparison and contrast between the Stoics, balancing Epictetus' optimism and confidence against the Emperor's uncertainty and pessimism, see Rutherford (1989: ch. 6).

There are three texts outside the *Discourses* and the *Manual* that purport to attribute the pantheistic expressions characteristic of Marcus to Epictetus: fragments 3, 4, and 8. However, at least two of these are most probably quotations from Musonius Rufus, and they are quite insufficient to modify the impression of Epictetus' theology that emerges from the discourses. Stoicism, as I have remarked before, was not a closed church, and it gains in interest when we let ourselves register the sympathies and inclinations of its individual spokesmen. In the main body of this chapter, I have preferred not to complicate the presentation by drawing comparisons between Epictetus and his near contemporary Stoics. But here is a brief report.

Seneca and Marcus Aurelius

Seneca's observations about God combine standard Stoicism with eclectic strands of Platonic dualism. The tenor of his comments also varies according to their context. I have already cited (p. 23) a passage from his early work *On Providence*, where he identifies God with the fated sequence of events. The main purpose of that essay is to defend the world's providential direction against the stock objection that this is incompatible with the occurrence of apparently random phenomena and the adverse experiences of 'good men'. Seneca writes too rhetorically for us to draw any clear conclusions from this work about his own religious experience. Although he echoes Cleanthes in calling the 'good man' God's 'true son and imitator', the point of Seneca's familial tie between man and God is not to underline their personal relationship, but to insist that, when good men experience hardship, this is evidence of how much God in testing them and giving them the opportunity to show their virtue, loves them like a true Roman father! One is inclined to say 'ugh!', but we had better not dismiss Seneca's sentiment as merely his own rhetoric; for Epictetus also speaks in a similar vein, when he calls God a tough 'trainer' (1.24.1), anticipating the language of muscular Christianity.

In the preface to book one of his *Natural Questions* Seneca treats the study of nature as the highest activity a person can engage in because it draws the mind 'upwards', making us ask questions about God and finally enabling us to learn that God 'is the world's mind; all that you see and all that you do not see' (13). The difference between us and God is that God is entirely 'reason' whereas we have mind as our 'better part'. Seneca's focus here is on God as the ground of natural order. In language that has strong Platonic overtones, he describes his project as one that enables the enquirer to transcend ordinary human concerns and free the mind from its shackles. Thereby the mind gains a cosmic perspective on the pettiness of a purely earth-centred view of life.

In the *Letters* Seneca frequently makes use of the lower/higher image, as when he characterizes the wise man as one who 'though he is stuck in his body, yet is absent from it in the best part of himself and directs his thoughts to the realm above' (65.18). Cosmology, however, is not Seneca's main concern in these writings. The theological theme he chiefly dwells on in them is the mind as our divine portion. One citation will suffice to show how close his expression of this doctrine can be to language Epictetus uses: 'A holy spirit [*sacer spiritus*] is seated within us, watching over and guarding our goods and evils' (41.2). However, Seneca's other-worldly leanings, drawing on Plato, and his preoccupation with the wise man lack the immediacy with which Epictetus frequently speaks of God.

Marcus Aurelius constantly invokes the cosmic perspective, but (as mentioned above) he rarely refers to God (singular) by name, preferring to talk of Nature or the Whole, and his conception of the world is unitary rather than couched in the dualistic terms that Seneca often uses. For Marcus, the most salient fact is the permanency and regularity of change. As a 'part of the Whole', he is destined, like everything else, to be reabsorbed into the flux of the elements, which is Nature's way of preserving the world in the most beneficial way. In Epictetus, by contrast, this cosmological perspective is rare, if not parenthetical, as when he wonders whether his students, in hearing from 'the philosophers' about the world's unity and the necessity of cyclical change, were merely bemused (3.24.9–10).

Marcus frequently refers to nature as governing reason or mind, and he follows the Stoic tradition in treating the individual person's mind as the 'divine' and guiding part, conferred by Zeus (v.27; cf. ii.1). But, although in the same context he says that someone 'dwells with the gods who at all times exhibits to them a soul satisfied with its apportioned lot', such a statement hardly changes one's general impression that Marcus' conception of God is minimally personalist. I share the view of MacIntyre (1967), who thinks that of all the Stoics Marcus is the one whose theology comes closest to a strict pantheism. Note especially iv.40: 'Think of the world as a single living being, a single substance and a single soul.' Unlike Epictetus, Marcus is most explicit and emphatic on universal determinism: see ii.3, iv.26.

In view of Epictetus' strong influence on Marcus, it is striking that their ways of talking about God, especially in the singular, tend to be strongly divergent. Would it be too bold to infer a difference here between their experience and status, or at least their temperaments? (For stimulating thoughts along these lines, see Rutherford 1989: 228–9.) I discuss the bearing of these divergences on their approach to ethics in the Further Reading and Notes to Chapter 7.

Socrates and Plato

For these influences on Epictetus' theology, see Jagu (1946: 116–18). On Socrates' religion, see McPherran (1996), and for excellent discussions of Plato's concept of 'becoming like God', and its resonance at Epictetus' date, see Annas (1999: ch. 4), and Sedley (1999).

Epictetus and Popular Religion

Epictetus undercuts the language and conventions of popular religion by transferring them into his own theology. Emotional collapse is 'impiety' because it flouts our God-given resources for coping with circumstances (1.6.39; cf. 2.23.2). The divination we should practise is the study of the world's and our own natures and not recourse to omens and augury (2.7; cf. 1.17.20). What we should offer sacrifices for is having the right desires (1.19.25), or restraining anger for thirty days (2.18.13). Lifeless images of gods are pointless when God's living works are available for contemplation (2.8.20; cf. 2.19.25), and, while all the mythological stories about Hades are nonsense, yet it remains true that the world is 'full of gods', as Stoically conceived (3.13.15). The supposed benefits of the agricultural divinity, Triptolemus, are as nothing compared with what Chrysippus has given us as a recipe for the good life (1.4.31).

CHAPTER 7

From Theology to Ethics

Rather than complaining, won't you thank the gods for permitting you to be on a higher level than everything that they have not made 'up to you', and for making you responsible only for what is 'up to you'?

(1.12.32)

7.1 ORIENTATION

In the previous chapter we saw how Epictetus' conception of a providential and personalist divinity decisively shapes his view of the capacities and limitations of human nature. God, he claims, given the way the world is inevitably structured, has done the best he can for every person. As rational minds housed in unavoidably vulnerable bodies, we are severely restricted in our direct power to influence external events. But we are responsible for what happens only to the extent that it results from our own judgements and decisions. What falls outside our agency, whether a natural event or the act or fortune of other persons, need not and should not affect our status and values as rational minds; so we should regard all such things as the way they had to be in this God-directed world. That world leaves us a mental and moral space that is exclusively and wonderfully ours, and the capability of filling it with the understanding that we are not alone but partnered by God.

This theology is Epictetus' principal reason for encouraging his students to face the world with confidence and serenity in every circumstance. What does it offer by way of guidelines for structuring a person's values and practical objectives in day-to-day life? If reliance on God is actually equivalent to exercising one's rational faculties well and is experienced as such, can God's partnership in the process be anything more than an edifying formula? Epicureans also placed unqualified faith in the value of good reasoning, but their gods remained aloof from every person's mind. If Epictetus' ethics is to be a meaningful combination of the autonomic with the theonomic, he needs to invest the divine law with a content and authority that a merely human standard would lack, and yet be, at the same time, intellectually compelling, emotionally satisfying, and practicable. To put this point differently, has Epictetus, in his ubiquitous appeals to God, succumbed to religiosity?

The temptation for agnostic moderns is to answer yes, but even if that were the case Epictetus would be no different from numerous thinkers of his time. Religious sensibility was prominent in his culture, whether pagan or Christian, and religiosity, with its implicit slur, is a historically crude term. The question is rather whether Epictetus' recourse to theology is a betrayal of his Stoic rationalism and Socratic dialectic. We need to consider, in response, whether, apart from personal faith, he had serious philosophical and pedagogical reasons for making God the starting point and constant underpinning of his philosophy.

This question is especially pertinent because this is not the way the main doctrines of Stoic ethics are presented and justified in some of the most detailed and authoritative of the surviving summaries.[1] Was Epictetus uncomfortable with such presentations and justifications? Did he have recourse to theology as the best way to authorize the truth of what all Stoics and their critics regarded as the school's central but hardest doctrine—that authentic happiness or human flourishing depends entirely on excellence of mind and character, with nothing else making a jot

---

[1] See Further Reading and Notes at the end of this chapter.

of difference? I shall argue in favour of these propositions, starting with a summary and critique of the earlier Stoic tradition.

7.2 LIFE IN ACCORDANCE WITH NATURE

Chrysippus had stated that 'the world's administration' is the
best and indispensable foundation for ethics (see p. 23); so
we can be confident that situating human nature within the
providential cosmic perspective was basic Stoic procedure.[2]
However, the official starting point of early Stoic ethics—the
concept from which the school's account of life in accordance
with nature began— was 'appropriation' (*oikeiôsis*): that is to say,
the instincts for self-preservation and for sociability that the
school's founders regarded as basic to every normal person's
innate motivations, and as *empirically* verifiable.[3] The providential plan of God or Nature is emphatically at work in *oikeiôsis*, but
you do not need to know that in order to find *oikeiôsis* plausible as
a basic datum of human nature; for an agnostic would be hard
pressed to dispute the fact that human beings, like other animals,
are endowed with instincts of the kind that Stoics attributed to
them. Theology mainly enters traditional Stoicism not as the
beginning or even as a part of ethics but rather as the culmination
of physics—the study of nature.[4]

To be more precise, the early Stoics favoured a 'bottom-up'
rather than a 'top-down' procedure for showing that their distinctive ethical principles—the supreme value of rationality or
excellence of character, and its sufficiency for complete happiness—are ingrained in human nature. Rather than specifying at
the outset a set of divine laws that reason requires us to obey, they
liked to start from the observable behaviour of all animals from
the moment of birth. What this behaviour shows, they argued, is
that animals are instinctually equipped with perceptions and

---

[2] That is equally clear from Cleanthes' *Hymn to Zeus* (see p. 153 above), and note
Cicero, *De finibus* III.73, where, *after* expounding Stoic ethics, Cato 'honours' the
school's ethics because 'one who is to live in accordance with nature must set out from
the entire world and its government'.

[3] For the main sources, with commentary, see LS 57 and 59D.   [4] See LS 26C.

drives that enable them to live in accordance with their specific natures. The nature of animals, then, is not simply their physical constitution but also the values and discriminations they need in order to be successful instances of the kind of animal they are. Exactly this pattern also pertains to human animals, at least initially. As infants, we too begin our lives, just like the other animals, by trying to make ourselves at home in our environment, and so we naturally assign positive value to everything that promotes this sense of belonging and negative value to the opposite. But as we mature and our minds develop, we gradually recognize that there is much more to our human nature than drives for bodily well-being or security and for association with our own kind. We become attracted to the mind and its powers, for their own sake, and, as this attraction grows, it leads us to diminish the value we initially assigned to bodily well-being and security, and to identify true goodness with complete conformity to reason; so that being at home in the world now becomes a function not of mere survival and sociability, but of understanding our identity as essentially rational beings, and living according to that understanding.

The crucial detail in this theory is the evolution of attraction from material well-being to intellectual and ethical values. At the end of the process, persons will (ideally) come to see that, while it is still natural and indeed reasonable to *prefer* materially advantageous things to their opposites and to take account of them in deciding how to act both self-interestedly and altruistically, such values are 'indifferent' relative to the incomparable and supremely *natural* value of rationality. Properly rational persons will make it their policy always to have the right (that is to say, rational) intentions, and they will identify their happiness with these intentions, irrespective of what events outside their control do to promote or frustrate them. In this way, persons will be in accordance both with their specifically *rational* nature and with God or the divine course of events.

From antiquity up to the present this theory has invited two main lines of criticism: first, over the coherence of deeming materially advantageous things to be both 'preferred' and yet 'indifferent' to happiness, and, secondly, over a shift in the

meaning of 'natural' from normal or regular (at the beginning of
the argument and the development) to right or proper (at the
end). Human beings do, as a matter of general observation, seek
out materially advantageous things at all stages of their lives; it
makes straightforward sense to call this behaviour natural, and
to treat it as analogous to the way other animals behave. It is also
plausible to say that human beings, unlike other animals, *naturally* acquire many further interests as their minds develop. But it
is not plausible to say that we 'naturally', i.e. regularly, evolve
into persons who view the attainment of materially advantageous
things with indifference or who identify our 'natural' good simply with rationality and excellence of character; so the argument,
which begins so promisingly, seems to end in equivocation.

I cannot prove that Epictetus felt the force of these criticisms,
but there are good reasons to think so. He was well aware of the
concept of *oikeiôsis*, and he draws on it more than once (see
p. 197), but it does not play a major role in justifying his principal
doctrines. He accepts the doctrine of so-called natural advantages and disadvantages, exemplified by health and illness
respectively.[5] However, he does not allow them to be respectively 'natural' and 'unnatural' in an unqualified sense (see
p. 201), and he never defines the human goal in terms of
'discriminating' between them, as some earlier Stoics had done.
Generally speaking, Epictetus speaks as though everything outside the mind's complete control is absolutely 'nothing to us'
(e.g. 1.4.27; 1.25.1). This is not to say that he gives that assessment to the 'use' of material things (2.5.1), or that he thinks we
should be negligent in regard to our health and external circumstances (1.2.37). That is certainly not his view, which is rather to
avoid assigning any vestige of unconditional value to things that
are 'not up to us'.

Epictetus' difference from his Stoic authorities can be broadly
summed up by saying that he proceeds *from* rather than *to* God.
The difference is not absolute, and it is by no means explicit in all

---

[5] Once, when citing Chrysippus (2.6.9–10) on the propriety of 'selecting' the former, in cases when the immediate future is unclear, and a second time in a paraphrase
of the same point (2.10.6). Yet he never uses the standard terminology 'preferred'
and 'dispreferred' (see LS 58) for things like health and sickness respectively.

of his arguments; but, even if we call his 'top-down' procedure only an emphasis, I think we can assume that it was strongly motivated by the judgement that it would make Stoic ethics more intelligible and appealing to his students than the traditional starting point in terms of *oikeiôsis* and the supposedly natural development from material goals to mental and moral objectives.

Like his predecessors, Epictetus is committed to the proposition that human nature is predisposed to grasp what Julia Annas (1993: 170) calls 'the moral point of view'. But he does not present the actual disposition as emerging in individuals out of their prior orientation to non-moral values and the instinctual drives he agrees that we share with other animals (see Section 6.7). Rather, he generally suggests that the moral point of view is part of our nature right from the start, but typically fails to develop properly as a result of the mistaken opinions we intrude, opinions that misidentify our happiness with acquiring those material advantages that earlier Stoics had called 'preferred indifferents'.

Instead of invoking and explaining this difficult concept, Epictetus grounds his ethics in numerous discourses simply on the distinction between what is 'ours' and 'what is not ours' (e.g. 1.1.10–14 = **16**; 2.16.27; 4.4.29; 4.7.35). The moral point of view is 'ours' and completely 'up to us'; material well-being, whether of our body or of anything else, is 'not ours' and 'not up to us'. Hence, if happiness is to be completely up to us, it must be grounded in the former and not in the latter.

But how can we be sure that this distinction is rigorously applicable? Why not suppose that I am incapable of premising my happiness on the moral point of view, or, alternatively, why suppose that material well-being is so precarious that I should eliminate it completely from my recipe for happiness? Epictetus, I surmise, thought that his best chance of consolidating the doctrines that exclude affirmative responses to these questions was to present them as foundational 'laws of nature'; that is to say, as laws of a divinity dedicated to engendering in human beings the resources to make themselves happy and serviceable to one another in whatever external state of the world they find themselves.

7.3 THEONOMIC FOUNDATIONS

Epictetus' favourite formula for the goal of human life is 'to follow the gods' (1.12.5; 1.30.4; 4.7.20).[6] This precept, he tells his students (1.12.1–6), makes sense only if the following propositions are false: (1) there are no gods; (2) there are gods, but they take no interest in the world; (3) there are gods whose interest is confined to the celestial realm; (4) there are gods whose interest extends to the earth and human affairs but only in a general way. It is the truth of a fifth proposition that is crucial to the applicability of his formula, namely: there are gods who care for human individuals and actually transmit their concern 'to me' (and also to any other person).

We know from Epictetus' arguments in favour of divine providence that he takes both parts of this proposition to be completely demonstrable: God's care for us as individuals is evidenced by his 'proclamations' via our own reason (3.13.12) or internal divinity (see Section 6.5). In the same vein, Epictetus tells a visitor from Rome:

The philosophers [i.e. Stoics] say that the primary thing to be learnt is that God exists and cares for the world and that he inevitably notices not only what one does but even what one intends or thinks.   (2.14.11)

In Epictetus' litany of false propositions, the second, the view of the Epicureans, is crucial. Their gods were notoriously uninterested in the world or in human affairs. Epictetus is at pains to emphasize his opinion that Epicurean theology with its heedless gods is disastrous to social cohesion and respect for moral principles (2.20). In sharp contrast to Epicurus, who looked to the fear of human punishment as the only sure deterrent against injustice, Epictetus gives his own endorsement to a belief in divine supervision that stretches right back to Homer and Hesiod. But for Epictetus, by contrast with this archaic belief,

---

[6] Although he attributes the formula to Zeno (1.20.15; and note Cicero, *De finibus* III. 73), he attaches it to his own slogan about 'making correct use of impressions', so he is hardly giving a verbatim citation but rather enrolling the Stoic founder as his authority.

divine supervision is tantamount to 'conscience', because of the coincidence he posits between the normative self and the divine.

Here, then, is a further reason for Epictetus' theonomic procedure—his concern to refute Epicurean laxness by insisting from the outset that moral principles are basic to the author of the universe.

Let us now consider in more detail the content Epictetus attributes to 'the laws of God'. He imagines a student, whom he has instructed in the thesis that 'nothing is of concern to us except our volition' (*prohairesis*), asking for guidance, and says to him:

95   What am I to prescribe to you? Hasn't Zeus already done that? Has he not given you things that are *yours*, free from impediment and hindrance, and things that are *not yours*, which are subject to impediment and hindrance? What guidance did you have from him when you were born, what kind of rule?

    Cherish completely what is your own, and don't seek after things that don't belong to you.

  Your integrity is your own; who can take it from you? Who but yourself will prevent you from using it? But how do you prevent it? When you are eager for what is not your own, you lose that very thing. Since you have these legacies and instructions from Zeus, what kind do you still want from me? Am I superior to him or more trustworthy?

                                               (1.25.3–5)[7]

In the sequel to this passage, Epictetus adds:

96   Adduce your preconceptions, adduce the philosophers' proofs, adduce what you have often heard, adduce what you have said yourself, adduce what you have read, adduce what you have practised.   (1.25.6)

Similarly:

97   What is the divine law? To cherish your own, not to lay claim to what doesn't belong to you, but to use what is given and not to long for what is not given. And when something is removed, to give it up easily and

    [7] See 1.17.27, where Epictetus denies that God would be God or truly providential if he had imposed any constraints on that part of himself that he has given to human beings.

immediately, grateful for the time you had the use of it—unless you
would rather cry for your nurse and your mummy!   (2.16.28)

And most succinctly:

98 This is God's law: if you want some good, get it from yourself.

(1.29.4).

The idea is that the uncertain student, by summoning up all
his experience, will be able to confirm the fact that he has been
innately equipped with an inalienable moral sense, or an understanding of the difference between 'mine' and 'thine'. Rather
than treating moral awareness as a a gradual development from
self-preservative instincts (*oikeiôsis*) to rational perfection, or as
a shift from general animal to specifically human values,
Epictetus builds it, or a *preconception* of it, into human nature
from the start of life.

I think that this highly optimistic assumption must be his
principal reason for tracing the 'laws' of life back to God. We
don't need God, *as distinct from ourselves*, to tell us what to do;
but we are able to tell ourselves what to do only *because of the way
our nature has been constructed*. And the author of our nature's
construction is God. Hence for Epictetus, the goal of 'following
God' is equivalent to 'living in accordance with nature' (1.26.1),
which was the standard Stoic definition of the good life.

If Epictetus' theonomic statements are largely translatable
into the dictates of normative human nature or reason, what further purpose do they serve? First and foremost, they provide the
assurance that human nature is invested with moral norms that
are neither arbitrary nor culturally relative but guaranteed and
explained by the actions of a supremely beneficent intelligence.

Secondly, Epictetus' ethics, with its constant refrain concerning what is and is not ours, only makes motivational sense on the
assumption that there really is, in the nature of things, a fundamental distinction between the power, responsibility, and value
attributable to our individual selves and everything else. The
hardest lesson of Stoic ethics, as I have said, is the ultimate
indifference of everything except rational (which is also to say

moral) excellence. Epictetus characteristically gives it a theonomic formulation, and he also draws powerfully on Socrates' claim that the only correct philosophical 'currency', for transacting desirable exchanges, is the intelligence constitutive of virtue (Plato, *Phaedo* 69a–b):

99 Pay attention to your impressions, keep a watchful eye on them. It's no little thing that you are guarding, but decency, integrity, robustness, serenity, the absence of pain, fear, and disturbance—to sum it up, freedom. What are you going to sell all these for? Look at what your purchase is worth.
But I shall not get anything comparable in return.
When you do get something, look at what you are taking in place of what you are giving up. I take modesty, he takes high offices of state [literally a tribunate or a praetorship], I take integrity. But I don't make a big noise where it is out of place. I will not stand up where I shouldn't. For I am free and a friend of God, with the purpose of obeying him willingly. I shouldn't lay claim to anything else. Not body, or property, or public position, or reputation—quite simply, nothing. For he does not want me to claim them. If he had wanted me to, he would have made them good for me. But he has not done so. I therefore cannot disobey his instructions.
Guard your own good in everything; and, for the rest, be satisfied with just what you have been given so long as you can exercise good reasoning in it. If not, you will have an unhappy life; you will be thwarted and impeded. These are the laws dispatched from God; these are his commandments. It is in these that you should make yourself an expert; make yourself subordinate to these, and not to the laws of Masurius and Cassius. (4.3.7–12)[8]

7.4 HAPPINESS, SELF-INTEREST, AND SOCIETY

Any readers who are new to the ethics of ancient philosophy may be puzzled by the way the discussion in this chapter has oscillated between talk of happiness and talk of morality. As modern philosophers or as ordinary persons, we typically think

---

[8] Masurius and Cassius were famous Roman jurists.

of morality and happiness as potentially in conflict. What I ought to do seems to have no necessary connection with what I may want to do, and my pursuit of happiness or well-being seems to be precisely what the moral point of view may require me to forgo. Ancient philosophers by contrast deny that happiness, when properly understood, and morality can ever conflict. On their conception of a good life, what I chiefly or (in the case of Stoicism) exclusively require, in order to achieve complete happiness (*eudaimonia*), is a virtuous character. Such a character will dispose me both to fare well from my own subjective perspective and to act objectively well in my relation to other persons.

This denial of a potential conflict between happiness and morality appears so counter-intuitive that we are tempted to think something must be wrong in either our or the ancients' understanding of the key terms involved. Hence it is often suggested that, although *eudaimonia* (the standard name for the ancient philosophers' 'goal of life') may be translated by 'happiness', it cannot mean what *we* mean by happiness; for one cannot actually be *happy* on the rack. Rather, we should take *eudaimonia* to signify the state of 'well-being' achieved by someone whose life is objectively admirable, notwithstanding its possible lack of emotional and material gratification.

As so interpreted, *eudaimonia* loses the modern connotations of subjective satisfaction but becomes intelligibly related to 'morality'. Alternatively, it is sometimes suggested that ancient ethics cannot properly be a 'moral' theory because its goal of *eudaimonia* makes self-interest and well-being, as distinct from duty or the good of others or disinterested love, the primary motivation of an excellent and personally fulfilling life.

In what follows I shall argue that Epictetus resists being pinned to either horn of the dilemma—either morality without real happiness, or happiness without real morality. However, if I am to succeed in persuading readers that this is so, I need to explain that his conception of happiness and unhappiness differs strongly in crucial respects from our ordinary thoughts about these conditions. That will be immediately evident from the second and third of the following three passages:

100 What is it that every human being seeks? To be in a robust condition, to be happy, to do everything as he wants, not to be impeded, not to be subject to compulsion. (4.1.46)

101 If someone suffers misfortune, remember that he himself is responsible. For God made all human beings with a view to their happiness, with a view to their robust condition [*eustathein*]. To this end he gave them resources [*aphormai*], giving persons individually some things for their own, and others not for their own. The things subject to impediment, removal, and compulsion are not their own, but the things not subject to impediment are their own. Among the latter, he included the possession [*ousia*] of goodness and badness,[9] as was right for one who cares for us and watches over us like a father. (3.24.2–3)[10]

102 It is impossible for happiness and longing for things not present to coincide. For that which is happy must possess everything it wants, resembling someone whose appetite is fully satisfied; no thirst or hunger can approach it.

Yet Odysseus longed for his wife and wept as he sat on a rock.
Do you accept Homer and his stories for everything? If Odysseus really wept, he must have been miserable. What genuinely excellent person is miserable? In truth the universe is badly governed if Zeus does not take care for his own citizens to resemble him by being happy.

(3.24.17–19)

Happiness, according to these specifications, involves the fulfilment of all desires that it is *reasonable* for human beings to have. Claiming that everyone wants 'to be in a robust condition', Epictetus characterizes happiness with the word *eustathein* whose connotations include health, stability, and tranquillity. This condition can be changelessly 'ours', he proposes, but only if we completely limit our desires and aversions to the domain in which we are capable of being autonomous—the domain of agency, rationality, judgement, and volition (*prohairesis*). For

---

[9] I translate *ousia* by 'possession' rather than by 'essence' or 'nature', as is generally done. 'Possession' is the better rendering in terms of context and thought, because Epictetus' point is precisely that goodness and badness are up to and internal to us. The alternative rendering, though compatible with this point, is too vague.

[10] 3.24 is one of Epictetus' longest discourses, with this extract occurring at its beginning. It is entitled *On the need not to be attached to things that are not up to us.* The chief point of Epictetus' argument is to rebut objections to the thesis that external contingencies must affect happiness.

that to be achieved, we need to detach our desires and aversions from everything that is not 'ours'—that is to say, our bodies and all external circumstances including even the material welfare of our family and friends.

Epictetus moves from the quite uncontroversial proposition—Everyone desires to be happy—to the highly contentious thesis that happiness in the strict sense is incompatible with even the possibility of misery or disappointment. For him, as for his Stoic predecessors, the official formulae for happiness and its opposite are absolute: either you are in a condition where your desires for the good are fulfilled, or you are not. You cannot be genuinely in the former condition if your state of mind and character include the possibility of disruption and frustration. Therefore happiness must be situated in those God-given mental 'resources' that equip us to make it a 'good' that depends only on our individual selves.

At this point something seems to be radically amiss. If Odysseus loved his wife, it was surely both natural and indeed reasonable to express his longing for her by grief. By contrast, it seems utterly unreasonable and unnatural to encourage persons to limit their desires to internal objectives where success can be guaranteed. Should we even want happiness under that condition?

I cannot offer a completely persuasive reply to this obvious objection. Yet, it would be a mistake to be led by such intelligible disquiet into dismissing Epictetus' conception of happiness as an outrageous mistake and anomaly. To understand where he is coming from, we need to situate his comment on Homer's Odysseus not only in Stoicism but also in the ethical tradition that goes right back to Socrates and Plato.[11]

Notwithstanding strong disagreements over particular values, all Greek philosophers treat real happiness as the condition that makes persons *godlike*, to the extent that this is humanly possible. Even Aristotle, who forcefully acknowledges human vulnerability

---

[11] The tradition continues right up to the time of Simplicius in the sixth century AD (see p. 206). We can be virtually certain that Epictetus did not believe that Odysseus was actually overwhelmed by grief; for he also, with reference to Homer again, treats him as an ideal Stoic (3.26.33–4).

to fortune, says that a truly virtuous person 'bears all the chances of life becomingly and always makes the best of circumstances . . . And if this is the case, the happy man can never become miserable—though he will not reach blessedness if he meets with fortunes like those of Priam'.[12] For Plato, Homer's representation of lamenting heroes and gods is not a fit subject for the young men of his *Republic* to read (III.388a), and the ideal Epicurean life promised long-term imperturbability. We have already noted how Epictetus cites Socrates as a model of emotional control, and in doing so he is typical of the way the Greek philosophical tradition took happiness to be incompatible with emotionalism.

There are strong cultural and linguistic differences here between our modern selves and the ancients. The happiness of the Greek philosophical ideal is not an everyday state of mind, which comes and goes like moods and feelings as one's reaction to circumstances changes, and it has nothing in common with our modern interests in excitement, ecstasy, or simple domestic comfort. Philosophical *eudaimonia* is a condition in which a person of excellent character is living optimally well, flourishing, doing admirably, and steadily enjoying the best mindset that is available to human beings. The Stoics in particular took the complete attainment of such a condition to be well-nigh impossible, yet so worth striving for that no human being who grasped its attractions would wish to settle for less.

Furthermore, in interpreting Epictetus' strictures on emotionalism, it is a mistake to take him to be asking: 'How can I avoid jeopardizing my tranquillity in all circumstances?', and simply responding: 'By practising detachment from everything that is outside my direct control.' Although he has a gift for acute psychological insight, he is not a quasi-modern analyst, offering purely psychological advice as it were, but a theologically centred philosopher. Tranquillity enters his argument not as its beginning but as the response to such questions as: How can I live in accordance with nature? How can I follow and obey God? How can I achieve the goodness and happiness that it is rational to pursue in a determinist and providentially structured world?

---

[12] *EN* 1.10.1101ᵃ6. King Priam of Troy, father of fifty sons whom he lost along with his realm, was a proverbial example for catastrophic change of fortune.

How can I put the resources God has given me to proper use? He gets to tranquillity as the content of happiness not by privileging this mental state *per se*, but because he takes it to be both the most subjectively satisfying condition available to us and also the condition that will best enable us to perform our social functions in a world governed by a benevolent deity.

We also need to take due account of Epictetus' ubiquitous concern to challenge his students by using language and examples that are calculated to jolt them out of any complacency with regard to bodily and external contingencies. His conception of happiness even reduces tragedy to mistaken reliance on the value and ownership of anything that is not strictly one's own and in one's own power. In the following passage, we hear first how a Stoic should respond to a tyrannical emperor. Then, drawing on Oedipus, the most famous example of tragic reversal, Epictetus starkly contrasts the sham happiness of regal prosperity with the contentment and autonomy that are available in principle even to someone who lacks material goods:

103   If only you remember what is yours, you will never claim what is another's.
    [The Emperor tells you]
        Take off the senatorial toga.[13]
    Look, I'm wearing the equestrian toga.
        Take that one off.
    Look, I'm wearing an ordinary toga.
        Take it off.
    Look, I'm naked.
        But you provoke my resentment.
    Take my pathetic body, all of it. Am I still afraid of the man I can throw away my body to?
        But [this other man] won't make me his heir.
    So what? Did I forget that none of these things is mine?
        How is it then that we call them 'mine'?
    Just as we do with the bed at an inn—if the innkeeper when he dies leaves you them. But if he leaves them to someone else, he'll have them

---

[13]   Roman rank was marked by the broad stripe of the senatorial toga, the narrow stripe of the equestrian or knight's toga, or the plain toga of the ordinary citizen. Epictetus' dialogue presupposes some tyrannical emperor, who could well be Domitian; see Starr (1949).

and you'll be looking for another one. If you don't find one, you'll sleep on the ground; but do so with confidence, snoring, and remembering that, whereas tragedies take their settings from the wealthy, kings, and autocrats, the only place for a poor man in a tragedy is as a member of the chorus. The kings start out from prosperity:

Festoon the palace.

Then about the third or fourth act [we hear]:

O Kithaeron, why did you receive me?[14]

Slave, where are your garlands, where is your diadem? Your body-guards are no help to you. So when you approach one of those types, remember that you are approaching a tragic character, not an actor, but Oedipus himself.

Yet that fellow is supremely happy: he's walking around with a crowd of people.

I too can line myself up with the crowd, and do the same.   (1.24.12–19)

Although Epictetus advances his prescription for happiness unequivocally, he also presents it as an ideal project from which his students should not be daunted because of its difficulty. A passage I have already excerpted (p. 111) merits repetition:

(47) Consider which of the things you proposed initially you have mastered, and which you have not, and how it gives you pleasure to remember some of them and pain to remember others, and if possible recover the things you have let slip. Those competing in the greatest contest should not fade out, but take the blows too. For our competition is not to do with wrestling or the pancration, where success or failure can make all the difference to a man's standing—and indeed make him [in his and the world's eyes] supremely fortunate or unfortunate—but over *real* good fortune and happiness.

What then?

Even if we fail here and now, no one stops us from competing again; we don't have to wait another four years for the next Olympics, but as soon as a man has picked himself up and renewed his grip on himself and shown the same enthusiasm he is allowed to compete. And if you give in again, you can compete again, and if once you win, you are like someone

---

[14] The line is spoken by Oedipus in Sophocles, *Oedipus Tyrannus* 1390, at the moment when he realizes that his parents exposed him as an infant on Mt Kithaeron, and thus he must be the unwitting murderer of his father Laius. Marcus Aurelius also cites the line (XI.6), and makes the tart comment: 'Even those who say "O Kithaeron" endure.'

who never gave in. Only, don't let sheer habit make you give in readily and end up like a bad athlete going around beaten in the whole circuit like quails that run away. (3.25.1-5)

In this elaborate passage the athletic simile, far from being merely decorative, throws important light on Epictetus' conception of happiness. We moderns tend to think of happiness as a psychological condition over which we have at best only partial control, but Epictetus presents it as a would-be achievement as distinct from being a merely psychological reaction or affect.

His competitive image needs careful scrutiny. He is not suggesting that happiness is a prize over which we are engaged in a contest with other people. Rather, the competition is with our individual selves, where what is at stake is our capacity to make the best use of every circumstance and to turn even unfavourable situations to good and robust effect.[15] Conventionally negative circumstances are to be interpreted, via the contest metaphor, as opportunities for training and for enabling happiness to prevail. Equally noteworthy is his insistence that, should we achieve happiness, that achievement cancels out all previous failures; which fits the Stoic doctrine that happiness does not depend upon duration or the aggregation of previous experience.

It should now be clear that, while Epictetus' conception of happiness is radically Stoic in its indifference to the favourable circumstances that any normal person, including Stoics, would in principle prefer for themselves, it does involve constituents of happiness that any normal person prizes: contentment, freedom, strength, making the best of oneself, fulfilling one's desires, and emotional stability are all central to the disposition that he calls *eudaimonia*.

The next question to ask is how this bears on his social prescriptions and his conception of morality. In a discourse entitled *How should we be disposed towards tyrants?* Epictetus asks why people in general are disturbed by such encounters, and responds:

---

[15] See e.g. 1.12.17; 2.2.21; 2.14.7.

104 It is not possible for that which is by nature free to be disturbed or impeded by anything except itself. Judgements are what trouble a person. For when the tyrant tells someone:

I will chain your leg,

the man who sets high value on his leg says:

No; pity me,

whereas the man who sets high value on his volition [*prohairesis*] says: If that seems to you more profitable, chain it.

You don't care?

I don't care.

I will show you that I am master.

How can you? Zeus has liberated me. Do you suppose that he was likely to enslave his own son? But you are master of my corpse; take it.

You mean that when you approach me, you don't attend to me.

No; I attend to myself. But if you want me to say that I attend to you too, I tell you that I do so in the way that I attend to my water jug.

This is not [egotistical] self-love [*philautia*]. Rather, it is the way creatures are made. They do everything for their own sake. Yes, even the sun does everything for its own sake and so too does Zeus. But when Zeus wants to be Rain-giver and Fruit-giver and Father of gods and men, you see that he cannot accomplish these works and earn these titles unless he is a public benefactor. And in general he has so constituted the rational animal's nature that it can attain none of its own goods unless it contributes something to the common interest.

Hence it is not antisocial to do everything for one's own sake. What do you expect? That someone should desert himself and his own interest? In that case, how could all creatures have one and the same starting point, namely—appropriation [*oikeiôsis*] to themselves?   (1.19.7–15)

This is one of the few passages where Epictetus invokes the standard Stoic doctrine of *oikeiôsis*. His predecessors, as I have mentioned (p. 182), made this concept of 'appropriation' basic to their ethics, using it to explain why animals in general and humans in particular are endowed with both self-regarding and sociable instincts. Did these earlier Stoics think of the latter instinct as an outgrowth of the former, or did they treat them as relatively or wholly independent of one another? Our sources on these difficult questions are complex and controversial. Epictetus acknowledges human beings' natural *oikeiôsis* for one another (3.24.11). But his position, as outlined above, implies that this operates only to the extent that it satisfies the principle of 'appropriation to oneself'. As he starkly puts it elsewhere (2.22.15–16):

105 It is a universal fact that every creature is appropriated to nothing so strongly as it is to its own interest. Whatever appears to it to be an obstacle to that interest, whether this be a brother or a father or a child or a beloved or a lover, the creature hates, rejects, and curses it. For its nature is to love nothing so much as its own interest.[16]

In **104** Epictetus starts from two antithetical illustrations of how self-interestedness may manifest itself. Confronted by a tyrant, a non-Stoic would probably and mistakenly identify his self-interest with bodily freedom. The Stoic, by contrast, situates his self-interest in his mental freedom, and hence rejects the tyrant's capacity to master *him* by chaining his legs. At this point, Epictetus invites the rejoinder that the Stoic's confrontational response to the tyrant exhibits egotistical self-love.

No, he responds. It is correct to say that the Stoic's behaviour is self-interested, but as such it is no different from the *natural* behaviour of every living being. In addition, so far from being simply egotistical or incompatible with 'the common interest', the Stoic's behaviour satisfies the following fundamental principle: the rational animal's nature is such that it can attain none of *its own goods* unless it contributes something to the common interest.[17] To give this thesis its strongest backing, Epictetus turns to cosmology, instancing the sun (which Stoics regarded as a divine entity) and Zeus as exemplary rational beings whose self-interested behaviour necessarily includes benefit to the world at large.

For a clearer account of how self-interest entails, or should entail, the moral point of view, we may turn to a passage that follows **105**:

---

[16] A few lines above **105** Epictetus illustrates this claim by citing the fratricidal quarrel of Polyneices and Eteocles (see p. 226 below) in a quotation from Euripides' *Phoenissae*.

[17] Epictetus does not spell out how the Stoic's resistance to the tyrant meets this condition; the unexpressed thought is presumably that society in general benefits from the Stoic's display of inner freedom.

106 If someone places his interest in the same pan of the scale where he places piety, the honourable [*to kalon*], country, parents, and friends, all of these are secure. But if he places his interest in one pan and his friends, country, relatives, and justice itself in the opposite pan, all the latter vanish, weighed down by his interest. For wherever 'I' and 'mine' are placed, to there the creature inevitably inclines: if they are in the flesh, the authority must be there, if in one's volition [*prohairesis*], there, if in external things, there.

Accordingly, if I am there, where my volition is, thus and only thus shall I be the friend and son and father that I should be. For this will then be my interest—to preserve my integrity, patience, abstemiousness, and cooperation, and to preserve my human relationships. But if I place myself in one scale and the honourable in another, then the doctrine of Epicurus wins, which states that the honourable is either nothing or only reputable opinion [*to endoxon*].[18] (2.22.18–21)

Epictetus now connects the universality of self-interested motivations with people's sense of their identity: we are drawn to 'wherever "I" and "mine" are placed' (cf. 1.22.12–16). If morality and other people's interests are to have a secure claim on me, they must not be in any competition with what I want for myself; but that can be assured only if I identify myself and my interest with the moral point of view (cf. 1.27.14). This is what Epictetus means when he specifies volition (*prohairesis*) as the only basis for personal identity that can guarantee dutiful behaviour. Precisely what *prohairesis* involves is the main subject of my next chapter. Suffice it to say that, in his present use of the term, he is referring to every person's share of divine reason, with all that that endowment provides for the correct understanding of the facts and values and choices essential to human excellence and happiness.

If I identify my interest with the moral point of view, is it still reasonable to call it *my* interest? Is there enough of me left to give substance to the thought that in cultivating the moral point of view I am still conforming to the general principle of universal self-interestedness? Three points need to be made in response to these challenges.

---

[18] Epictetus probably has in mind the saying of Epicurus, often quoted against him, that 'I spit on the honourable [*to kalon*], unless it brings pleasure' (H. Usener, *Epicurea* 512).

First, Epictetus insists that the disposition in which we identify with the moral point of view is at the same time the disposition that generates the freedom and tranquillity and stability that
make for our happiness as individual persons. There are not two
dispositions, a self-interested one and an altruistic one, but a single attitude that treats concern for others as integral to concern
for oneself.

Secondly, Epictetus devotes far more attention to instructing
his students in self-improvement than he gives to advising them
on specific social roles. As we have already seen, he treats the latter as a topic that is secondary to the primary topic of training
one's desires and aversions (see Section 4.4). We could say that
Epictetus places duty to oneself as the top priority. It is not given
to everyone to be a resplendent benefactor of mankind; but,
while it is one's primary function to improve oneself, this should
not be at the expense of neglecting one's social relationships
(4.10.12–13).

There is a third point, which is no less crucial. Epictetus is a
strong naturalist; he thinks that a person's interests are not simply up to him or her to determine, but are factually set by the
kind of rational beings that we are. Basic to that nature, he holds,
is not only our human identity in terms of volition (*prohairesis*)
but also our being 'world citizens'.[19]

107 You are a citizen of the world and a part of it, not one of the subordinate
parts [like the domestic animals] but one of the foremost; for you are
capable of understanding the divine administration and of reasoning
out what follows from it.
What is the profession of a citizen?
To treat nothing as a purely private interest and to deliberate about
nothing as though one were detached [from the world as a whole], but
as the hand or the foot, if they had reason and the capacity to attend to
the world's [natural] constitution would never exercise impulse or
desire except by reference to the whole.[20]   (2.10.3–4)

108 What is the meaning of the statement that some external things are
natural and others unnatural?

  [19] On 'world citizen', see Section 9.2.
  [20] His use of the foot example here and in **106** is modelled on Chrysippus; see
2.6.10.

It is as though we took ourselves to be detached beings. For while I admit that it is natural for the foot to be clean, yet if you take it as a foot and not as something detached, it will be appropriate for it to step into mud and trample on thorns, and sometimes be amputated for the sake of the whole. Otherwise it will no longer be a foot.

That is the way we should also view ourselves. What are you? A human being. If you view yourself as something detached, it is natural for you to live to old age, to be wealthy, and healthy. But if you view yourself as a human being and a part of some whole, for the sake of that whole it is appropriate for you now to be sick, now to set sail and take risks, now to be in need, and maybe even die before your time. Why then are you upset?

Don't you know that, just as the former [the putative foot] will no longer be a foot [if it is detached], so you [if detached] will no longer be a human being. For what is a human being? The part of a community, first the community of gods and human beings, and secondly of the one called closest to that, which is a small copy of the universal community.

(2.5.24–6)

In these passages we see how Epictetus continues to revise conventional concepts of self-interestedness and to relate his own view of what that entails to a proper grasp of one's essential human identity. He argues that our identity is so irreducibly social, both globally and locally, that we cannot achieve our own good unless we see ourselves as integral parts of the world in general and of our society in particular. Hence, while there is such a thing as 'my' interest, it is no more detachable from the communities of which I am a part than my foot is detachable from the functions I require it to serve. The implication is that, if you isolate your own interest from these social 'wholes', you turn yourself into the equivalent of a detached limb, and therefore cease to be a functioning person with any genuinely human interests as such.

These are predictable thoughts for a Stoic to voice. Yet, Epictetus verges on heterodoxy when he claims, at the start of the last passage, that 'natural' and 'unnatural' are evaluative distinctions that pertain only when we look at our lives and objectives in 'detachment' from our social and global contexts. In saying this, he appears to offer his own interpretation of the standard Stoic doctrine concerning the 'preferred' and 'dispreferred' indifferents (see p. 184). As I understand that doctrine, orthodox Stoics would say that the cleanliness of a foot is 'naturally preferable' even in circumstances that make it impossible or that require me, for the sake of a more pressing objective, to accept dirt and discomfort. Epictetus seems to be saying that it is as natural, or at least as 'appropriate', *in practice* (as distinct from abstractly), for one's foot to be dirty, and therefore the so-called preferred indifferents are inadequate guidelines for influencing one's conduct as a well-reasoning local and world citizen.[21]

If this is his point, it fits his general reticence concerning the doctrine of preferred indifferents. In addition, it recalls the heterodoxy of the early Stoic Aristo, who rejected this doctrine on the following grounds: 'In the face of the different circumstances, neither those which are said to be preferred prove to be unconditionally preferred, nor are those said to be dispreferred of necessity dispreferred.'[22] The theme of **108** is the 'difficult but not impossible project' of 'using' one's material circumstances 'carefully' while at the same time remaining completely unconcerned about the value of the materials and the results of their use:

109   This is what you will see skilful ball players doing. None of them cares about the ball, as if that were something good or bad, but only about throwing it and catching it. That's what athletic skill and technique and speed and good judgement consist in. Whereas I myself cannot catch the ball, even if I stretch out my coat, the expert catches it if I throw it. But if we throw or catch the ball with anxiety and fear, what fun is left, how will a player be in good form [*eustathêsei*], and how will he keep his eye on the sequence of the game? One will say 'throw', another will say 'Don't throw', and a third, 'You've had your turn'. That wouldn't be a game but a brawl.   (2.5.15–17)

With this telling image, Epictetus likens happiness and the moral point of view to the interactions of an expert athletic team.

---

[21] Cf. 1.2.14: in the abstract, life is preferable to death and pleasure to pain, but such values are not commensurable with the value one should set on one's own worth.

[22] See LS 58F. Dobbin (1998: 205) aptly notes how Epictetus (1.25.3–4) also echoes Aristo in rejecting the necessity and efficacy of classifying moral rules in a set of precepts. Sorabji (2000: 170) observes Epictetus' stress on the indifference rather than the value of the 'preferred indifferents'.

Each member of the team focuses on his own role in the collaborative performance, using his turn with the ball well, and not interfering with the other players' turn. Athletic skill requires concentration on the game's essentials, focus on the right moment, and expert anticipation. None of these is compatible with anxiety or concerns about the state of the ball.

So in the game of life, Epictetus suggests, we should reflect on an extreme case—Socrates' 'ball-playing' expertise. What was the ball Socrates had to play with at his trial?

110 Imprisonment, exile, drinking poison, loss of wife, leaving orphaned children. These were the context of his game, but none the less he deftly played and handled the ball. So too we should deploy the ball-player's consummate skill, but also his indifference as to its object, a mere ball. For it is unconditionally incumbent on us to be skilful in our handling of any external material, but rather than making it part of ourselves we should treat it, whatever it is, as the context for displaying our skill. (2.5.19–21)

More is involved in Epictetus' ball-game image than he sets out in my excerpt. Lives, he suggests, resemble team games in being social encounters governable by their members' specific skills, but they are also necessarily finite occasions, with unpredictable eventualities and conclusions. Individual players trip or fall sick, but the game continues. Yet, as individuals we also have the option of declining to continue our participation 'when it ceases to please' (1.24.20). With this and other euphemisms (the 'open door' that gives exit to the 'smoky room' (1.25.18)), Epictetus acknowledges the Stoic doctrine that suicide could be justified under intolerable material circumstances. But he goes out of his way to give this doctrine a theological endorsement:

111 If you [God] send me to where human beings cannot live in accordance with nature, I shall depart—not in disobedience to you, but as though you were signalling the retreat. I do not abandon you, heaven forbid! But I see that you have no need of me. But if a life in accordance with nature is granted me, I shall seek no other place than where I am or other people than those I am with. (3.24.101–2)

As so often, Epictetus blends his Stoicism with an unmistakable allusion to Socrates. While granting the conditional propriety of suicide, he also mimics Socrates' famous quotation of the saying that no one should leave the guardhouse until God has given the signal. In its context (Plato, *Phaedo* 62b–c) Socrates' remark is both an argument against arbitrary suicide and an acknowledgement that one's death, as in his own judicial case, can be timely and divinely mandated. By attaching the conditional justifiability of suicide to Socrates' famous statement, Epictetus contrives to remain loyal to both camps. In the light of Roman attitudes and examples, it is a great exaggeration to say that 'the final recourse of suicide recurs at intervals through his pages like a tolling bell'.[23] Epictetus shows none of Seneca's fascination with suicide, nor does he treat it, like Seneca, as the supreme test of a Stoic's freedom.[24]

Our next task is to study the skills that Epictetus proposes that his students can acquire to enable them to play the game of life in ways that are inwardly satisfying and outwardly admirable.

FURTHER READING AND NOTES

Life in Accordance with Nature

Modern scholars have differed over the role assigned to cosmic nature, as distinct from human nature, in the foundations of early Stoic ethics: for bibliographical details see under 'Stoicism', p. 36. To some extent the debate has been at cross purposes, because any interpreter must accept that, since human nature was taken to be a 'part' of cosmic nature, both natures must be involved. The issue, as expressed by Annas (1993: 160), is whether the early Stoics 'give a priority within ethical theory to cosmic nature', taking the understanding of this nature to be a foundation for knowledge of our final end, or whether they start simply from what it is humanly natural to do and to value, reserving the cosmic perspective to later.

[23] Oldfather (1925–8: i, p. xxv).

[24] Apart from warning his students against suicidal distaste for their bodies (see p. 159 above), he describes his successful efforts to restrain a friend from starving himself to death 'for no reason' (2.15.4–12).

This question again, in my opinion, invites some misunderstanding, because what the evidence shows is that they made use of both procedures (compare DL VII.85–9 with Cicero, *De finibus* III.17–22; and see Inwood in Algra 1999: 675–6). However, I completely agree with Annas that it is important to explore the differences of emphasis accorded to the two kinds of nature in our evidence, and to be sensitive to differences between the early and the later Stoics on what she well calls 'the point of view of the universe'. See also Long (1996*a*: 152–5).

Annas and those like her who are uncomfortable with basing ethics on cosmic nature give special weight to the Ciceronian text cited above; and I draw primarily on this passage on pp. 182–3. The 'point of view of the universe' is certainly not made primary in Cicero's treatment (or indeed in some others), and in my main text I have argued that this, or, as I would prefer to say, the lack of priority assigned to God/Nature, did not satisfy Epictetus. Actually, I think that the main point of the Ciceronian text is not to provide foundations for the truth of the school's principal ethical claims but to show how people *naturally* (as the argument claims) come to acquire moral motivations that accord with the principles of Stoic ethics. But Epictetus, I have argued, looks as much to God for explaining the origin of moral 'preconceptions' as for authorizing the content of moral principles.

Annas (1993: 161) finds 'the point of view of the universe' (PVU) more prominent in Marcus Aurelius and Epictetus than in earlier Stoics. So far as Marcus is concerned, I completely agree. PVU, she suggests (1993: 175), particularly involves 'two strategies'. One, which she calls 'only a part', is an invitation 'to abstract from one's own viewpoint', and to see ourselves as 'merely a part of a larger whole'. The other, which she calls 'alienation', is an invitation to 'see things as they are', as distinct from according them normal human significance. I am not sure if I understand the difference between these two strategies, but they or this outlook are extremely prominent in Marcus, and give his meditations their strong air of resignation and melancholy (see p. 178 above).

On the other hand, in Epictetus not only is PVU, as distinct from the perspective of a personalist God, quite rare (much more so than is acknowledged in Annas's qualification (1993: 176 n. 62)—for a few instances, see p. 155 above), but also his principal use of the 'being a part' strategy is to elevate human identity by treating it as participant in the divine administration.

Happiness, Self-interest, and Society

For salient texts illustrating early Stoic thought on these subjects, see LS 57, 64, 66. The concept of *oikeiôsis* is treated in LS 57, and for further discussion see Pembroke in Long (1971*b*), Striker (1983), Annas (1993), and Frede (1999*a*). Epictetus' specific conception of social *oikeiôsis* is excellently discussed by Inwood (1996).

The fullest Stoic treatments of happiness are Seneca, *De vita beata*, *De constantia sapientis*, and *De tranquillitate animi*. In the early sections of the first of these works, Seneca prefigures Epictetus in emphasizing, as the features of happiness, unbroken tranquillity, freedom, peace, harmony, and high-mindedness (*magnitudo animi* in Latin; *megalopsychia* in Greek). Happiness as tranquillity is discussed and criticized by Striker (1990). For a comprehensive study of the eudaimonist tradition of ancient ethics, see Annas (1993), and for Stoicism in particular Long (1989), which focuses on Epictetus, and Cooper (1996). Long (1993*b*, 2001) explore the bold claims of Greek ethics concerning rationality's capacity to fashion and empower the self. Simplicius, in his commentary on the *Manual*, endorses the conception of happiness I have identified as the dominant view in Greek philosophical ethics (see I. Hadot 1996: 221–2), and he also describes it as 'invulnerable, because it provides no entry-point for harmful things' (224.1), asking us to note 'how Socratic' it is (230.27).

For bibliography on society and appropriate actions, see p. 257.

Life as a Game

See Xenakis (1969: ch. 2) and Striker (1996*b*: 309–11).

Suicide

In addition to the passages cited on p. 203, Epictetus refers to this option in the following places: 1.25.20; 2.1.19; 3.8.6 ('God has left the door open for you'); 3.13.14 ('When God does not provide the necessities, he signals the retreat'); 3.22.34. For treatments of suicide in the Stoic tradition, see Rist (1969) and Griffin (1986), and for Kant's criticism of Stoicism on this issue, see Seidler (1983).

CHAPTER 8

Autonomy and Integrity

You are not flesh or hair but volition; if you keep that beautiful, then you will be beautiful.

(3.1.40)

8.1 RATIONALITY, SELF, AND PERSON

In almost every discourse Epictetus tells his students to focus on God's special gift to human beings. The essence of goodness, meaning beneficial activity, is God (see p. 144), who has given each person a portion of himself. Epictetus characterizes this divine endowment in the following ways: the reasoning and self-studying faculty, the faculty that can make correct use of impressions, and the faculty of positive and negative impulse and of desire and aversion.[1] He also calls it 'me' (i.e. the self) and *prohairesis*, which I have translated by 'volition' in the citation at the head of this chapter and in most of the word's earlier occurrences in this book. Because any rendering of this term is controversial, for the time being I shall leave it untranslated, in order to avoid begging too many questions. But, however *prohairesis* is translated, it is Epictetus' favourite name for the purposive and self-conscious centre of a person.

---

[1] See pp. 63, 129.

Epictetus is at pains to emphasize three points about our rational faculty. First, it is quite distinct from the flesh and blood of the body; secondly, in a further contrast with this bodily material, it is given to us to be 'ours' and to be *naturally* free, unimpeded, and unconstrained; and, thirdly, it includes not only intellect but also the capacity to be motivated to act as a consistently rational being.

In making the first point, Epictetus is not claiming that the rational faculty is non-physical. As we have seen (Section 6.4), his contrast between body and mind is not a metaphysical contrast between two distinct modes of being, but it is, none the less, a dualistic conception, with close affinities to the philosophical soul's detachment from the body recommended by Socrates in Plato's *Phaedo*. Unfortunately, Epictetus thinks, most of us misunderstand our proper relation to our bodies, and so, by identifying with them and by pursuing or avoiding external things that are not 'ours', we doom ourselves to frustration, lack of freedom, unhappiness, and moral imperfection, all of which are misuses of rationality.

If we could consistently understand that nothing except our rational faculty is truly 'ours', this self-identification, when its implications are properly grasped and put into practice, would render us completely autonomous, capable both of achieving everything we desire and avoiding everything to which we are averse; and it would also render us morally excellent. How so? What is the connection between rationality, autonomy, happiness, and moral excellence; and what kind of autonomy is in principle inalienably ours?

To approach these big questions, I offer a sample of texts that highlight Epictetus' special word, *prohairesis*. First, the beginning of a discourse addressed to someone engaged in a lawsuit:

112 Watch out, you who are engaged in litigation, for what you want to secure and where you want to succeed. For if you want to secure the natural condition of your *prohairesis*, you are completely safe and completely at ease; you will have no problem. What else do you care about if you want to secure the things that are completely in one's power [*autexousia*] and naturally free, and if you are content with

them?[2] Who has authority over them, who can remove them? If you want to be a person with integrity, who will stop you? If you want to be free from impediment and compulsion, who will compel you to have desires and aversions that don't accord with your judgements? Well—the judge will treat you in ways that are thought to inspire fear. But how can he make you experience them with aversion?

Therefore, when desire and aversion are up to you, what else do you care about? This should be your introduction, this your narrative, this your proof, this your victory, this your peroration, and this your public testimonial. (2.2.1–7)[3]

Next, towards the conclusion of a discourse concerning the correct analysis of our rational faculty, Epictetus imagines someone consulting an interpreter of Chrysippus on what the Stoic principle of living in accordance with nature involves. The interpreter responds as if he were a seer interpreting signs in the entrails of a sacrificial animal:

113   My friend, you have a *prohairesis* that is by nature unimpeded and unconstrained. This is inscribed here in the entrails. I will prove it to you, first in the sphere of assent. Can anyone prevent you from assenting to a truth?

No one can.

Can anyone compel you to accept a falsehood?

No one can.

Do you see that in this sphere you have a *prohairetic* faculty that is unimpeded, unconstrained, unhindered? Come now, is it different in the sphere of desire and impulse? What can overcome an impulse except another impulse? What can overcome a desire or an aversion except another desire or aversion?

Yet if someone threatens me with the fear of death, he does constrain me.

What constrains you is not the threat but your decision that it is better to do something else rather than die. Once again, then, it is your judgement

---

[2] The term *autexousios* is one of Epictetus' distinctive expressions for the mental things that are entirely 'up to us'; cf. its use in his long discourse on freedom (4.1.56, 62, 68, 100). Musonius Rufus (fr. 12) had applied the term to a master's belief in his absolute authority over a slave. For its later usage, especially in Christian writers, see Bobzien (1998: 355).

[3] The words 'introduction', etc., all allude to the standard components of a courtroom speech. Epictetus continues 112 by paraphrasing Socrates' words to one of his companions before his trial, as reported by Xenophon, *Apology* 2–5.

that compelled you; that is to say, *prohairesis* compelled *prohairesis*. For if God, in taking from himself his very own part, which he has given us, had constructed it to be impeded or constrained by himself or by something else, he would no longer be God or caring for us as he should. These are the signs I find in the entrails: If you so wish, you are free; if you so wish, you will blame no one, accuse no one, and everything will be in accord both with your own intelligence and with God's.

                                (1.17.21–8; see also p. 91 above, and cf. 4.1.69)

And now a third excerpt from a discourse on progress, drawing a contrast between the proper way to achieve this condition and book learning:

114   *Where is progress?*
If any of you, withdrawing from external things has turned to concentrate on his *prohairesis*, working and toiling at it, to make it harmonious with nature, elevated, free, unimpeded, trustworthy, and respectful; and if he has learnt that no one who desires or shuns things that are not up to him can be trustworthy or free, but is inevitably changed and tossed about with them, and inevitably subjects himself to other people who have the power to provide or withhold those things; and if, lastly, when he gets up in the morning he secures and keeps a watch on these principles, taking his bath and dining like a trustworthy and respectful person, and similarly working at these fundamentals in every material circumstance, as a runner or a voice trainer does in his sphere of activity.

    This is the one who is making genuine progress, the one who has not travelled in vain.   (1.4.18–21)

8.2 VOLITION

There are three intimately related themes in **112–14**: the achievement of success and security, the freedom of impediments to one's will, and moral progress. In each case, the central concept is *prohairesis* and its characterization as 'naturally' unimpeded and unconstrained. What does Epictetus mean by *prohairesis* and by this characterization? The question, which has been keenly debated, is of great interest, for the way it is answered not only decisively influences the interpretation of

Epictetus but also the history of the idea of the will, especially the idea of a free will.

One thing is quite clear: Epictetus is the only Stoic according to our record who made *prohairesis* a key term. Earlier Stoics did have a use for the word (see p. 220), but they almost certainly did not employ it extensively or with the broad scope that Epictetus adopts. They typically referred to rationality via their standard term for the human mind, *hêgemonikon*, which literally means 'governing faculty'. The human *hêgemonikon* is the seat of rationality and the centre of the person; and in virtue of being these things it is one's epistemic and moral disposition. Epictetus also uses the term just like this. In many cases too he specifies it in ways that are identical to what he says about *prohairesis* in 112–14, especially the need to secure its 'natural' condition (3.5.3; 3.6.4; 3.9.11), and also its not being controllable by another (4.5.4). In addition, he makes it clear that *prohairesis* involves assent and impulse (113), which are basic faculties of the *hêgemonikon* in Stoic doctrine.

This congruence could suggest that the terms are synonymous in Epictetus, but I do not think this is right. Although they overlap in their referent, so far as human beings are concerned, *hêgemonikon* does not *mean* rationality; it is a term that applies to the souls of animals who lack rationality as well as to human beings. Epictetus confines *prohairesis* to humans and God; it is God's special gift of a rational, self-scrutinizing, and motivating faculty. *Prohairesis* rather than *hêgemonikon* is Epictetus' preferred term, and we must assume that he had strong reasons for this preference.

Rather than opting for synonymy, we should take *prohairesis* to refer to the human mind in just those capacities or dispositions that Epictetus constantly maintains to be completely 'up to us' and free from external constraint. Does that not apply to the human *hêgemonikon* too? Epictetus' implicit answer to this question is no, because the mind, as so designated, also includes our capacity (*phantasia*) to be presented with sense impressions and other kinds of thoughts that simply 'befall' us. We are not autonomous over the mere occurrence of impressions, or at least over the occurrence of those impressions that simply depend upon the way our sense organs are affected by the external things within their range. What is up to us is how we interpret such information, and the truth and value we attribute to it.

As we have seen, Epictetus associates with *prohairesis* his cardinal rule—the requirement to make *correct use* of our impressions. How we use them is up to us, because it falls within the purely internal domain of judgement, assent, and impulse. These faculties, of course, belong to the *hêgemonikon*, but because the mind, as so designated, includes our capacity to receive impressions and thus be externally affected, I conclude that Epictetus chose the term *prohairesis* to pick out the human mind in this more restricted aspect: 'us', so to say, in just those respects that are dependent on nothing that we cannot immediately judge, decide, and will, entirely by and for ourselves.

In my sample of passages Epictetus associates *prohairesis* with 'the things up to us', as distinct from external things; and he often calls these two types of thing *prohairetika* and *aprohaireta*, with the latter term signifying that everything outside the scope of *prohairesis*, including our bodies, is 'not up to us'. He did not invent a terminological and conceptual link between *prohairesis* and 'what is up to us'. Rather, he had the illustrious precedent of Aristotle.

In his ethics, Aristotle adopted the term *prohairesis* to signify what he calls 'the deliberated desire of things that are up to us' (*EN* III.1113^{a}10). In a further analysis of the term Aristotle calls *prohairesis* 'either desirous intellect or intellectual desire, and this sort of starting point for action is a human being' (*EN* VI.1139^{b}4).

Aristotle does not mean that everything human beings do is done on the basis of *prohairesis*. People sometimes act against their better judgement on the basis of ignorance or under the influence of emotion or appetite. Nor does he mean that *prohairesis* guarantees a morally correct decision. Vicious as well as virtuous persons act on its basis. However, *prohairesis*, because it combines thought and desire, is the proper starting point for action in all cases where we need a rational decision procedure on the best means to achieve our goals. It will direct us to actions that are 'up to us'—that is, 'things that it is within our power to do'—and it is itself a voluntary capacity, initiated by ourselves and not by anything external. Aristotle defines virtue as a '*pro-hairetic* disposition', and he judges it to be a better criterion for moral character than action.

The standard translation of Aristotelian *prohairesis* is choice, though 'decision' is sometimes adopted instead. Both terms are clearly appropriate, because our characters are shaped by the kinds of choices or decisions that we make. By defining *prohaire-sis* as he does, Aristotle draws attention to the complex structure of volition and thought that practical reasoning may be taken to involve. He proposes that we act or should act only after we have first (the *pro* prefix means 'before') deliberated about the best way to fulfil our desires.

It is unlikely that Epictetus studied Aristotle at first hand. But his own concept of *prohairesis* betrays unmistakable traces of the Aristotelian concept. The crucial points of similarity include (1) the idea of practical reason, or reason in action, as the integration of thought and desire; (2) the restriction of this faculty to 'things that are up to us'; and (3) the connection between *prohairesis* and moral character. In Epictetus' usage, however, *prohairesis* has also taken on a range of functions that are quite distinct from the Aristotelian precedent, owing to the differences between Aristotelian and Stoic psychology.

As a Stoic, Epictetus accepts the school's standard doctrine that the human mind is rational through and through.[4] In con-trast with Plato and Aristotle, who divided the mind into rational and irrational faculties, he takes all desires and emotions to be true or false value judgements made by the mind as a whole. Human beings frequently behave 'irrationally', but such behav-iour is due not to the intervention of a mental faculty other than reason but to the malfunctioning of reason itself. Hence, as he never tires of saying: 'It is not things that disturb people but their judgements about things' (*Ench.* 5). For an Aristotelian, *pro-hairesis* comes into play only when persons are attempting to organize their practical activities according to rational princip-les. In Epictetus *prohairesis* is at work throughout every person's

---

[4] For Posidonius' deviation from this model of the mind, see p. 164.

waking life. It is the basis for everything that is 'us', our character, our judgements, our motivations; for whenever we want anything or try to do anything, we are always, however imperfectly, exercising our rational faculty; we are always motivated by reasons and by what we *judge* to be desirable or undesirable.

Notwithstanding these differences over psychology, Epictetus completely endorses Aristotle's strong conceptual tie between *prohairesis* and 'what is up to us'. We cannot, he is saying, take responsibility for every impression that is presented to us; for impressions are typically generated by external conditions over which we have only limited control. What we *are* always in a position to do is to decide what to make of any impression, and whether or not to give it our assent. That is standard Stoicism, but earlier Stoics did not designate the *autonomous* functions of the mind by a single term in order to distinguish them collectively from its function as a receptor of impressions. Hence, I suggest, the principal motivation for Epictetus' adoption of the term *prohairesis*. He proposes that our judgements, our ways of interpreting the world, are the critical factor in how we fare, and that they depend on nothing that is not 'up to us'.

It will be helpful, before proceeding further with the analysis of *prohairesis*, to review a discourse that illustrates why the 'correct use' of impressions serves as a description of Epictetus' entire educational agenda. What we need to appreciate, in studying this text, is that the term impression (*phantasia*) covers anything at all that 'appears' to us—any thought or object of awareness, ranging from the simplest perceptions such as 'here is a dog' to such complex thoughts as 'money is highly desirable' or 'death is not an evil'. Human impressions, as conceived by Epictetus and earlier Stoics, generally have this propositional structure, which is to say that they are either true or false. Human beings are naturally inclined to accept all impressions that appear true (see p. 100). Yet, because apparent truth is far from equivalent to actual truth, he takes the task of judging and interpreting impressions to be the critical test of human rationality, consistency, and moral character.

Epictetus begins the discourse entitled *How should we fight against impressions?* by observing that habits are established by the corresponding actions. He continues by making a similar point about our passions:

115 Once you have a passion for money [i.e. have the impression that money is extremely valuable], if reasoning is brought to bear to make you aware of the harm, the passion abates and our governing faculty is restored to its original authority. But if you bring nothing to bear by way of remedy, it will no longer return to that state, but when it is next inflamed by the corresponding impression it is kindled with passion more quickly than before.

And if this happens regularly, the next stage is a hardening of the skin, as it were, and that ailment confirms the avarice. For the person who has had a fever and then recovered is not in the same state as he was before the fever unless he has been completely cured. Something like this occurs with the soul's passions. Certain traces and weals are left within it, and unless one erases them well, the next flogging in the same place generates wounds rather than weals. So if you wish to be free from passion, don't feed your habit, and present it with nothing to make it grow . . .

Today when I saw a good looking boy or woman I did not say to myself:

If only I could have sex with her and *Her husband is a happy man.*

For to call the husband happy is to say the same of the adulterer. And I don't draw a mental picture of what comes next—the woman with me, getting undressed, and lying down by my side. I pat myself on the head, and say:

Well done, Epictetus, you have solved a clever puzzle in logic, much cleverer than the Master argument.[5]

But if the girl is willing, and nods to me and calls for me, and if besides she clutches me and presses me close and I hold back and win, I have solved a greater puzzle than the Liar argument . . .

How is this to happen?

You must want to be pleasing just to yourself, you must want to appear beautiful to God. Make it your passion to become pure in the presence of your pure self and in the presence of God . . .[6] Go back to Socrates and observe him as he lies down with Alcibiades and makes light of that

---

[5] On the Master argument, see 2.19.1–10. Like the Liar paradox (see p. 116 above), it was a classic conundrum of Stoic logic. Epictetus refers to it, like the Liar, as a temptation liable to distract his students from the more urgent task of mastering their desires and aversions.

[6] 'Pure self' is a striking expression, probably referring to a person's internal divinity; see Section 6.5.

man's beauty.[7] Consider what a victory he knew himself to have won, a truly Olympic one . . . so that one might, by the gods, rightly greet him 'Hail, you wonder', not like those rotten boxers and all-in wrestlers and their like, the gladiators.

With such opposing thoughts you will conquer the impression and not be dragged off by it. But for a start, don't be carried away by its vividness, but say:

Wait for me a bit, impression; let me take a look at you and what you are about, let me test you.

Next, don't let it lead you on by painting a picture of what comes next. Otherwise, it is off and away, taking you wherever it wishes. Instead, confront it with another impression, a fine and noble impression, and dismiss this foul one. If you accustom yourself to this kind of training, you will see what shoulders you will get, what sinews and strength; but at present you are all philosophical jargon, nothing more.

(2.18.8–12, 15–18, 19, 22–6)

In this discourse, as frequently elsewhere (see 2.22.6; 3.3.17; 3.22.5–6; 3.25.6), Epictetus shows why he connects autonomy with the 'correct use of impressions'. Anyone, irrespective of intention or moral character, may experience the sexual allure of a beautiful body, but what we do with that impression is up to us, meaning how we describe it to ourselves and what value we assign to the thing itself. Impressions as such are causal only in the sense that they make us aware of their objects; but by assenting to them, as in saying 'Here is something I want for myself', we surrender our own agency and put ourselves in the position of being 'conquered' or 'disturbed' or 'dazzled' by them.

The outcome of such assent is an ailment of rationality or a passion.[8] Nor is it likely to be only that. Along with loss of autonomy we may well allow the impression to make us pursue unethical objectives, such as an adulterous relationship, and so suffer loss of integrity.

Epictetus' crucial point is that impressions have only the effects that we permit them to have. What we are really motivated by is

---

[7] An allusion to Plato, *Symposium* 218d, where Alcibiades recounts his inability to seduce Socrates.

[8] The treatment of the passions as ailments is standard Stoicism. See further Section 9.3.

not the vivid or attractive or frightening look of impressions (as we are inclined to suppose) but our own wants and priorities, which are the value judgements we make.[9] Tempted as we may well be by an alluring impression, we have the power to confront it by picturing alternatives and so provide ourselves with a range of options.

In the present discourse Epictetus does not actually use the word *prohairesis*, but he implies it when he says such things as 'If you wish to be free from passion', or 'I don't draw a mental picture of what comes next', or 'You must want to be pleasing to yourself'. In 112–14 we found Epictetus characterizing *prohairesis* in just these ways, as for instance: 'Look at what you want to secure;' 'If you so wish, you are free;' 'Desire and aversion are up to you.'

Prohairesis by its nature, he reiterates, is unhindered and unconstrained, but that does not mean that we, who are *prohairesis*, cannot misuse our natures and so constrain it. In that case, however, as he says in 113, *prohairesis* has compelled *prohairesis* because it can be impeded only by itself (3.19.2); that is to say, we have hindered and constrained ourselves by our own voluntary abrogation of autonomy. All turns on what we 'want'—self-generated freedom from external constraint and from consequential disturbance, or self-inflicted enslavement to externals and the passions that ensue.

The natural or proper condition of *prohairesis*, then, is complete autonomy. Persons with this kind of *prohairesis* desire nothing they cannot obtain and are averse to nothing they cannot avoid because they restrict their desires and aversions to those things that are entirely up to them; these are the only genuinely good and bad things that there are. Good and bad things are entirely up to them because they are dispositions of the *prohairesis*; for goodness simply is a *prohairesis* disposed to treat rational autonomy as God's prescription for human excellence and happiness, and to treat everything external as indifferent. Badness, conversely, is nothing but a *prohairesis* that falls short of this prescription.

[9] For Epictetus' acknowledgement of uncontrollable 'shocks', see p. 253.

We can now address the questions of how best to translate *pro-hairesis* and what its natural freedom entails. Favoured transla-tions include moral purpose, moral character, and moral person. *Prohairesis* certainly encompasses purpose, character, and person, but 'moral' is a misleading intrusion. When we attribute morality to someone, we generally imply that they are ethically well motiv-ated, but the quality of someone's *prohairesis*, as in Aristotle's use of the term, can be bad as well as good. The inclusion of 'moral' is also misleading because its connotations are unavoidably coloured by later ethical traditions; in its usage by these traditions, 'moral' is too closely tied to the ideas of social duty and obligation to fit Epictetus' primary concern with the achievement of happi-ness in terms of mental freedom and tranquillity.

Choice or decision (standard translations of the Aristotelian concept) clearly pertain to Epictetus' use of *prohairesis*, but these terms are primarily associated with particular acts or policies and so they are less apt to capture the sense of a person's entire voli-tional mentality. I have occasionally translated the term by 'will' in contexts where any other translation seems perverse. 'Will' has the advantage of conforming to Epictetus' language (e.g. 'If you will, you are free'), but, like 'moral', will suffers from the misleading accretions of later philosophy and it could incorrect-ly imply that Epictetus envisions a faculty called 'the will' that is distinct from assent and impulse.

Prohairesis is what makes us agents or beings capable of for-mulating objectives and trying to put them into practice. Agency would be a better translation than mentality, because it calls attention to Epictetus' insistence that everything we can actually *do* is a function of our *prohairesis*. But agency is also misleading for a reason I take to be central to Epictetus' liking for this word.

Consider the following passage, the context of which is the thesis that our acts of assent and impulses are never *necessarily* impeded by anything external, including even a tyrant's threats and chains. Epictetus' interlocutor is not yet convinced:

116   *What if I have the impulse to take a walk and another person impedes me?*
What part of you will he impede? Surely not your assent?

No; but my body.
Yes, as he would impede a stone.
Let that be so; but the fact is that I don't walk.
And who told you;
It is your function to walk unimpeded?
What I was telling you is that the only unimpeded thing is the impulse.
Wherever there is a need for the body and the body's cooperation, you
have long ago heard that nothing is your own. (4.1.72–3)

According to this remarkable passage, Epictetus is saying that
something is 'ours' or 'up to us' only if it *cannot* be externally
impeded. Taking a step can be externally impeded. Therefore,
even when we voluntarily walk, we should not say that the only
causal factor was our *prohairesis*, because our body's parts do not
strictly belong to 'us' and so do not fall within the unequivocal
scope of our agency.[10] In order for something fully to depend on
us, Epictetus claims, it must be the kind of thing that is in our
power under all possible circumstances, including bodily para-
lysis or a tyrant's seizure of all our limbs. The only kinds of thing
that qualify are the two mental functions of *prohairesis*, assent
and impulse.

Epictetus' response to his interlocutor may seem depressingly
inconsequential or worse. The fact that I cannot be prevented
from wanting to walk, even when my legs fail to function, looks
like the truism that desires can be frustrated by not issuing in the
intended actions. But plainly that is not Epictetus' point. In
order to grasp his point, we need to distinguish the purely
mental acts of assent and impulse from the purposive bodily
movements with which they are connected whenever circumstances permit. Rather than taking the bodily movements to be a
person's actions and evidence of agency, Epictetus takes them to

---

[10] The walking example recalls a disagreement between Cleanthes and
Chrysippus: Cleanthes had called walking 'the vital breath [*pneuma*] dispatched from
the mind right into the feet', whereas Chrysippus had called it 'the mind itself'
(Seneca, *Letter* 113.23), on which see Inwood (1985: 50–1). Epictetus' detachment of
prohairesis from the bodily actions to which volition is directed seems to indicate his
preference for Cleanthes' account: i.e. the mind as such remains detached from the
foot much as we might distinguish the brain from the nerves that transmit its mes-
sages to other parts of the body.

be only contingently related to our agency as such, the thing that is irreducibly up to us, our *prohairesis*.

The crucial claim, then, is that nothing outside our individual selves has ultimate authority over what we want or do not want. Epictetus presents this capacity as the basic fact about the self. It is a claim concerning our power as agents, but as agents of our minds' behaviour rather than of what we can do to bring about changes in the external world. Ordinarily, we regard what people do, in the sense of how they move their bodies purposefully, as evidence of their choices. Epictetus would surely agree. But, since our actions in this sense and our intentions cannot be guaranteed to coincide (though they normally will), Epictetus locates the essence of the self in the mental processes and dispositions that necessarily precede every bodily action; for *prohairesis* literally means 'pre-choice' or 'choice before choice', which is how the term is defined in early Stoicism.[11]

It should now be clear why I favour volition as the translation of *prohairesis*. This term comes as close as we can get to Epictetus' claim that the essence of the self is our decision-making, purposive, and evaluative disposition. Volition suits the fact that *prohairesis* is what persons can be held fully responsible for and what is up to them. In addition, this word has the advantage of not begging questions concerning the mind's autonomy. When we characterize persons in terms of their volitions, we do not thereby adopt a view concerning the undetermined freedom of their will; for we take people to have volitions irrespective of whether these are predetermined or independent of antecedent causation. Epictetus does attribute autonomy to *prohairesis*, but that is an attribute that he seeks to prove rather than something he builds into his basic use of this word.

8.3 THE FREEDOM OF THE WILL?

Since *prohairesis* is the faculty of volition and is 'naturally unhindered and unconstrained' (1.17.21), there is clearly a sense in which Epictetus takes persons to have a capacity for *free* will, but

[11] *SVF* iii.173; see Inwood (1985: 240–2) for the insignificance of the term in early Stoicism.

in what sense? The question has been much discussed, but, thanks especially to the excellent work of Susanne Bobzien (1998), we need not pursue it at length here (see also p. 230 below). It is virtually certain that Epictetus' concept of a free will, far from requiring the will's freedom from fate (i.e. a completely open future or set of alternative possibilities or choices), presupposes people's willingness to comply with their predestined allotment. The issue that concerns him is neither the will's freedom from antecedent causation nor the attribution to persons of a completely open future and indeterminate power of choice. Rather, it is freedom from being constrained by (as distinct from going along with) external contingencies, and freedom from being constrained by the errors and passions consequential on believing that such contingencies *must* influence and inhibit one's volition.

A free will in this sense is not the actual condition of every person, as would be the case if Epictetus were an indeterminist. Although it is every person's natural or normative condition, it is achievable only by those who attend to his constantly repeated injunction to focus one's desires and aversions exclusively on things that fall within the scope of one's volition. Consequently, the free will that Epictetus promulgates is not a universal psychological datum but an arduous project that is equivalent to mastery of Stoic philosophy:

117 The unconstrained person, who has access to the things that he wants, is free. Whereas he who can be constrained or necessitated or impeded or thrown into anything against his will is a slave.

Who is unconstrained?

The person who seeks after nothing that is not his own.

What are the things not one's own?

Everything that is not up to us to have or not to have, or to have thus and so qualified, or thus and so disposed. Therefore the body is not one's own, nor its members, nor property. If, then, you attach yourself to any of these things as if it were your own, you will pay the appropriate penalty of one who seeks after things that are not one's own. The road that leads to freedom, and the only release from enslavement, is to be able to say wholeheartedly: Lead me, Zeus and you, Fate, wherever you have ordained for me. (4.1.128–31)[12]

---

[12] These last words are a citation of Cleanthes; see p. 23 above.

In this passage, Epictetus construes freedom or autonomy as a mindset that cannot, in its outlook on its own future, be subject to frustration because it wants nothing that it cannot be assured of securing. What it wants is 'its own' or 'up to itself'—that is to say, its conformity to rationality, with all that that implies concerning the correct use of the impressions representing where one is situated in the world. That external situation, taken by itself, is not 'one's own' because it falls outside one's volition. But genuinely free persons will accommodate themselves to it, whatever it is, with the understanding that it cannot involve anything they do not want because their wants are determined by nothing outside themselves.

This is the one passage where Epictetus mentions freedom and fate in the same context. Notably, his focus is not on the causal history of the free person, asking how that person's autonomy is related to the network of causes signified by fate, but future oriented. To the extent that Epictetus connects freedom with fate, he does so by treating the autonomous person as someone who voluntarily complies with a predetermined situation rather than by asking how a causal nexus can be compatible with a capacity for assent that is completely unconstrained.

8.4 INTEGRITY AND FREEDOM

In Chapter 7 we saw how Epictetus draws on his concept of volition (*prohairesis*) in order to reconcile the universality of self-interested motivations with altruism and social obligations. To repeat a passage that I translated in that earlier context:

(106) Wherever 'I' and 'mine' are placed, to there the creature inevitably inclines: if they are in the flesh, the authority must be there, if in one's volition, there, if in external things, there.

Accordingly, if I am there, where my volition is, thus and only thus shall I be the friend and son and father that I should be. For this will then be my interest—to preserve my integrity, patience, abstemiousness, and cooperation, and to preserve my human relationships.

(2.22.19–20)

In my earlier comments on this passage (p. 199), I took Epictetus to be saying that, if morality and other people's interests are to have a secure claim on me, they must not be in any competition with what I want for myself; and hence, to assure that, it is necessary to identify oneself and one's interests with the moral point of view. I am certain that this is Epictetus' point in this fundamental passage, but a big question remains to ask—namely, the connection he posits between identifying oneself with one's *prohairesis* and integrity. How is morality guaranteed by limiting one's volition to unfrustratable internal objectives as distinct from states of one's body and external things? In order to elucidate and to answer this question, we need to study Epictetus' concept of integrity.

I use 'integrity' to translate such words as *aidôs*, *pistos*, and *gennaios*, two or more of which Epictetus typically uses in conjunction. The noun *aidôs* and its adjectival form *aidêmôn* had long been used to signify one or more of the following attitudes— shame, modesty, moderation, respect for public opinion, and regard for other persons' dignity. *Aidôs* is what Achilles lacks when he drags Hector's corpse around the tomb of Patroclus, and it is what inhibits Phaedra from revealing her adulterous passion for Hippolytus. Persons motivated by *aidôs* may simply be inhibited by fear of social disapproval or by concern to maintain their reputation, but *aidôs* can also signify self-respect and the internalized respect for moral norms that we call conscience. *Pistos* describes someone who is trustworthy, loyal, and creditable. *Gennaios* means noble or honourable in either the social or ethical sense that these words have in English.

These are familiar ways of referring in Greek to the virtuous attitudes towards family and fellow citizens commended in Latin by such everyday words as *pietas*, *fides*, and *honestas*. Traditional Stoicism had elaborated classifications and definitions of *aidôs*, *pistos*, and so forth, but Epictetus does not invoke these refinements or presuppose them.[13] Rather, we should take

---

[13] There was a technical use of *aidos* in Stoicism, to signify a species of 'caution' (*SVF* iii.432), which in turn was one of the three so-called good feelings (*eupatheiai*). For references and discussion, see Kamtekar (1998); and for 'good feelings' see p. 244 below. According to the theory underlying these expressions, *aidôs* presupposes perfect rationality and would be confined to the ideal sage. But none of this pertains to Epictetus' use of the term.

him in his use of these words to be signifying a range of ordinarily approved qualities that, unlike the special virtues of the ideal sage, will resonate well with his students and fall within their experience and aspirations. In the case of *aidôs*, as with *prohairesis*, Epictetus has taken a word that had a restrictedly technical use in traditional Stoicism and made it central to his own ethical discourse—with the difference that *aidôs*, unlike *prohairesis*, was a term as familiar in Greek as shame or respect in English.

As I have mentioned, Epictetus regularly couples *aidôs* with other words; and these include not only *pistos* and *gennaios*, but also *eleutheros*, 'free', and *atarachos*, 'undisturbed'. All of these fall within his concept of integrity, but before asking what freedom has to do with that, we need to consider what Epictetus means by characterizing *aidôs* and *pistos*, and so on, as 'natural':

118 God has entrusted yourself to you, and says:
I had no one more trustworthy than you. Keep him for me in his natural state, respectful [*aidêmôn*], trustworthy [*pistos*], high-minded, unperturbed, unimpassioned, undisturbed. (2.8.23)

119 Do we not have natural respect?
We do.
Is the person who loses this not penalized, deprived of nothing, losing nothing that belongs to him? Do we not have a natural trustworthiness, a natural affection, a natural benevolence, a natural patience with one another? Is the person who allows himself to be stripped of these things unharmed and undamaged? (2.10.22–3)

120 How are we endowed by nature? As free, as honourable [*gennaioi*], as respectful. For what other animal blushes or has an impression of what is shameful? (3.7.27)

In a discourse that deals with the compatibility of caution with confidence, Epictetus reverses conventional attitudes by arguing that caution is appropriate concerning things that are up to us (*prohaireta*) and confidence in regard to external contingencies that fall outside this sphere. He now charges himself and his students with reversing these priorities:

121 Where death or exile or pain or ill repute are concerned, there is the context of our running away and our agitation. Therefore, as is to be expected with people who err over what is most important, we turn our natural confidence into audacity, desperation, recklessness, and shamelessness, while we turn our natural caution and respect [*aidêmon*] into cowardice and abjectness, full of fears and anxieties. (2.1.10–11)

According to orthodox Stoicism, human beings are endowed with instinctual impulses for virtue or with 'seeds' of virtues, but the full actualization of this potentiality requires the knowledge and consistency of the ideal sage. Epictetus, as we have seen (p. 33), is reticent concerning this uncompromising doctrine. Instead, and in keeping with his focus on progress rather than achievement, he treats his preferred terms for ethical excellence and integrity (*aidôs*, etc.) as 'natural' faculties or equipment, including among them even courage, which was one of the traditional quartet of cardinal virtues (1.6.28–9, 37–43). We should not presume him to be saying that fully-fledged Stoic virtue is an innate faculty that people can simply choose to access, but we should not presume, either, that he is merely rephrasing the doctrine about innate impulses for virtue. The integrity that Epictetus urges his students to cultivate appears to be an innate moral sensibility.

From the fact that we 'naturally' have this sensibility, it neither follows that we adequately understand its proper application nor that we cannot misuse it. Like any faculty, our innate integrity requires rigorous training in order to guide our 'properly' human actions. Without the understanding of Stoic values (see **122**), we are liable to make radical mistakes about what we respect and fear. It is our 'profession', as human beings, to transcend the brute behaviour of non-rational animals, and we do so by conforming to our rational nature. That requires us to treat ourselves in a manner analogous to the way craftsmen cultivate their professions:

122 Each thing is augmented and preserved by the corresponding actions, the carpenter by carpentry, the grammarian by grammar. But if someone gets the habit of writing ungrammatically, his craft must be undermined and destroyed. In the same way the respectful person is preserved by respectful actions, and destroyed by disrespectful ones.

(2.9.10–11)

Epictetus' central point is that lack of integrity is a deviation from our nature's norms. We are not born morally neutral. Under this highly optimistic conception, moral progress is essentially a matter of trying to become true to our essential, God-given selves. To put it another way, lack of integrity is a self-inflicted loss, a failure to make proper use of what is ours from the start.

Having now studied the 'naturalness' Epictetus attributes to integrity, we may ask about his rationale for so strictly associating it with freedom and tranquillity. The analysis of this question requires us to notice how he treats integrity and freedom as interentailing; for both alike are 'natural', 'belonging to us', 'up to us', 'independent of externals', 'in our interests', and 'socially beneficial'. Here are two of the most revealing passages:

123 [In response to someone who complains of being inactive]

At this moment I [Epictetus] am being summoned to do something. I am leaving now in order to pay attention to the proportions that I ought to observe, to act with integrity [*aidêmonôs*], securely, without desire and aversion towards externals; and further, I pay attention to other people, to see what they are saying and doing, not in order to criticize or mock them, but to focus on myself in case I am making the same mistakes. (4.4.6–7)

124 Everything everywhere is perishable and easy to attack. Whoever sets his heart on any such things must be disturbed, discouraged, a prey to anxiety and distress, with desires that are unfulfilled and aversions that are fully realized. Therefore, are we not willing to secure the only safety that has been granted to us, and by giving up the perishable and slavish domain work at those things that are imperishable and naturally free? Don't we recall that no one does injury or benefit to another, but that the cause of each of these things is a judgement? It is this that does harm and wreckage; this is battle and civil strife and war.

What generated Eteocles and Polyneices was simply this—their judgement concerning dominion and their judgement concerning exile, taking the latter to be the worst of bad things and the former to be the greatest of goods. This is everyone's nature, to pursue the good and to avoid the bad, and to consider him who deprives us of the one and inflicts us with the opposite as a foe and a plotter, even if he is a brother or a son or a father; for nothing is more closely related to us than the good.

So if these things are good and bad, no father is dear to his sons or brother to brother, but everything is full of wars, plots, and informers. But if correct volition is the only good and incorrect volition the only bad thing, what place is left for battle and contention? About what things? About things that are nothing to us? With those who are ignorant, with those who are unfortunate, with those who have been deceived about what really matters?

Socrates kept this in mind, as he lived in his own house, putting up with his wife's ill temper and his insensitive son. What was her purpose in being shrewish? So that she might pour all the water she liked over his head, and stamp on the cake [he had been given by his friend Alcibiades]. But what do I care if I judge that these things have nothing to do with me? Volition is my function, and neither tyrant nor master will constrain me against my will, nor the multitude the individual, nor the stronger the weaker. For this is God's gift to each person, free of impediment. These judgements generate love in the household, concord in the community, peace among nations, gratitude to God, and complete confidence, since they treat of things that are not one's own, things of no importance.

We, however, while we are capable of writing and reading this, and praising what we read, are far from being convinced by it. So the saying about the Spartans—lions at home, but foxes at Ephesus—will apply to us too: lions in class, but foxes outside. (4.5.27–37)

There is no ethical concept in 123–4 that we have not already encountered in Epictetus' discourses, so they provide excellent material for consolidating our grasp of his moral psychology. Rather than treating the moral point of view as a disposition that is distinct from self-concern, he presents it as all of a piece with the natural or proper understanding of one's human identity. That identity is one's volition or *prohairesis*, the only inalienable thing that we have and that we are. It is in virtue of *prohairesis* that we are capable of conscience and self-consciousness— knowing ourselves, reflecting on who we are, and reasoning about how we should organize our lives.

Volition, in Epictetus' philosophy, has an essential monitoring aspect that manifests itself in people's innate propensity to feel shame, respect others, and conform to social norms. However, the focus of the monitoring to which he directs his students is not convention or public opinion but their own characters and the values central to Stoic philosophy. What he repeatedly urges them to respect and to keep faith with is exclusively their own normative selves (see texts on pp. 110, 139, 189); that is to say, their autonomous volition and ideal indifference to the way the world treats them.

How is this an ethical recommendation and how does it bear on freedom and tranquillity? In **124** Epictetus traces the errors of the fratricidal brothers, Eteocles and Polyneices (the unfilial sons of Oedipus), to their identifying their interests with achievement of dominion and avoidance of exile. In consequence of this, they simultaneously surrendered their autonomy, forfeited tranquillity, inflicted war on their people, and flouted elementary norms of fraternal integrity. Epictetus' fundamental claim is that any allocation of unconditional value to external contingencies or possibilities is both an abrogation of self-respect (esteeming indifferent things above one's rationality and internal goodness) and a certain recipe for lack of integrity in one's behaviour towards other people.

As we have seen, Epictetus is largely silent concerning the traditional Stoic virtues and their analysis as epistemic dispositions confined to the ideal sage. Instead, he highlights the qualities I have collectively called integrity, treating them as 'natural' not only in the sense of being proper to human excellence but also as faculties with which people are innately equipped even though they typically fail to acknowledge and utilize them (1.12.30). This shift does not betoken a weakening in his understanding of what the Stoic life in accordance with nature demands at the limit. But that infallible ideal is not his theme in the discourses. Their purpose is rather to encourage his students to acknowledge that they are already equipped with the resources to make significant progress in a genuinely Stoic way of life. What matters is what they want for themselves—to live as free and self-respecting persons, in harmony with the world's divine direction, or to live as slavish and anxious creatures, approximating to non-rational animals.

My discussion of the passage treating Eteocles and Polyneices should have helped to show that the self-concern Epictetus recommends is not only compatible with philanthropy but actually requires it. Even so, some of his comments can give the impression that he recommends his students to practise a detachment that is much too self-absorbed to count as a morally commendable attitude. Questions then remain about how the ideas presented in this and the previous chapter relate to his second 'topic' of philosophy—our appropriate responses and behaviour towards other people. That is the theme of Chapter 9.

FURTHER READING AND NOTES

Rationality, Self, and Person

Stoic philosophy of mind, which I outline in the first part of this chapter, is a complex subject. For a selection of the basic texts, see LS 53; and for detailed discussion Long (1982b), Inwood (1985), Annas (1992), Long (1999). In Long (1991) I discuss Stoic philosophy of mind with particular reference to concepts of the self, as reflected in Epictetus' slogan about 'making correct use of impressions' and his use of the term *prohairesis*. For the through-and-through rationality of the mind, including its emotional states, see Frede (1986); for self-perception as the primary datum of animal (including human) life, see Long (1993a); for the Stoic concept of 'owning oneself', see Long (1997).

Volition and the Freedom of the Will

The most detailed studies of Epictetus' concept of *prohairesis* are Dobbin (1991), and Dragona-Monachou (1978-9), both of which emphasize comparison with Aristotle's use of the term. See also Dihle (1982), Kahn (1988), Gourinat (1996), and Sorabji (2000). It has generally been supposed that the freedom Epictetus attributes to *prohairesis* is not freedom from fate or antecedent causation, but Dobbin (1991) argues that Epictetus, in claiming that not even God can constrain *prohairesis*, 'appears to introduce a clear break in the causal nexus dependent on Zeus and also called fate by the Stoics' (p. 121). Dobbin's argument, which sees Epictetus as responding to Peripatetic criticism of Stoic determinism, is carefully formulated, but I do not find ultimately compelling.

The claim that even Zeus, the universal causal agent, cannot constrain a person's assent does not entail that assent is independent of antecedent causation. What it entails is that nothing including Zeus can constrain a person's volition in the sense that persons can be forced to have different wants from those that they do have: that is, volition by its very nature is not subject to coercion, which leaves the question of its causation entirely open (so Bobzien 1998: 335). However, the volition of the perfected Stoic completely coincides with the will of Zeus, and, since that volition is itself a part of Zeus, Epictetus leaves no room for a freedom that is actually independent of divine causation.

The question of where Epictetus stands in regard to free will has been explored with great effectiveness by Bobzien (1998). She argues, to my mind quite convincingly, that his concept of *prohairesis* and 'what depends on us' is not advanced as a 'compatibilist' contribution to the classic issue of freedom versus determinism (a topic of physics for Chrysippus) but as ethical guidance, to enable people to discriminate between the mental realm of 'things that depend on us' and everything that falls outside that realm. In my treatment of this topic I have broadly accepted her account.

Integrity

Epictetus' treatment of *aidôs* and the other terms I group under the concept of integrity is the subject of an outstanding article by Kamtekar (1998). She shows in convincing detail how Epictetus diverges from traditional Stoicism, and she makes an excellent case for interpreting *aidôs* as a notion like 'conscience'. I have not attempted to incorporate all of her insights in my own treatment, but I recommend her study as one of the best accounts of Epictetus' educational philosophy.

Although Epictetus never refers to the Middle Stoic Panaetius, his focus on integrity, as involving 'decent' or 'becoming' or 'scrupulous' conduct, recalls Cicero's presentation of Panaetius' ethics in the second part of *De officiis* book I. There Cicero, in discussing the virtue of moderation, deals especially with decorum. Cicero's account of decorum has more to do with good manners than with the rigorous self-scrutiny that concerns Epictetus, but that may be his own intrusion rather than the legacy of Panaetius. In any case, Panaetius prefigured Epictetus in developing a Stoic ethics for 'progressives' (as distinct from would-be sages) and he emphasized, just like Epictetus, the innate moral sensibility of human beings (see Cicero, *De officiis* 1.14). We find further common ground between Panaetius and Epictetus in the latter's treatment of social roles (my Chapter 9).

CHAPTER 9

Appropriate Actions and Feelings

Do not hesitate to sympathize verbally with a [distraught] person, and even, if the occasion arises, share in the person's groans. But take care not to groan also within yourself.

(Ench. 16)

9.1 ORIENTATION

Epictetus bases his entire instruction on the premiss that the things that are 'up to us' (volition and integrity) are the only domain of goodness and happiness. It is on the perfection of these mental dispositions that our education should primarily concentrate, with the object of trying to ensure that our desires and aversions are properly directed, effective, and not liable to afflict us with emotional disturbance, undermining our *natural* performance as rational beings. This field of endeavour (which he calls the first topic—see Section 4.4) tells us the true identity of a human being as such, differentiating us from non-rational animals and aligning our human faculties and potentialities with the divine author of our being.

However, it tells us nothing about our contingent identities as individual persons of a particular time and place with corresponding roles and relationships and personalities.

Epictetus' concept of 'innate' integrity presupposes our sociability, but, if the exercise of reverence and trustworthiness is an essential part of our human identity, we need to know who we are quite specifically and what is incumbent on us as parents, siblings, and citizens, and as persons engaged with others in careers and leisure pursuits. Study of these secondary identities is what Epictetus calls his second topic.

We have already encountered his general description of what this involves (p. 115). Like earlier Stoics, he says it deals with 'what is appropriate' (*kathêkon*), but he immediately adds: 'For I ought not to be unmoved [*apathês*] like a statue, but I should maintain my natural and acquired relationships, as a dutiful man and as a son, brother, father, and citizen' (3.2.4).[1] 'Unmoved' was the Stoics' standard word for a mentality from which all 'irrational' emotions, such as envy, dread, anxiety, or lust, are absent. Epictetus himself uses the word in just this way, so to gauge his meaning in the present passage the crucial words are 'not like a statue'. He is not advising his students to be emotional in their human relationships, but he *is* telling them to be open enough to other persons to be affected by the relationships in which one stands to them—not to be stony or impervious. His explicit linkage between 'what is appropriate' and 'not being unmoved' is unparalleled in other Stoic authors.

What feelings or degree of feeling Epictetus advocates are questions for later. My first subject in this chapter is his treatment of the connection between our primary identity as human beings and the conduct appropriate to us in our secondary roles.

9.2 HUMAN PROFESSIONS AND ROLES

In a discourse entitled *How to discover a person's appropriate acts from his identifications* (*onomata*), Epictetus begins by addressing a student:

---

[1] I translate *eusebês* by 'dutiful', taking it to refer to more than religious piety (its literal meaning), and to resonate against the Latin word *pius*, which covers religious, familial, and civic obligations.

125 Study who you are. First of all, a human being, that is, one who has nothing more authoritative than volition [*prohairesis*], but who holds everything else subordinate to that while keeping it unenslaved and sovereign.

Consider, then, from what creatures you are separated by possessing reason. You are separated from wild beasts, you are separated from sheep. (2.10.1–2)

We should carefully notice that Epictetus does not tell the student that he *should* identify himself with autonomous volition. He advances this as the primary and factual identification of human beings as such. Here, as frequently elsewhere, he uses the term human being (*anthrôpos*) with the normative connotation of what members of our species *properly* are. Under this description, those who fail to identify themselves with autonomous volition and the moral character that it betokens are not properly human; they are not 'professional' human beings (see p. 110). Vestiges of this notion persist today in our use of the term 'inhuman'. But *we* reserve that word for instances of wickedness. For Epictetus, by contrast, 'human being' is an identity so honorific and demanding that most of us would fall far short.

In the immediately following sentences, which I have already excerpted (p. 200), Epictetus amplifies this primary identification by telling his student to regard himself as 'a citizen of the world' and a 'principal part of the world' with the capacity 'to understand the divine administration and to reason about its consequences'. Then, using the word *epangelia*, that means literally 'proclamation' or 'profession', he asks what that is in the case of a citizen, and responds:

126 To treat nothing as a purely private interest and to deliberate about nothing as though one were detached, but as the hand or the foot, if they had reason and understanding of the [world's] natural constitution, would never exercise impulse or desire except by reference to the whole.

(2.10.4)

World citizenship is a concept with a complex Stoic background. Stated briefly, it involves the idea that the world is providentially organized to be the proper habitation of human beings, whose possession of divine rationality, construed as the prescriptions of *correct* reasoning, makes them participants with God in a shared law and therefore a shared community, irrespective of their local nationalities and interests.[2] Epictetus, however, co-opts the concept for his favourite theme of moral and psychological readiness for anything: world citizenship (or, what comes to the same, 'kinship with God') is a status that should provide people with equanimity and resolution in every circumstance, including the prospect of death and disease.[3]

He invites his students to regard all their contingent situations and vicissitudes as quasi-political roles, assigned to them by higher authority with a view to their playing their proper part in that authority's excellent world administration. His requirement that his students review their identity asks them to begin by treating their general outlook on the world as analogous to the elite Roman ideology of public service.

Excerpts from two other discourses will illustrate how the role of world citizenship should influence persons' conception of their local identity. Having outlined the 'divine administration' and the requirement to adapt to it rather than to wish it different (see p. 153 above), Epictetus continues:

127   *Is it possible to escape from people?*
How could it be?
     But is it possible by associating with them to change them?
And who grants us that?
     What else is there, then, and what resource can we find for dealing with them?
This sort of resource, whereby they will do what seems good to them, but we shall even so be in conformity with nature. Yet you are unhappy and discontented. If you are alone, you call it isolation, and if you are in company, you call people plotters and robbers, and you find fault with your parents and children and brothers and neighbours. Yet when you are alone, you should call it peace and liberty and regard yourself as like the gods; when you are in a group, you should not call it a crowd and a

---

[2] For a full account of the 'cosmic city', see Schofield (1991).
[3] See 2.10.5–6; 3.24.10–12; and cf. 1.9.1–9, where he unhistorically puts 'citizen of the world' into Socrates' mouth.

throng and an unpleasantness, but a festival and a gathering, and so accept everything cheerfully.

What, then, is the punishment for those who don't accept?

To be just as they are.

Someone doesn't like being alone.

Let him be in isolation.

Someone doesn't like his parents.

Let him be a bad son and moan.

Someone doesn't like his children.

Let him be a bad father.

Throw him in gaol!

What gaol? You mean where he is now. For he is there against his will, and wherever someone is against his will, he is in gaol. Just as Socrates was not in gaol because he was there willingly. (1.12.18–23)

And now:

128 Having received everything including your own self from another [i.e. God], are you annoyed and critical of the giver if he takes something away from you? With what identity and for what purpose have you come? Was it not God who brought you in? Did he not show you the light? Did he not give you fellow workers, and sensory faculties, and rationality? As what did he bring you in? Was it not as a mortal? Was it not as someone to live with a little portion of flesh upon the earth and to be a spectator of his administration and to join in his procession and festival for a short while? Aren't you willing, then, for the period granted you, to be a spectator of the procession and the festival, and then, when he leads you forth, to go, after prostrating yourself and thanking him for what you have heard and observed?

No; I wanted to go on with the festival.

So the initiates would like their initiation to continue, and probably too the people at Olympia would like to see other athletes. But the festival has an end. Leave and depart, like a grateful person, like a reverent person. Give your place to others. They too need to be born, just as you were born, and once born they need space and dwellings and provisions. But if the first ones don't give way, what is left over? Why are you insatiate? Why do you not have enough? Why do you crowd the world?

(4.1.103–6; see p. 169 for 4.1.108–9)

With such vivid passages Epictetus exemplifies the identity and emotional disposition appropriate to a 'world citizen'. Shortly after **125** and **126** Epictetus details the 'professions' of various specific 'roles':

129 Next, keep in mind that you are a son.
What is the profession of this role?
To regard all your [material] possessions as your father's, to be completely obedient, never to criticize him to someone else or say or do anything to harm him, but to be deferential in everything, cooperating with him as far as possible. Next, be aware that you are also a brother. Obligatory to this role too are deference, compliance, politeness, never laying claim against him to anything outside your volition, but conceding such things gladly in order that you may have the better of it in the domain of your volition. For consider what it is to obtain his gratitude in exchange for a lettuce, maybe, or a chair—how much you have gained.

Next, if you are some city's councillor, keep that in mind; your youth, if you are young; your old age, if you are old; being a father, if you are a father. For each of these identifications, when it is reflected upon, underwrites the appropriate actions. But if you go off and criticize your brother, I tell you: You have forgotten who you are and what your identification is.   (2.10.7–12)

As with the term 'human being' (*anthrôpos*), Epictetus treats family relationships, public office, and stages of life as *normative* identifications that specify the conduct appropriate to each designation. To be a real son, one must be filial, to be a real brother, one must be fraternal; the blood relationship by itself is insufficient to identify one in these ways.

If appropriate conduct requires us to be completely unassertive and considerate in our relationship with other persons, how does that square with Epictetus' constant injunction to care only for 'what is mine' and to be indifferent to 'externals'? The essence of his answer is contained in his remark that a genuinely fraternal brother 'has the better of it in the domain of his volition'. Epictetus means that the moral and emotional benefits to oneself from being considerate vastly outweigh the value of any material items one concedes to others.

We are asked to regard the relationships in which we stand to other people not as external states of affairs but as constituents of our personal identity and hence as falling within the realm of our essential self or our volition. To recall a key passage from an earlier chapter (p. 199): 'If I am there, where my volition is, thus and only thus shall I be the friend and son and father that I should be.'

The correct performance of one's social roles—Epictetus' second topic—is both outwardly and inwardly oriented. It is outward in what it requires by way of sensitivity to the dignity and claims of other persons, but what it is about other persons that should concern us is not how they treat us, nor who they are and how they fare independently of us, but only how we dispose ourselves in relation to them. The relevant relationship is entirely one-sided: us in relation to them, not them in relation to us. That is because, as Epictetus views the basis of proper relationships, they should be entirely translated, like everything we deal with, into the domain of our volition and integrity.

130 For this reason goodness has priority over every relationship. Even my father is of no concern to me but only goodness.

Are you so hard?

Yes; that is my nature. This is the currency God has given me. Accordingly, if goodness is different from honourableness and justice, that is goodbye to father, brother, country, and all such things. Am I to pass up my own good, in order for you to get yours, and give way to you? In exchange for what?

I am your father!

But you are not my good.

I am your brother!

But you are not my good. Yet, if we locate goodness in correct volition, the actual maintenance of such relationships becomes a good, and also, one who gives way over certain externals acquires the good.

My father is seizing my property.

But he is not injuring *you*.

My brother will get the main part of the land.

As much as he wants. He won't be getting any of your integrity or your fraternal attitude. Who can rob you of this property? Not even Zeus. For he did not wish to, but he made it up to me, and gave it as he has it himself, unhindered, unconstrained, unimpeded. (3.3.5–10)

To take the measure of this startling passage, we need to combine it with Epictetus' earlier comments on the role of being a son. There he claimed that there should be no limits to filial respect. Here, contrary to first appearances, he is actually making the same point. We do not choose our parents (1.12.28), and some parents do not deserve that title (3.18.5), but what matters about parents, so far as their children are concerned, should be not how they treat us but how we treat them. We are not accountable for how our parents and other relatives behave (1.12.33). In that respect they are of no concern to us and to our own integrity. If, however, we allow their treatment of us to become a matter of concern, we are liable to jeopardize the integrity that is one of our most valuable possessions.

There is clearly a strong and coherent link between Epictetus' introverted recommendations and his social prescriptions. Whether we are trying to make progress on cultivating our autonomy (his first 'topic') or on improving our ways of dealing with other people, we are expected continuously to dwell on the importance of making correct use of our impressions, of treating that as central to our human identity, and of relegating to God everything that falls outside the things that are 'up to us'. Epictetus prefers these general principles, like the prescribed roles of father, son, and so forth, to casuistry or to ranking duties in order of priority. He does, though, recognize that human beings differ greatly in their propensities and that insight into one's individual character is an essential element of the training he recommends:

131 People differ in what they regard as reasonable and unreasonable, just as they do in the case of good and bad and what is or is not in their interests. That is especially why we need education, to learn how to fit our preconception of the reasonable and the unreasonable to particular instances, in harmony with nature.[4] But for judging what is reasonable and unreasonable we use not only our assessments of external things but also [our assessments] of what fits our individual role.

One person finds it reasonable to handle [another person's] chamber pot, on the sole consideration that if he does not do so he will be flogged and deprived of food, whereas if he does it he will not undergo anything harsh or painful. But for someone else it is not only unbearable to handle the thing himself; he cannot even stand another person's doing so. If you ask me:

---

[4] For the concept of correctly fitting preconceptions to particular cases, see p. 80.

Shall I handle the pot or not?
I shall tell you that getting food is more worthwhile than not getting it, and being flogged is less worthwhile than not being flogged. So if you measure your concerns by these criteria, go ahead and handle it.
But that would be beneath me.
That is something for you, and not for me, to bring to the question. Because you are the one who knows yourself, how much you are worth to yourself and at what price you sell yourself. For people differ in the prices at which they sell themselves.

(1.2.5–11; for 1.2.1–4, see p. 98 above)

In the sequel to this passage Epictetus offers examples of heroic persons who preferred death or the risk of death to compromising their self-respect. He contrasts them with those who 'by calculating externals one by one come close to forgetting their *specific* role' (1.2.14).

This train of thought could suggest that in **131** he is criticizing someone (presumably a slave) who serves his master by ministering to his sanitary needs, and commending a person who is revolted by anyone's doing such a thing.[5] But I do not think this is quite his point. Epictetus is not endorsing the conventional indignity of performing that trivial function (something a Stoic should regard with indifference), but using it as the measure of a person who will do anything to avoid freedom from bodily pain. His point, then, is that, in deciding what it is right or reasonable to do, we are never simply assessing material gains or losses; we are also, whether we acknowledge it or not, putting our individual characters on the line and implicating them in our judgements of reasonable behaviour. How people act, especially when critical choices have to be made, reveals their sense of values and thereby the value they assign to themselves.

Epictetus cannot tell anyone what a person is worth in the person's own eyes, but he is entitled to argue that when we weigh up the material advantages or disadvantages of any contemplated action we are also engaging in a trade-off with our characters.[6] It

---

[5] Seneca (*Letter* 77.14) tells of how a young Spartan captive not only refused to perform this servile task but even dashed out his brains to prove his freedom.

[6] For further discussion, see Kamtekar (1998), who shows how the text I have been discussing relates to Epictetus' concept of integrity (*aidôs*).

is up to us to decide 'who we want to be' (3.23.1), but we cannot be anything worthwhile unless we consistently act in accordance with the standards pertaining to the roles of our choice. Overriding everything else is the human 'profession' not to act like a wild or domestic animal, and, in addition to that, our individual pursuits set us standards to live up to, whether as craftsmen or athletes or philosophers and so forth (3.23.2–6).

He imagines himself being asked: 'How shall we each become aware of what fits our role?' (1.2.30), and offers two responses. First, he suggests that special endowments, such as a Socratic aptitude, are intuitively obvious to those persons who have them, equipping them, subject to arduous training, for 'what is great and exceptional' (see 4.8.41–2) More generally, persons should make an assessment of their qualifications and potentials, and adopt the corresponding role:

132 You are a calf; when a lion appears, do your own thing; otherwise you
     will be sorry. You are a bull: go out and fight; for that befits you and you
     are capable of doing that. You have the ability to lead the army against
     Troy: be Agamemnon.   (3.22.6–7)

The criterion of one's 'role' is both the rational norm of human nature—a general standard to try to live up to—and also one's personality and qualifications that one should not try to exceed by attempting things beyond one's present powers (cf. *Ench.* 37; 1.27.8).

As a second response, Epictetus reverts to his trading image:

133 Consider simply at what price you sell your volition. If nothing else,
     friend, don't sell it for little . . . Because I lack talent, shall I give up
     practising? I pray not. Epictetus will not be superior to Socrates, but if
     I am not too bad, that is enough for me.[7] For I shall not be Milo either,
     and yet I do not neglect my body; nor Croesus, and yet I do not neglect
     my property. In a word, we do not give up any practice because we
     despair of perfection.   (1.2.33–7)

     [7] As generally interpreted, the text here makes Epictetus say, 'If I am not inferior
     to Socrates'. That cannot be right, for then he would be putting himself on the same
     level. Several scholars have emended the text, to avoid this statement. I retain it as
     transmitted, but take the words *ou cheirôn* to mean 'not too bad', i.e. as a modest self-
     assessment.

The allusion to Milo is interesting because Aristotle had referred to this famous Greek wrestler when explaining his ethical doctrine of 'the mean between two extremes, relative to us' (*EN* II.1106^{b}3): Milo, as a wrestler, requires much more food than a novice athlete. This illustrates the fact that the quantities appropriate to individuals can all be 'intermediate' (not too much or too little) while varying in particular magnitude relative to the needs of individuals.

Aristotle draws on this concept for his definition of ethical excellence: 'a disposition concerned with choice (*hexis prohairetikê*), lying in a mean relative to us, this being determined by reason and in the way the intelligent man would determine' (*EN* II.1106^{b}36). Aristotle's doctrine, in essence, is that virtues exhibit rational choice within a spectrum of behaviour and feeling that avoids excess and deficiency; and in order to achieve the virtues, we need to make an assessment of our own proclivities. 'For some of us tend to one thing, some to another . . . We must drag ourselves away to the contrary extreme; for we shall get into the intermediate state by drawing well away from error' (*EN* II.1109^{b}2–6).

Epictetus offers exactly similar recommendations in a context dealing with the need to combat bad habits:

134 I have an inclination for pleasure. I will throw myself in the opposite direction, beyond the intermediate point, for the sake of training. I have a disinclination for work. I will focus and train my impressions on this objective, with a view to eliminating my aversion to everything of the kind . . . And so some people must practise more on some things, and other people on other things.   (3.12.7–8)

This is not an original thought, as the close parallel with Aristotle shows.[8] I draw attention to it in order to register Epictetus' sensitivity to basic differences between people. He expects his students to take account of their own temperaments and personalities in applying his pedagogy to themselves.

---

[8] The Aristotelian 'intermediate' does not figure in Epictetus' accounts of good character states; but cf. Cicero, *De officiis* I.129, which does invoke it and may depend on the Stoic Panaetius. For Panaetius' probable influence on Epictetus' treatment of roles and character, see p. 257.

Epictetus' emphasis on intentions as distinct from outcomes, on internals rather than externals, may have given the impression that he takes little interest in people's observable behaviour. Actually, the reverse is true. He regularly exhorts his students to 'reveal' themselves, not in the sense of parading or showing off, but of publicly revealing their progress and education, exemplifying and witnessing to their Stoic commitments (1.4.13; 1.29.33; 2.1.31; 3.9.6). His pedagogy is aimed at their performance. I use this word advisedly, because it ties in with his language of role playing. He adverts to the theatre, not only to exemplify bad models of behaviour, such as the fratricidal pair Polyneices and Eteocles, but also as a 'staging' metaphor of life itself:

135 Remember that you are an actor in a play, whichever play the dramatist chooses, whether short or long. If he wants you to play the part of a beggar, be sure to act it skilfully, and similarly with the parts of cripple or official or private citizen. For your function is to play the assigned role well, but the choice of the role is another's [i.e. God's].   (*Ench.* 17)

136 A time will soon come when the tragic actors will think that their masks and boots and costumes are themselves. Friend, you have these things as [mere] material and plot.[9] Say something, so we may know whether you are a tragic actor or a jester. For both of these have everything else in common. Hence, if someone should remove the performer's boots and mask, and stage him like a mere ghost, has the tragic actor vanished, or does he remain? If he has a voice, he remains. That's what it's like here.
  Accept this provincial governorship.
  I do, and having accepted it I show how an educated man behaves.
  Strip off the senatorial toga, put on rags, and come forward in that role.[10]
  Well then. Have I not been granted a fine voice?
  In what role are you now mounting the stage?
  As a witness summoned by God, who says: 'Go and bear witness for me; for you are worthy to be produced as a witness by me'.   (1.29.41–7)

---

  [9] 'Plot' translates *hypothesis*, correctly rendered so by Souilhé (1948–65) but missed by English translators.
  [10] 'Rags' is almost certainly an allusion to the Cynic costume, which fits Epictetus' following comments on playing the part of a divinely appointed witness. On being stripped of the senatorial toga, see p. 194.

The theatrical image of life goes back to early Stoicism and beyond, but in Epictetus' marvellous use of it (see also 4.1.165; 4.7.13) we may detect his sensitivity to the performative demands of elite Roman culture. His students, as we have seen, were the sons of families in the upper echelons of society and expected to distinguish themselves as officials, soldiers, and so forth. Elite Romans were generally raised to be intensely ambitious and many of them were obsessed with the external accoutrements of rank and office.

Epictetus buys into the concept of performance, but he inverts its ideological conventions by proposing that every role persons find themselves occupying is equally apt as the setting for them to distinguish themselves. Thus, in the second excerpt above, the stage costume corresponds to external contingencies and the voice to the authentic self. The point is then: what reveals persons is not their appearance and the station in life they happen to occupy (their dramatic plot, as it were) but entirely how they perform and speak in these roles.

Epictetus vivifies the performance of Stoicism by frequently invoking the kinds of public arena already familiar to his students or by picturing occasions they are likely to encounter in the future: Caesar's court, religious festivals, grand dinner parties, the amphitheatre, gymnasia, baths, military campaigns, athletic contests, lawcourts, and, less likely but possibly, prisons and places of torture or execution. The personages as well as the settings he selects for making his points in the discourses offer a panorama of Graeco-Roman life: slaves, family members, friends and neighbours, business associates, high officials, models of fortitude, and the reverse. Every situation, he proposes, mundane or exceptional, is equally germane to his students' performance of Stoicism and to their showing in action what they have learnt as distinct from 'spewing out' their lessons:

137 Those who have merely ingested the principles want to spew them out immediately, as people with a weak stomach do with their food. First, digest them, and then you will not do this. Otherwise, what was decent matter really becomes vomit and inedible. But after having absorbed them, show us some resulting change of your governing faculty, in the way that athletes display their shoulders, as a result of their training and diet, and those who have absorbed crafts the results of their learning. The builder does not come and say:

Listen to me lecturing on building.

He gets his contract for a house, builds it, and shows that he has the craft. You should act in the same sort of way: Eat like a human being, drink like a human being, and so too, dress, and marry, and father children, and play your roles as a citizen; put up with abuse, and an inconsiderate brother, father, son, neighbour, fellow-traveller. Show all this to us, so that we can see what you have really learnt from the philosophers. (3.21.1–6)

Epictetus' philosophy of action is designed to equip his students with an art of living for all seasons: 'It is circumstances that reveal people' (1.24.1). Accordingly, he makes Socrates a model of cleanliness and forbearing husband and father (4.5.33; 4.11.19) as well as the model of a courageously principled death.

9.3 FEELINGS AND PASSIONS

Throughout its history Stoicism has been popularly characterized as a philosophy that is tantamount to emotional repression, a mentality not only egoistically unimpassioned but also insensitive towards the fortunes, whether good or bad, of other people. We do not associate Stoicism with attitudes that express themselves in such feelings as 'I am really happy for you' or 'I am sad for you', or in excitement or anxiety over what happens to loved ones and to friends. Yet, the unimpassioned mentality (*apatheia*) of the ideal Stoic is not equivalent to a complete absence of emotion. As I said at the beginning of this chapter, it signifies a mind that is free from 'irrational' passions such as lust, craving, anger, dread, jealousy, envy, irritability, and worry. The Stoics set against these 'morbid' emotions a category of attitudes that they called 'good feelings' (*eupatheiai*), classifying these under three broad headings—joy, caution, and well-wishing. Under these headings they included such attitudes as cheerfulness, sociability, respectfulness, kindness, and affection.

Like the 'passions' the 'good feelings' are 'impulses' (*hormai*), which means they are the psychological mechanism of action, launching our positive or negative responses to everything we experience. What differentiates a good feeling from a passion is the quality of a person's judgement and disposition, together with the object of the feeling or passion. Good feelings are the impulses of fully rational persons, based on correct judgements concerning the spectrum of Stoic values. Hence they are characterized by positive affect towards genuine goodness (moral excellence), negative affect towards genuine badness (moral weakness), and indifference to everything else. Passions, by contrast, are faulty judgements manifested in 'excessive' or 'irrational' impulses. They are prompted by giving highly positive or highly negative value to things that are essentially indifferent: worldly success or failure, sensual pleasure or pain, and, in short, everything outside the mind's direct and sure control.

The inclusion of 'good feelings' in the Stoics' mental repertoire shows that their philosophy did not countenance extirpation of all emotions. Where does Epictetus stand on this issue? In line with his general avoidance of technicalities, he does not advance an explicit theory of the emotions, and he never refers to the concept of 'good feelings' by this official name. Implicitly, however, he strongly endorses a wide range of what we today would call positive emotions or affects: family affection, gratitude, cheerfulness, joy, and enthusiasm; and he devotes an entire discourse to showing that 'caution' (*eulabeia*), which was one of the cardinal 'good feelings' of orthodox Stoicism, is entirely compatible with self-confidence.[11] A reader who did not know the antecedent Stoic tradition would form the impression that cheerfulness and family affection are central to the outlook that Epictetus hopes to encourage in his students even though their achievement of these attitudes will not strictly qualify for the 'good feelings' of the ideal Stoic.

As to the passions or 'morbid emotions', he completely accepts the following propositions that were central to the Stoic tradition. First, such mental states are due not to the intervention of

[11] See **121**, p. 224. Stoic doctrine did not admit a 'good feeling' corresponding to the 'irrational' passion of grief or mental pain, and Epictetus follows suit.

an irrational faculty (for the mind contains no such thing), but to erroneous judgement or misuse of reason. Secondly, morbid emotions are correctible if those subject to them have the will to acknowledge that their faulty desires and aversions fall within the domain of their volition and potential autonomy. The implication of both these propositions is that the cause of morbid emotions is not external situations as such but *ourselves* in as much as we misdescribe and misjudge those situations, and affect ourselves accordingly.

Epictetus draws on these propositions when he interprets Medea's resentment of Jason as a radical misjudgement of the harm Jason was doing to her (see p. 76); likewise when he interprets the man terrified by the threat of fetters as confusing his alienable legs with his potentially inalienable self (see p. 218). But he develops the same line of thought concerning emotions people typically feel concerning other people's condition as well as their own:

138 If we we see someone grieving, we say:
>   *He's done for,*
a consul and we say:
>   *The happy man,*
an exile and we say:
>   *The unfortunate one,*
a beggar and we say:
>   *Poor person, he has no means of eating.*
These are the bad judgements we need to eliminate and to concentrate on. For what are weeping and sighing? A judgement. What is misfortune? A judgement. What are strife, quarrelling, blaming, accusing, impiety, fooling around? They are all judgements, nothing more; judgements, moreover, that treat things falling outside volition as being good and bad. If only someone transfers his judgements to the domain of his volition, I guarantee that he will be in a good and firm condition, howsoever things are around him.   (3.3.17–19)

At face value these critical observations concerning emotional responses to other people appear thoroughly repellent, like the criticism of Odysseus for weeping for his lost Penelope (see p. 191). If the price of being 'in a good and firm condition' is refraining from sympathy with those less fortunate, what humane person would go for it? But before we settle for that response, we need to be sure that it adequately interprets Epictetus' point and pays due allowance to his rhetoric. His focus in this passage is not on the plight of the mourner or the beggar any more than it is on the qualities of fathers and sons when we consider how we should treat them. Epictetus is warning his students against becoming emotional voyeurs of other people's situations when they could and should, instead, focus on their own powers and area of moral responsibility. So I suggest the following interpretation.

To be a beggar is not, of itself, to be in a bad condition, and it may not be viewed as such by the beggar himself. If our response to seeing a beggar is simply the emotion of pity, we jeopardize our volition as far as the beggar and ourselves are concerned. In this, as in all situations, we should not surrender ourselves to first impressions or gut reactions, but ask such questions as: 'How should I position my moral character and integrity with regard to this person?', or 'What is required of me, as a would-be philanthropic individual, in relation to this person?'

Epictetus' claim that passions are faulty judgements fits his insistence that we should always be extremely scrupulous in our use and interpretation of external impressions. He is emphatically not saying that we should not help beggars or mourners. His point is, rather, that our responses to others should be based upon a correct understanding of Stoic values: what matters about the beggar, so far as we should be concerned, is how his hunger affects *our* responsibility to treat any other person philanthropically. Instead of saying to him or to ourselves 'poor you' (which he may well resent) and merely indulging our heartstrings, we should convert our impression of him into a question about whether his situation offers us an opportunity and an obligation to do the best we can to act kindly and generously; that is to say, we should translate an external situation, indifferent in itself, into the moral and first-person question: 'What, if anything, should *I* be trying to do about this?'

Epictetus' refutation of the would-be loving father (see p. 77) makes this point with superb clarity and forcefulness. The father was so emotionally distraught by the plight of his sick daughter that, instead of supporting her, he left home and did not return until he learnt that she had recovered. Emotions can, as in this case, debilitate people from actively assisting those they claim to love, and thus stand in the way of effective philanthropy.

'How am I to become affectionate?' (3.24.58–62). Epictetus answers this question by urging self-reliance and abstention from all criticism of God or fellow human beings. His essential point is that affection requires us to be consistently positive in our attitude to those we love, to regard ourselves as 'fortunate' in having them, for as long as that is vouchsafed, but not to repine if and when they are taken away, and even to prepare oneself for such eventualities:

139 Whenever you are devoted to something, don't regard it as irremovable but as belonging to the class of things like a jar or a drinking glass so that when it is broken you remember what it was and are not disturbed. So in the case of love, if you kiss your child or your brother or your friend, never let your thoughts about them go all the way, and don't allow yourself to be as elated as your feeling wants, but check it and restrain it, like those who stand behind triumphing generals and remind them that they are human. Just so, remind yourself that what you love is mortal and not something that you own. It has been given to you for the present, not as something irremovable and permanent, but like a fig or a grape, at the appointed time of the year. If you long for it in winter, you are foolish. So too, if you long for your son or your friend, at a time they are not granted to you, be sure that you are longing for a fig in winter. For the relation of winter to a fig is the relation that every event in the world has to the things that the same event takes away.

Furthermore, at the very moment you are taking joy in something, present yourself with the opposite impressions. What harm is it, just when you are kissing your little child, to say:

Tomorrow you will die,

or to your friend similarly:

Tomorrow one of us will go away, and we shall not see one another any more? (3.24.84–8)

Chilling must again be one's first response to this passage. Can it possibly square with Epictetus' requirement that we not be 'statue-like' (see p. 232) in our relationships? Two rejoinders are immediately in order. First, when reading this and numerous other 'consolatory' texts from classical antiquity, we need to acknowledge the radical differences between modern life expectancy and health care and the conditions in Epictetus' day; we moderns, at least in the affluent countries, can afford to be relatively confident about the survival of our loved ones. Secondly and more importantly, I take this passage to recommend not a restriction of affection, but an admittedly stark appreciation of the vulnerability of what one loves; we should not expect more of it than is reasonable and thereby misuse it in the present and be emotionally unprepared in the future.

It remains true, of course, that Epictetus' recommendations are chiefly grounded in his providential theology. Believing, as he does, that it is a profound error to attribute badness to anything for which human beings are not responsible, he advances confidence in the divine rationale of all outcomes as the only secure basis for emotional health:

140 When you have Zeus as your leader and align your wishes and desires with him, why are you still afraid of failing? Attach your desire to wealth and your aversion to poverty: you will not get the former and you will get the latter. Similarly with health, public office, honours, native land, friends, children—in sum, with anything that falls outside your own volition. Attach your desires to Zeus and the other gods. Hand them over to them, let them take charge of them and regiment them. How, then, will you be unhappy? But if, poor fellow, you are subject to resentment, pity, envy, and fearfulness, and spend every day bewailing yourself and the gods, how can you continue to say you have had an education? (2.17.23–6)

To interpret this text, we need to remember that Zeus, the Stoic name for God, is not only the external author of the world but also each person's internal 'divinity' or, what comes to the same, the voice of perfectible rationality. Surrendering oneself to Zeus, then, is not a recipe for resignation or passivity. It is a metaphor for a mentality that makes the best of actual eventualities as distinct from wishing for things to be different from how they are independently of ourselves, wasting mental energy on frustration and disappointment.

That is Stoicism as we have always known it. I will not comment further on its theological underpinnings because they are untranslatable into any secular context of modernity. What I turn to now is Epictetus' analysis of emotional pathology and his recommended responses when we encounter situations that typically provoke anger and resentment.

9.4 EMOTIONAL PATHOLOGY AND TOLERANCE

On the one hand, he completely rejects the idea that people are passive victims of disturbing emotions. Love did not drive the father of 1.11 (see p. 77) to abandon his sick daughter; he ran away because he wanted to shield himself from anguish. His timidity was due to his misjudgements of how a loving father should behave. Because all emotions are judgements and functions of our volition, they are 'up to us' and therefore not necessitated by anything external.

But Epictetus is equally insistent that people are necessarily motivated by their conceptions of what they take to be good or bad for themselves. Medea's anger towards Jason, motivating her to kill her children, was a terrible misjudgement of her own interests. She acted quite deliberately and yet, Epictetus says: 'As long as she is deceived about her real interests, what else has she to follow except what appears to her to be true?'

I have already commented on the Socratic antecedents of Epictetus' assessment of Medea (p. 76). The Socratic principle that Epictetus invokes is often described as the principle that 'No one sins willingly'. But that slogan is ambiguous and liable to misrepresent Socrates' claim completely. It does not mean that people are not responsible for wrongs they commit or that their actions are involuntary from their point of view as agents. What it means is that, if wrongdoing is construed Socratically as bad for the doer, it is never strictly perceived as bad at the moment of action, by those who do wrong. You cannot really mean it if you say with Milton's Satan: Evil be thou my Good. To act at all is to be motivated, however mistakenly, by a desire for good or an aversion to bad where good and bad are construed as beneficial and harmful to oneself.

Hence, following Socrates again, Epictetus traces the source of wrongdoing and emotional disturbance to inconsistency and to holding incompatible beliefs or attitudes: wanting to possess something genuinely good or to avoid something genuinely bad, and at the same time applying these values to items that are indifferent, or even treating what is genuinely good as bad and vice versa. According to this analysis, a wrongdoer is like everyone in wanting what is good for herself, and so, when she errs, she does not do what she wants to do, or at least what she would want to do if she understood that the goodness on which happiness depends is excellence of character.

On the basis of this rationalistic analysis of human motivations and error, Epictetus proposes that we never have any sound reasons for being angry or censorious. In a remarkable passage, he even advances an argument against capital punishment:

141   *Shouldn't this brigand and this adulterer be executed?*
Don't ask this, but rather:
> *Shouldn't that person be executed who has gone astray and erred over the most important things, blinded not in vision, which discriminates between black and white, but in the intelligence, which discriminates between good and bad?*

If you make your point like this, you will recognize how inhumane it is, just as if you were saying:
> *This blind man or this deaf man should be executed.*

For if loss of the most important things is the greatest harm, and what is most important in each person is correct volition, and someone is deprived of this, why are you still angry with him? My friend, if you must go against nature in your response to the plight of another person, pity him rather than hate him. Give up this retaliation and hostility.

(1.18.5–9)

A few lines later Epictetus argues that criminal behaviour is not simply due to the moral ignorance of the criminal. The victims of crimes are also responsible if they overvalue their material possessions, providing criminals not only with tempting opportunities but also with bad role models:

142 *Why are we angry?*

Because we set such store on the things they steal from us. If you stop setting store on your clothes, you won't be angry with the thief. Stop setting store on your wife's beauty, and you won't be angry with the adulterer. Recognize that the thief and the adulterer have no place in the things that are yours; their place is elsewhere and outside the things that are up to you . . . But as long as you set store on these things, be angry with yourself rather than them.

For just think: you have fine clothes, but your neighbour does not. You have a window, and you want to air your clothes. The other person, in his ignorance of what the human good is, has the impression that it consists in having fine clothes, just as you do too. So he's going to come and take them, isn't he? If you show a cake to greedy people and gobble it down all by yourself, aren't you inviting them to snatch it? Don't provoke them, don't have an open window, don't air your clothes.

The other day I had an iron lamp next to my household gods. Hearing a noise at the window, I ran down and found that the lamp had been stolen. I reflected that the one who took it had a quite intelligible motive. So what? Tomorrow, I say, you will find a lamp made of cheap pottery.[12] (1.18.11–16)

The almost genial tolerance Epictetus recommends his students to show towards criminals is a consequence of his general position concerning the human 'profession'. We are not responsible for anything that falls outside our own volition, and so it is not for us to tell other people how they should behave in relation to our individual selves or even to react with anger when they help themselves to our possessions. That is for them to decide. But we have responsibilities *to* them, not only in the specific areas of family and civic relationships but also in the values we exhibit and in the charity we should show to those whose outlook is different.

With a jesting allusion to the Stoic paradox that the transition from folly to ideal wisdom is instantaneous, he asks: 'Have you been so suddenly converted to wisdom [that you are harsh with other people]?'[13] This question occurs just before **142**, and probably continued (the manuscript is defective at this point) with

[12] Epictetus' lamp became so famous that this, or another lamp that he had, was sold to an admirer for a very large sum; see Dobbin (1998: 171).

[13] For this Stoic doctrine, see LS 61STU.

words like those I print in brackets. The ideal sage was traditionally unforgiving and pitiless, but Epictetus' allusion to him here
is an ironical way of telling his students why their own condition
does not justify their having such attitudes.[14]

Epictetus would not be a Stoic if he thought that the proper
way to help a distraught person is to 'feel' that person's pain. The
task of a Stoic comforter is not to become upset oneself but to try
to assuage the afflicted person. But, as we see in the passage
printed at the head of this chapter, Epictetus does recommend
'showing' sympathy in words and even 'sharing in another's
groans', provided that one does not 'groan within oneself' (*Ench.*
16).

What are we to make of this controlled empathy? There are
two sides to Epictetus' recommendation. First, an outward
acknowledgement of the distraught person's distress, putting
oneself in the other's position; and, secondly, an inward refusal
'to be carried away by the impression' that the other's situation is
objectively 'bad'. Inwardly, comforters should say to themselves: 'It is not what has happened that is crushing this person
but the person's judgement about what has happened.'

Epictetus admits that no one, including the ideal sage, can fail
to react emotionally to quite unexpected shocks, such as a thun-
derclap or sudden news of some catastrophe (fragment 9). Such
things can happen too rapidly for any reflection or judgement to
intervene. But he does not take such uncontrollable reactions to
count against the difficult Stoic doctrine that dread and other
debilitating passions fall within the scope of our volition. Even a
wise man will blench under a sudden shock, but blenching is not
an instance of dread, as the Stoics define that passion: 'judging
that something terrible is looming.' Having experienced a terri-
fying shock, the wise man 'does not assent to such impressions or

[14] See 2.22.36. Epictetus begins 2.22 with an argument that no one but the wise
man is capable of love. The style of this argument is relatively formal, prompting me
to think that Epictetus is presenting his students here with official Stoic doctrine, on
which he then elaborates in his characteristic way. In his commentary the ideal sage
disappears. Epictetus plainly thought that much that passes under the name of love
does not deserve that word, but it would be a mistake to think that he regarded the
moral conditions for loving that he proposes in this discourse to be beyond his students' powers. On the wise man's love, see Stephens (1996*b*).

add that judgement to them, but rejects them and finds nothing
to dread in them'.

Stoic comforters, then, will allow for shocks, but they will take
prolonged distress and other passions to be self-inflicted, deriv-
ing not from events directly but from people's misjudgements
about the harm or benefit they are experiencing or expect to
experience.

Nothing better illustrates Epictetus' commitment to this doctrine than his startling reduction of the two Homeric epics to the
'misuse of impressions':

143   The *Iliad* is nothing but an impression [*phantasia*] and the use of
impressions. Paris had an impression of abducting the wife of
Menelaus, and Helen had an impression of following him. If Menelaus
had had the impression that it was an advantage to be robbed of such a
wife, what would have happened? We would have lost not only the *Iliad*
but the *Odyssey* as well.   (1.28.12–13)

Paris's lust for Helen, Helen's compliance, and Menelaus's
desires for revenge were all instances of misjudging the value of
what their impressions or thoughts presented to them.

Emotional health or, what comes to the same for Epictetus, the
'correct use of impressions' is implicated in all four of the themes
I have focused on in this book—freedom, judgement, volition,
and integrity. I conclude this chapter and the main part of the
book with an extended analysis of how he combines all of these in
a discourse on everyday social behaviour (4.13). This text will
also bring us back to his Socratic styles of argumentation.

9.5 RESPONDING TO OTHER PEOPLE'S CONFIDENCES

144   Whenever we think that a man has talked straightforwardly to us about
his own business, we ourselves are somehow induced to express our
secrets to him, and we think that this is straightforwardness.   (4.13.1)

After this opening sentence, Epictetus suggests that people reci-
procate confidences for three reasons:

1 We think non-reciprocation is unfair (4.13.2).
2 We think non-reciprocation will give the impression that we aren't straightforward (4.13.2–3).
3 We think we can safely trust persons who have apparently trusted us (4.13.4).

Each of these reasons is like the beliefs that Socrates typically elicits from his interlocutors in Plato. Epictetus now undermines the cogency of these reasons, with a view to showing that what they reveal is not straightforwardness but rashness.

As regards 3, we have no good reason to trust persons we do not know. As regards 1, reciprocity would be required only if we had made that a condition of the conversation in advance. It may be the case that the relationship is non-reciprocal precisely because the first confidence giver is untrustworthy.

At this point Epictetus proposes that the criterion for speaking to someone straightforwardly should be quite independent of the three proposed reasons: it should be based entirely upon one's impression of the other person's integrity and judgements or principles. If that condition is satisfied:

145 I shall not wait for you to entrust your own affairs to me; I will come myself and beg you to hear mine. For who does not want to use a fair vessel? Who looks down on a kindly and trustworthy adviser? Who would not gladly welcome persons to share the burden of his difficulties? (4.13.15–16)

Now, the imaginary interlocutor returns to the reciprocity point: I do trust you, but you do not trust me. Epictetus responds: either it is false that you trust *me*, because I find that you blab to everyone, including complete strangers; or, if you do trust me, it is because you find me trustworthy and not because I have shared any confidences with you. Epictetus concludes that entrusting a confidence is no evidence of the speaker's integrity, and therefore the listener is under no obligation to respond in kind. What confidences require is integrity, and for that, he elucidates, we need to be shown someone whose character is such that the person says:

146 I care only for what is my own, the things that cannot be impeded and are by nature free. This property, pertaining to goodness, I have, but let the rest happen as it is granted to me; I don't differentiate.   (4.13.24)

These are the last words of the last discourse that survives from Arrian's collection. For Epictetus, as we have repeatedly seen, nothing in life is too trivial for his doctrines to apply to. Or to put it another way, he finds every occasion apt for exemplifying his paramount principle that what matters beyond everything else is the way we care for our rational autonomy and integrity.

In this chapter I have tried to show that Epictetus' instruction includes charity towards others, including even criminals, and a sympathetic understanding of their motivations. Epictetus was as convinced as any Stoic that *passionate* attachments to any non-moral goods, including even our own loved ones, are incompatible with our making the best use of our only secure powers—our rational autonomy and integrity. But the context in which we are expected to deploy these powers is precisely our families and a fully engaged social and civic life. There is no hint of ascetic withdrawal from the world in Epictetus' discourses, no suggestion that, in order to safeguard our tranquillity, we should disengage from the ordinary business of life or erect barriers between ourselves and other people. Much of the reason for Epictetus' devotion to Socrates was precisely that great paradigm's civic centredness and his resolute acceptance of the conditions under which he found himself living in Athens.

FURTHER READING AND NOTES

Human Professions and Roles

In Cicero's *De officiis* 1.107–15, four roles (*personae*) are attributed to each human being: (1) human identity as such, (2) individual physique and personality, (3) contingent identity, exemplified by social status and wealth, and (4) choice of career and (would-be) area of excellence. Cicero almost certainly derived this scheme from Panaetius (see Gill

1988, 1993; Dyck 1996). Epictetus may well have been influenced by this scheme, but his deployment of it or something like it is more fluid. In 2.10 (pp. 233, 236 above) he focuses on (1) and (3); in 1.2 (p. 238 above), on (2) and (4). And in 3.23 (p. 240 above) on (1) and (4). On roles in Epictetus see Long (1983: 162–7), Kamtekar (1998: 147–52), and Gill (2000a). On theatrical images in Greek philosophy generally, see Long (1993b: 153). Gill (1990a) is a good account of the human being as an ethical norm.

Epictetus makes 'appropriate action' the second of his three 'topics' (3.2.4), but he hardly gives any exposition of the term *kathêkon*; for his skeletal and obscure division of *kathêkonta* into three types, see 3.7.25 with discussion by Bonhöffer (1894: 205–6). Epictetus says that 'in general they are measured by our relationships' (*Ench.* 30), and at 3.7.26 he lists as the principal ones: 'citizenship, marriage, having children, honouring God, caring for parents: i.e. in general, exercising desire and aversion, and negative and positive impulse, in the way that we ought to do each one of these.' The examples of relationships are in line with the Stoic tradition (cf. DL VII.108), but by summing them up with the sentence 'i.e. in general . . .' Epictetus in effect assimilates this 'second' topic to his 'first' (see my remarks on p. 126, where I argue that the distinction between the two topics is procedural rather than substantive).

The Stoic tradition had drawn a sharp distinction between *kathêkonta* in general, which are within any person's capacity to perform, and 'perfectly performed *kathêkonta*', to which the name *katorthômata* was assigned. The latter require the rationality of the ideal sage. Epictetus never refers to this distinction, in keeping with his frequent reticence concerning ideal wisdom. In earlier Stoicism *kathêkonta* include such self-regarding actions as looking after one's health and one's property. Epictetus probably refers to these when he specifies 'those pertaining to existence' (3.7.25), and he says of himself that 'I don't neglect my body or my property' (1.2.37). But the *kathêkonta* that he treats in the discourses fit his stated focus on social relationships.

There is a large scholarly literature on *kathêkonta*, which is the theme of Cicero's *De officiis*, based upon the work of Panaetius. For a selection of the primary texts, see LS 59. Recent treatments include Cooper (1996) and Inwood and Donini (1999).

Feelings and Passions

Release from dangerous and debilitating emotions had been part of the agenda of ancient ethics from its earliest days, but in the Hellenistic and Roman period philosophy was virtually identified by the rival schools' promises to deliver peace of mind: see Nussbaum (1994), Braund and Gill (1997), Sihvola and Engberg-Pedersen (1998), and especially Sorabji (2000). The early Stoic theory of the passions was the most ambitious attempt to identify these mental states with mistaken judgements. Stoics wrote copiously on the causes of the passions and on what could be done, by argument and training, to 'cure' those subject to them. Seneca's three books *On Anger* are the most extensive treatment of a single passion, and see Cicero's *Tusculan Disputations* for a broader but more summary account. On early Stoic theory see LS 65 for a selection of texts and the outstanding article by Frede (1986).

On the Stoic concept of 'good feelings' (*eupatheiai*, p. 244), see Inwood (1985). The evidence on these, as contrasted with the 'morbid' passions, is sketchy, probably because the conditions that they signified were assimilated to the mentality of the ideal sage. Seneca, however, makes quite a lot of this paragon's joy (e.g. *Letter* 59).

Several of Epictetus' discourses start from themes that had become standard in the Stoic tradition: anger (1.18; 1.28), contentment (1.12; 1.29; 4.4), anxiety (2.13), depression (3.13), and fear (3.26; 4.7). But he is much less concerned with particular passions than with the overall mentalities that make people either susceptible to emotional disturbance or capable of being free and unimpeded. Rather than treating passions as a special topic of ethics, Epictetus approaches them as symptoms of every mind that is out of touch with its own God-given potential and proper outlook on the world. The tolerance that he recommends towards wrongdoers is strongly echoed by Marcus Aurelius: see *Meditations* II.1; IV.3; V.25; etc.

On Epictetus' treatment of uncontrollable shocks (p. 253) and its Stoic background, see Inwood (1985: 175–81) and Sorabji (2000: 375–84).

Epilogue: The Afterlife of Epictetus

My chief aim in writing this book has been to present Epictetus in his own time and place, but I hope I have also succeeded in showing why his practical philosophy has never lacked readers and admirers. The authenticity of his voice, even when he presents theological and psychological ideas that we cannot endorse, is palpable. His moral seriousness and sharp observations transcend history. They are the principal reason why his work has been a real presence throughout the nineteen centuries of its existence. What are the forms that this presence has taken, and where do we or should we position Epictetus today? In this concluding chapter I offer some answers to these large questions.

Stoicism as a widely taught, lived, and living philosophy probably survived the death of Epictetus by no more than 100 years. The philosophers of later antiquity turned increasingly to the interpretation of Plato and Aristotle, and even these powerful movements soon came under pressure from the momentum of Christianity. The official attitude of the early Church to all Greek philosophy was disapproving, but there are clear traces of Stoicism in the Pauline books of the New Testament, and formative Christian thinkers, especially the Alexandrians Clement (*c*.150–220) and Origen (*c*.185–254), appropriated much of it, particularly in the field of ethics. In the period 200–600

Epictetus' name occurs sufficiently often to show that influential Christians esteemed him as a virtuous pagan. They transmitted anecdotes and even composed verses, praising his excellence and 'free' character, notwithstanding poverty, lameness and slavery. Origen himself drew a striking contrast between Plato and Epictetus. Whereas Plato, he writes, 'is only in the hands of those reputed to be scholars, Epictetus is admired by ordinary people who have the urge to be benefited, and who perceive improvement from his words' (*Against Celsus* VI.2).

The 'words' Origen mentions are likely to have been largely confined to the *Manual*, rather than extending to Arrian's full record of the *Discourses* with which we have been chiefly concerned in this book. The fame and influence of the *Manual* in later antiquity are evident from the remarkable fact that Simplicius, the great Neoplatonist commentator on Aristotle, composed an enormous commentary on the work (see p. 273), one of the few surviving commentaries on any ancient philosopher other than Plato or Aristotle. For Simplicius, writing at Athens in the sixth century, the appropriate readers of Epictetus' *Manual* are not fully-fledged philosophers, dedicated to asceticism and the highest reaches of a contemplative life, but rather:

those who want to be genuine human beings, eager to regain the nobility of their ancestry, with which God has graced humans beyond the non-rational animals—persons who are eager for their rational soul to live as it is by nature, ruling the body and transcending it, using it not as a coordinate part but as an instrument. It is to such persons that ethical and political virtues, the virtues promoted by these statements, belong.
(I. Hadot 1996: 195; my translation)

Simplicius introduces his commentary by praising the *Manual* in words similar to, and probably influenced by, Arrian's prefatory letter to the *Discourses* (see p. 39): 'The statements are very urgent and stirring: in fact all who are not totally deadened are goaded by them and become aware of their own passions and roused to correct them, some more than others. Yet anyone not affected by the statements could only be set straight by the courts of Hades' (I. Hadot 1996: 193; my translation).

Starting with Poliziano's translation of the *Manual* into Latin (Bologna, 1497), this standard summary of Epictetus' teaching was soon available in almost every European language. The work was modified specifically for monastic use with changes that included replacing the name of Socrates with that of St Paul. Fresh versions of the *Manual* appeared very frequently throughout the period 1550–1750, especially in English, French, and German, and it was partly translated into Chinese by a Jesuit missionary, who took the work's affinity to Confucianism to help prepare its readers for conversion to Christianity. Most of the early translators of the *Manual* were Protestants who typically read and corrected Epictetus through the medium of their religion, and there were poetic summaries of the work. The full *Discourses* were first edited by Trincavelli (Venice, 1535), but they were not available in English until 1758. In that year Elizabeth Carter published a translation that remained the standard English version prior to the work of Oldfather (1925–8).

Carter (1717–1806) was an extraordinary woman. Her father, an Anglican clergyman, had taught her Greek and Latin, and she mastered many other languages by herself. Her close friends included Samuel Johnson (himself an admirer of Epictetus), Samuel Richardson, Thomas Secker, who became Archbishop of Canterbury, and many other literary luminaries. She declared that she preferred Plato and Socrates to the Stoics, but a woman friend induced her to translate Epictetus' *Discourses*. The completed work earned her the princely sum of £1,000 and financial independence.

Carter appended to her translation a summary of Stoicism (see Carter 1910: pp. ix–xxv). Like many of her contemporaries and early modern predecessors, she combined appreciation of the Stoic doctrine of divine providence and 'excellent rules of self-government and social behaviour' with strong criticism of their theological errors, 'arrogance', and 'insults to human nature . . . by enjoining and promising a perfection in this life of which we feel ourselves incapable'. Had Carter been asked to write a defence of Stoicism, she would almost certainly have declined. What clearly attracted her to her task as translator was an empathy she felt for

Epictetus specifically: 'It is hardly possible to be inattentive to so awakening a speaker as Epictetus. There is such warmth and spirit in his exhortations; and his good sense is enlivened by such a keenness of wit, and gaiety of humour, as render the study of him a most delightful as well as profitable entertainment' (Carter 1910: p. xxv). The record of Elizabeth Carter's life shows her to have been a highly independent and eccentric personality and one of the most accomplished women of the eighteenth century.

Her translation of the *Discourses* was an instant success, but it would have made still more impact if it had appeared 100 years earlier, to supplement the ubiquitous but overly sententious *Manual*. By the middle of the eighteenth century, Epictetus' influence in Europe, though still considerable, had begun to decline, partly as a reaction against the extreme popularity of the *Manual* throughout the preceding two centuries. That popularity had been greatly assisted by the neo-Stoic writings of Justus Lipsius (1547–1606) in the Netherlands and Guillaume du Vair (1556–1621) in France.

Lipsius' most influential work, published in 1584, was *On Resolution* (*De constantia*). He invokes Seneca and 'the divine Epictetus' as the inspiration for his project—to strengthen the mind against anxiety and external problems. Using the form of a dialogue between himself and a mentor called Longius, Lipsius is instructed to think that the chief enemies of mental resolution are 'false goods and evils'. In regard to externals, he should ask himself (as Epictetus would have asked) whether he has really lost something. With reference to Stoic providence and determinism, Lipsius is told to acknowledge that natural phenomena are controlled by an 'eternal and divine law'. Rather than adopting a position on the religious and political factions of the troubled times, Longius urges Lipsius to cultivate 'voluntary and uncomplaining endurance of all human contingencies'. The instrument for this cultivation is 'a good mind' or the rationality that we derive from God. Lipsius puts numerous objections to his mentor, based on the premiss that the advice he is being offered is not consistent with human nature (a standard criticism of Stoicism, echoed, as we just saw, by Carter), and all of these objections are countered.

This work by Lipsius owed its contemporary appeal to numerous cultural and political circumstances extraneous to Epictetus and ancient Stoicism. But it was authentically Stoic and specifically in tune with Epictetus in its emphasis on the mind, judgement, and interiority as the domain of authentic human goodness and tranquillity. Lipsius made no attempt to replicate Epictetus' vivid challenges and memorable images; but many of his numerous readers probably became acquainted with the *Manual* through reading him and also through reading du Vair, who had translated that work into French in 1586 and popularized it in *La Philosophie morale des Stoiques*, which was translated into English by Thomas James under the title *The Moral Philosophie of the Stoicks* (1598).

Epictetus' renown and influence were probably at their greatest during the first half of the seventeenth century. A striking instance of his presence occurs in a short essay by Pascal (1623–1662): 'Discussion with Monsieur de Sacy' (see Pascal 1995: 182–92). In this work Pascal, who was a fervent Jansenist Christian, contrasts Epictetus as a Stoic with Montaigne, whom he treats as a Pyrrhonian sceptic. He praises Epictetus for his excellent understanding of 'man's duties' and for 'seeing God as his principal aim'. To support this judgement, Pascal cites several passages from the *Manual*, including:

Remember that you are here as a player, and that you are playing whichever character in a play the director chooses to give you. If he gives you a small part, then play it accordingly; if he gives you a long one, then play it accordingly; if he wants you to be a beggar, you must do it with all the simplicity ['grace' would be a better translation] you can muster, and so on. It's your task to act well the character assigned to you; the choice is another's. (*Manual* 17)

Following this and other citations, Pascal continues:

There, sir, is the knowledge of this great thinker who has understood the individual's duty so well. I'm tempted to say he would deserve adoration, if he had also realized the individual's powerlessness . . .[but] he becomes lost in the presumption of what we are able to do. He says that God gave man the means to fulfil all his obligations; that these means are within our power, that we must look for happiness through things that we are capable of, since that is why God gave them to us; that property, life, and esteem are not in our power and do not therefore lead to God. Our spirit cannot be forced to believe what is false, nor our will to love something which makes it unhappy. These two powers are, therefore, free, and it is through them that we can become perfect; man through these powers can know God perfectly, love, obey, and please him, cure himself of all his vices, acquire virtue, and thereby become saintly and God's friend. These wickedly proud principles lead man into other errors, such as that the soul is part of the divine being, that pain and death are not evils, that we can commit suicide when we are so afflicted that we have to believe God is calling us, and there are still more.

For Pascal, as for Carter and numerous others, the standard charge against Stoicism was its profoundly 'arrogant' doctrine of human perfectibility, which not only, in their eyes, erased the necessary gap between divine and human excellence but also undermined the redemptive message of Christianity. Readers of this book will note that Pascal has accurately reported several of Epictetus' central themes, but the charge of arrogance (though intelligible from Pascal's theological perspective) will hardly stick for a more detached reader. As we have repeatedly seen, the main focus of Epictetus' teaching is not on perfection or ideal wisdom, but on shaping and improving the mindset of ordinary persons like ourselves. He assumes that we are fallible, as he admits himself to be; but he is profoundly committed, contra Pascal, to the optimistic belief that we are innately and (as he would also say) 'divinely' equipped to live well, even in unfavourable situations, if we make our thoughts and desires, and not our circumstances, responsible for how we fare and act in relation to ourselves and our associates.

It is Descartes (1596–1650), Pascal's contemporary, who captures the essence of Epictetus' prescriptions in his *Discourse on Method* (see Descartes 1931: i. 95–7). After describing his intention to question all opinions other than 'clear and distinct ideas', Descartes writes: 'In order that I should not remain irresolute in my actions while reason obliged me to be so in my judgements, and that I might not omit to carry on my life as happily as I could, I formed for myself a code of morals for the time being which did not consist of more than three or four maxims.' His first maxim

could be described as moderate conventionalism—obedience to
the laws and customs of his country, adherence to the religion he
had been brought up in, and provisional acceptance of 'the most
moderate opinions'. The second maxim invokes consistency and
resoluteness in action, notwithstanding the uncertainty or mere
probability of the opinions he chooses to act upon. The third
maxim deserves to be quoted in full:

My third maxim was to try always to conquer myself rather than fortune, and to alter my desires rather than change the order of the world,
and generally to accustom myself to believe that there is nothing
entirely within our power but our own thoughts: so that after we have
done our best in regard to the things that are without us, our ill-
success cannot possibly be failure on our part. And this alone seemed
to me sufficient to prevent my desiring anything in the future beyond
what I could actually obtain, hence rendering me content; for since
our will does not naturally induce us to desire anything but what our
understanding represents to it as in some way possible of attainment,
it is certain that if we consider all good things which are outside of us
as equally outside of our power, we should not have more regret in
resigning those goods which appear to pertain to our birth, when we
are deprived of them for no fault of our own, than we have in not possessing the kingdoms of China or Mexico. In the same way, making
what is called a virtue out of a necessity, we should no more desire to
be well if ill, or free, if in prison, than we now do to have our bodies
formed of a substance as little corruptible as diamonds, or to have
wings to fly with like birds. I allow, however, that to accustom oneself
to regard all things from this point of view requires long exercise and
meditation often repeated; and I believe that it is principally in this
that is to be found the secret of those philosophers who, in ancient
times, were able to free themselves from the empire of fortune, or,
despite suffering or poverty, to rival their gods in their happiness. For,
ceaselessly occupying themselves in considering the limits which were
prescribed to them by nature, they persuaded themselves so completely that nothing was within their own power but their thoughts, that
this conviction alone was sufficient to prevent their having any longing
for other things. And they had so absolute a mastery over their
thoughts that they had some reason for esteeming themselves as more
rich and more powerful, and more free and more happy than other
men, who, however favoured by nature or fortune they might be, if
devoid of this philosophy, never could arrive at all at which they aim.

Descartes's ancient philosophers are not only the Stoics in general but also Epictetus in particular.[1] That is clear from his comments on thoughts as the only things that are entirely in our power, on making one's desires conform to one's situation, and from the tone of the entire passage. Descartes offers an extraordinarily accurate and appreciative synopsis of Epictetus' philosophy. Instead of voicing the stock contemporary criticisms concerning Stoic pride and impracticality, he grasps and approves the psychological rationale of Stoicism, while acknowledging, as Epictetus repeatedly does, that no one can begin to live accordingly without unremitting exercise and reflection.

Descartes's sympathy for Epictetus is a powerful testimonial from the greatest seventeenth-century philosopher. Turning to the eighteenth century, we find Joseph Butler (1692–1750) drawing directly on Epictetus' first discourse in support of what Butler calls the faculty of 'conscience, moral reason, moral sense, or divine reason'. Butler, bishop successively of Bristol and Durham, was a friend of Archbishop Secker, whom Carter consulted on her translation of Epictetus, and he himself probably knew her. In his celebrated *Sermons* Butler draws on Stoicism in order to identify a foundation for moral philosophy that would be independent of revelation or divine law. He finds it in an account of the human 'constitution' or 'nature', the authoritative component of which he takes to be conscience, or:

a capacity of reflecting upon actions and characters . . . and on doing this, we naturally and unavoidably approve some actions, under the peculiar view of their being virtuous and of good desert; and disapprove of others, as vicious and of ill desert. That we have this moral: approving and disapproving faculty is certain from our experiencing it in ourselves and recognizing it in each other.[2]

He then notes: 'This way of speaking is taken from Epictetus [1.1] and is made use of as seeming the most full, and least liable to cavil.'

---

[1] Descartes's close reading of Stoicism is reflected in his recognition (contrary to most popular accounts of the philosophy) that they attributed intellectual joy, as distinct from bodily emotion, to their wise man. See Descartes (1931: i. 290).

[2] See section 1 of Butler's *Dissertation on the Nature of Virtue*, in his collected works, edited by W. E. Gladstone (Butler 1896).

Actually, in the context Butler cites (see p. 62 above), Epictetus is as much concerned with the autonomy and reflexive capacities of reason as with its approving and disapproving functions. But what Epictetus says elsewhere concerning human beings' innate conceptions of good and bad and concerning 'natural integrity' shows that Butler has appropriated an important element of the discourses. Exactly like Epictetus, he takes our 'reflective' principle to be superior to everything else, with the consequence that we can act in accordance with nature only by conforming to its dictates. This, he says, is the meaning of the expression 'reverence yourself'.

For what Epictetus could mean to an Enlightenment thinker, the best example known to me is Anthony Ashley Cooper (1671–1713), the third Earl of Shaftesbury. In his published work (which was extremely influential) Shaftesbury anticipates Butler in treating human beings as *naturally* benevolent as well as self-interested. This thesis has a Stoic pedigree, but Shaftesbury's Stoic affinity emerges most clearly in his unpublished reflections. In the manner of Marcus Aurelius he composed an extensive series of reflections under the general heading of 'The Philosophical Regimen' (*Askemata*) (see Rand 1900: 133, 137). These consist in the main of questions and answers to himself, peppered with and inspired by quotations from Marcus and Epictetus. The collection is too extensive and informal to lend itself to summary, but the following example is representative, taken from the section called 'Natural Self'.

Know but this self only and what self is indeed, and then fear not to say 'No one is dearer to me than myself' and 'This is father and brother and relative and country and God'.[3] For this is the only piety, the only friendship. Take it the other way, and good-bye to all.[4] With the first weary fit (if there be nothing else in the case) it will be 'Stuff all, what care I? And let it go as it will'; thus stretching, yawning, common weariness, or heaviness, before so much as a sigh comes. But if something harder than usual come across, then (with sighs) 'Why was I born? What is this life? These mortals? This world and all this ado? What

---

[3] Shaftesbury refers in Greek first to Epictetus 3.4.10 and then gives a Greek paraphrase of such passages as 2.17.24 and 2.22.18, for the second of which see p. 199 above.

[4] By 'the other way', he means taking the self to exclude father, brother, etc.

good of all? What justice or wisdom? Why was I made thus? Why made at all? Why anything made? How? Or by whom? For what necessity? What end?' . . . 'Can anyone expel me from the world?'[5] To be despatched, made way with, sent out of the world: terrible! But whither? Where there is world still, or no world? For, if there be any, it is the same still, or better; if there be none, it is no harm, and so no fear . . . What am I? A particular mind, and acting principle? Over what? Over a particular body, senses etc.? To what end? To that which the general mind has appointed, and for so long as it has appointed that I should use such a body and such senses.—But they may be taken from thee.—Let them be so.—But thou art lost then thyself.—How lost?— By having no longer a body and senses to take care of? If I have nothing to take care of, what is anything to me? If there be anything afterwards, I shall be concerned then as now; and all will be well. If there be nothing, all is well still; this is all. I am discharged.

When we move to nineteenth-century Britain, such direct appropriations of Epictetus become harder to trace. Mathew Arnold praises Epictetus and Marcus Aurelius, calling them 'the great masters of morals' (Arnold 183: 345–7). Yet, like Carter, he finds them lacking in the 'warmth' and 'light' of Christianity. Quoting Epictetus' prayer (actually Epictetus' citation of Cleanthes, see p. 23 above) 'Lead me, Zeus and Destiny, whithersoever I am appointed to go', Arnold comments: 'The fortitude of that is for the strong, for the few; even for them the spiritual atmosphere with which it surrounds them is bleak and gray.'

In North America, however, Epictetus was widely valued in his own terms. His emphasis on autonomy and freedom resonated well with the non-conformist individualism of Emerson and Thoreau, but they were drawing on a tradition that went right back to the early days of colonialism. John Harvard's will, written in 1638, bequeathed a copy of Epictetus (presumably the *Manual*) to his newly founded college, and Stoic texts were well represented in the College of William and Mary, from which Thomas Jefferson graduated in 1762 (see Lawson 1979, 179–81). He included Carter's translation in a reading list he drew up for a friend, and he ordered the entire Greek text of Epictetus for his

---

[5] Epictetus 3.22.22.

newly founded University of Virginia. In a letter of 1819 he
wrote: 'Epictetus has given us what was good of the Stoics; all
beyond, of their dogmas, being hypocrisy and grimace . . . I have
sometimes thought of translating Epictetus (for he has never
been tolerably translated into English).'

For even greater appreciation we may turn to Walt Whitman
(see Allen 1979, 43–52). Towards the end of his life he told his
friend Horace Traubel: 'Epictetus is the one of all my old cronies
who has lasted to this day . . . He is a universe in himself. He sets
me free in a flood of light—of life, of vista . . . I do not remember
when I first read the book. It was far, far back . . . It was like being
born again.' In his poem of 1860, 'A Song of Joys', he wrote:

> O while I live to be the ruler of life, not a slave,
> To meet life as a powerful conqueror,
> No fumes, no ennui, no more complaints or scornful
>   criticisms,
> To these proud laws of the air, the water and the ground,
>   proving my interior soul impregnable,
> And nothing exterior shall ever take command of me.

Whitman is far too complex and original to be called a neo-Stoic,
but in 1891, a year before his death, he told another friend that
the Stoics 'are especially needed in a rich and luxurious, and even
scientific age'. Theodore Dreiser in his early novel *Sister Carrie*
(1900) could assume that his readers would catch the general significance of Epictetus' name; for he wrote: 'It is the unintellec-
tual miser who sweats blood at the loss of a hundred dollars. It is
the Epictetus who smiles when the last vestige of physical welfare is removed' (Dreiser 1999: 434). Anthologies and fresh
translations of the *Manual* ensured Epictetus a position in the
reading lists of college campuses throughout the twentieth century, and he acquired startling prominence in the USA with the
publication of Tom Wolfe's novel *A Man in Full* (1998).

In this book, largely set in Atlanta, a young and thoroughly
decent Californian converts Croker, a ruthless 60-year-old
tycoon, facing financial ruin, to Stoicism. The young man,
Conrad, undeservedly imprisoned, has escaped from the Santa
Rita gaol as a result of an earthquake. While a prisoner, he had

discovered Epictetus in a book called *The Stoics*, which he had
been sent mistakenly in place of a thriller by his favourite author
entitled *The Stoics' Game*. He rapidly comes across such passages from Epictetus as the following: 'We must die. But must
we die groaning? We must be imprisoned, but must we whine as
well? What say you, fellow? Chain me? My leg you will chain—
yes, but my will—no, not even Zeus can conquer that' (Wolfe
1998: 398).[6] Conrad is fascinated, and asks himself how he could
apply Epictetus' lessons 2,000 years later amongst his fellow-
prisoners. He memorizes lots of Epictetus, and succeeds in over-
coming the verbal and physical assaults of an especially brutal
antagonist. At the end of the book, Conrad encounters Croker,
and tells him about the Stoic Zeus and Epictetus. Croker had
been on the point of clinching a deal that would have saved him
from bankruptcy at the cost of compromising his Georgian sense
of honour. Instead, he disavows all interest in wealth, parrots
Epictetus to the bemused Atlanta elite, and walks away from
everything that had previously defined his life. Finally, we hear
that he has become a highly successful televangelist, with a programme called 'The Stoic's hour'.

Wolfe's conclusion seems ironical, in keeping with the satirical wit that pervades his novel. Yet, the large role he assigns to
Epictetus together with the admirable character of Conrad are
clearly offered as a challenge to the wealth, luxury, and corruption of the book's other characters, and thus as an indictment,
albeit tongue in cheek, of modern excess. Wolfe was inspired by
the actual experience of Admiral James Stockdale, who has
described how remembered maxims from Epictetus were his
only hold on self-respect when he endured several years of solitary confinement in a Vietnam War prison cell.[7]

The response to Epictetus has always been strongly influenced
by the preconceptions and situations of his readers. In antiquity Christians and non-Christians alike were impressed by

---

[6] Wolfe's quotations from Epictetus are taken from Oates (1940). The reference
here is to Epictetus 1.1.22, p. 63 above.

[7] See Stockdale (1993), with excerpts in Gill (1995: 347–9). Stockdale was the
vice-presidential running mate of Ross Perot in the 1992 US presidential election.

his intense concentration on the mind's capacity for self-improvement and for liberation from unethical impulses. When the early modern era dawned, the *Manual* became a standard supplement to the New Testament and doctrinal Christianity. Its principles were too heterodox and autonomous for many to accept without demur, but they offered a powerful antidote to the pressures of secular and theological authority. Highly independent thinkers such as Descartes, Shaftesbury, and Butler found it possible to bracket their Christian beliefs and draw directly and unapologetically from Epictetus. In the nineteenth and twentieth centuries, Epictetus has served as an advocate of self-reliance and integrity for those who have no official religion as their filter.

What are the prospects for Epictetus in the new millennium? His unqualified faith in divine providence, which helped his appeal to earlier centuries, will not serve him well. Associated with that doctrine is the central Stoic thesis that the only good and bad things in the completely strict sense are states of mind as distinct from external conditions and the consequences of actions. No Stoic, least of all Epictetus, intended this thesis to disoblige persons from doing everything they can to live philanthropic lives, but his discourses are unacceptably insensitive to the damage that circumstances, many of them amenable to rectification, regularly inflict on those who are powerless to help themselves. Epictetus offers no political policies or general strategies for improving living conditions and legal safeguards. The often repeated criticism that Stoicism is a philosophy only for the strong is hard to rebut.

What I propose, as the most promising response on Epictetus' behalf, is that he offers all of us, as individual persons, an extraordinary challenge. His discourses are an invitation to ask whether we have mental and emotional and ethical resources that we have not properly grasped—untapped and perhaps unconscious resources that can equip us to become more self-aware and more determined to make the best of ourselves, whether in mundane situations or ones that are severely testing. Some of us may find that we have these resources, others may not or may do so only to a limited extent. About this difference between persons he is ruthlessly frank. He does not presume that his Stoicism will work well for everyone, but he is convinced that it is worth everyone's while to respond to his challenges and to see what each can do with them.

The Epictetus of this millennium will not be a moral philosopher offering universally valid principles for every human being. As a practical rather than theoretical thinker, he is not in tune with the main currents of academic philosophy. Rather, as Henry James wrote, 'Let us take Epictetus as we take all things in these critical days, eclectically', as I have presented him in this book, appropriating what we find helpful and effective, and discarding what fails to fit our preconceptions—but only after we have given him the chance to help us rethink our priorities and possibilities (see Beattie 1979: 70). As his literary legacy shows, Epictetus has the inimitable language, intensity, and passionate seriousness we associate with the greatest writers. His vigour, wit, and peremptory injunctions will assure him readers who, whatever they think of Stoicism, will find Epictetus himself as benevolently demanding as his original students found him to be.

Here, to end, is a characteristic excerpt from the *Manual* (51) that needs no commentary.

How long are you going to wait before you demand the best for yourself and in no instance bypass the discriminations of reason? You have been given the principles that you ought to endorse, and you have endorsed them. What kind of teacher, then, are you still waiting for in order to refer your self-improvement to him? You are no longer a boy but a full-grown man. If you are careless and lazy now and keep putting things off and always deferring the day after which you will attend to yourself, you will not notice that you are making no progress but you will live and die as someone quite ordinary. From now on, then, resolve to live as a grown-up who is making progress, and make whatever you think best a law that you never set aside. And whenever you encounter anything that is difficult or pleasurable or highly or lowly regarded, remember that the contest is *now*, you are at the Olympic games, you cannot wait any longer, and that your progress is wrecked or preserved by a single day and a single event. That is how Socrates fulfilled himself by attending to nothing except reason in everything he encountered. And you, although you are not yet a Socrates, should live as someone who at least wants to be a Socrates.

FURTHER READING AND NOTES

On Epictetus and early Christianity, see Bonhöffer (1911) and Arnold (1911), who is particularly helpful in identifying Pauline affinities to Stoicism. Christian adaptations of the *Manual* are excellently edited and discussed by Boter (1999); see also Spanneut (1962, 1969). I. Hadot (1996) is an edition of Simplicius' commentary on the *Manual*; an English translation of this work by T. Brennan and C. Brittain is forthcoming from Duckworth.

Oldfather (1927, 1952) provides meticulous details on editions, translations, adaptations and studies of Epictetus. For the Chinese translation of the *Manual* made by the Jesuit missionary Matteo Ricci in the early seventeenth century, see Spalatin (1975) and P. Hadot (2000: 156–7).

The modern reception of Epictetus is generally studied in conjunction with the influence of the other Roman Stoics. For the period 1500–1700, including discussion of Lipsius and du Vair, see Zanta (1914), Oestreich (1982), Morford (1991), and Barbour (1998). On Lipsius specifically, see Saunders (1955). Taylor (1989) discusses Epictetus and neo-Stoicism within a much broader context. See also MacIntyre (1981, 1988).

For Descartes's ethics, see Marshall (1998), who cites a curiously disparaging comment by Leibniz: 'We need only inspect the incomparable manual of Epictetus and the Epicurean of Laercia [Diogenes Laertius] to admit that Descartes has not much advanced the practice of morality' (see Leibniz 1989: 241). Marshall (1988: 55 n. 4) finds Descartes's third maxim, which I have quoted, the centre of Descartes's 'more developed moral theory'. I cannot agree with him that it is closer to du Vair than to Epictetus; it draws quite specifically on Epictetus' fundamental distinction (1.1) between the things that are in our power and the things that are not.

Elizabeth Carter's writings have been edited by Hawley (2000, which includes Carter's complete translation of Epictetus). Gaussen (1906) is a chatty memoir of Carter's life.

For my comments on the reception of Epictetus in America I am heavily dependent on the excellent set of essays in MacMillan (1979).

Tom Wolfe's extensive use of Epictetus in *A Man in Full* attracted considerable journalistic attention when the book first appeared. *The Chicago Tribune* of 22 Jan. 1999 ran a piece headed 'Epictetus the Stoic is Hot Again Thanks to Tom Wolfe'; for other newspaper coverage, see the *New York Times*, 2 Jan. 1999: 'The Stoics have a Stand on

Everything, even on Dinner Parties and Sex', and the front page article of the *Los Angeles Times*, 11 March 1999, headed 'A New Season of Reason'. In an interview, published in the *San Francisco Examiner Magazine*, 29 Nov. 1998, Wolfe tells of how he 'came across an account of an ordeal by an American pilot shot down in Vietnam [James Stockdale]. I remember him saying that if he had not taken a philosophy course at the Naval Academy he would never have survived the ordeal—and the only name that came back to him was Epictetus.' Either Wolfe's source or his memory is in error because Stockdale learned his Epictetus at Stanford University; see Gill (1995: 347). For further reference to Epictetus in recent American literature, see J. Higgins, *Thunder Point* (1994: 143).

Academic study of Epictetus has notably increased during the past few years in company with the strong revival of research on Hellenistic and later ancient philosophy. Contemporary interests in concepts of the self are a further stimulus for fresh readings of Epictetus. Foucault (1988: 37) credits Epictetus with pioneering techniques of self-examination that culminate in Freud. Books that do not name Epictetus but have striking affinities to his way of connecting integrity with robust consciousness include Bruner (1990) and Beebe (1992).

GLOSSARY

Italicized terms are Greek. The references to pages are selective, being intended to direct readers only to pages where the terms are strongly marked in Epictetus' text or explained in my discussions.

WHO'S WHO: STOICS AND OTHERS

Stoic philosophers and other significant figures are described below, apart from Epictetus, Arrian, Xenophon, and Musonius Rufus, who are more fully treated in chapters 1 and 2. For further details, see the *Oxford Classical Dictionary* (3rd edn., 1996) and D. Zeyl (ed.), *Encyclopedia of Classical Philosophy* (Westport, Conn. 1997).

ANTISTHENES of Athens, c.445–360 BC, devoted follower of Socrates and author of Socratic dialogues that have not survived; reputed to have inspired the Cynicism of Diogenes.

ARISTO of Chios, fl. early to mid-3rd century BC. Unorthodox Stoic pupil of Zeno.

ARISTOTLE of Stageira, Macedonia, 384–322 BC. Plato's greatest pupil, and founder at Athens of the Lyceum or Peripatetic school.

AULUS GELLIUS, c. AD 130–80. Roman encyclopaedist.

CHRYSIPPUS of Soli, Cilicia, c.280–208 BC. The third head of the Stoa at Athens, and the school's most voluminous writer; the standard authority for later Stoics.

CICERO, 106–43 BC. Roman orator, statesman, and Academic philosopher; major source of information on the fragmentary work of Stoic and other Hellenistic philosophers.

CLEANTHES of Assos, c.331–232 BC. The second head of the Stoa at Athens; wrote in verse as well as prose. His *Hymn to Zeus* is the only complete work surviving from early Stoicism.

CLEOMEDES, fl. second century AD. Stoic author of astronomical handbook.

DIOGENES LAERTIUS, fl. c. AD 200. Compiler of lives and doctrines of Greek philosophers, and a major source for early Stoicism.

DIOGENES of Sinope, fl. mid-4th century BC. Founding father of the Cynic movement.

DIO of Prusa (also called Dio Chrysostom), mid 1st to early 2nd century AD. Greek orator and self-styled Cynic philosopher.

EPICURUS of Athens, 341–271 BC. The founder of Epicureanism, sometimes called the Garden.

EUPHRATES of Tyre, d. *c.* AD 120. Stoic philosopher, probably pupil of Musonius Rufus, and well known to Epictetus.

HIEROCLES of unknown origin, fl. 2nd century AD. Stoic writer on ethics.

MARCUS AURELIUS ANTONINUS, AD 121–80. Roman Emperor 161–80 and author of Stoic *Meditations*.

PANAETIUS of Rhodes, *c.*185–110 BC. Head of the Stoa at Athens from *c.*129; spent time in Rome as close friend of leading figures there.

PLATO of Athens, 427–347 BC. Founder of the Academy at Athens and the effective creator of philosophy as a distinct discipline.

PLOTINUS perhaps of Lycopolis in Egypt, AD 205–70. Neoplatonist philosopher.

PLUTARCH of Chaeroneia, *c.* AD 45–125. Platonist philosopher, educational theorist, and biographer; major source of information on early Stoicism, of which he was highly critical.

POSIDONIUS of Apamea, Syria, *c.*135–50 BC. Stoic philosopher, pupil of Panaetius, and domiciled in Rhodes; cultivated numerous scientific interests and gave Stoicism a closer affinity to Plato and Aristotle.

PYRRHO of Elis, *c.*365–270 BC. Founder of Sceptical movement, and figurehead of the revived Pyrrhonism familiar to Epictetus.

SCEPTICS, a name adopted by neo-Pyrrhonist philosophers by the time of Epictetus. He also mentions and attacks ACADEMICS, referring to those Platonists after Plato himself who interpreted his dialogues sceptically, as invitations to suspend judgement about everything.

SENECA, *c.* AD 1–65. Roman Stoic, tutor and adviser of the emperor Nero, and author of works in philosophy and science, and tragedies; compelled to commit suicide on Nero's orders.

SIMPLICIUS of Cilicia, 6th century AD. Neoplatonist commentator on Aristotle, and author of commentary on Epictetus' *Manual*.

SOCRATES of Athens, 470–399 BC. Moral radical and dialectician, who wrote nothing; the main speaker in most of Plato's dialogues. Executed on charges of irreligion and corruption of youth.

ZENO of Citium, Cyprus, 334–262 BC. Founder of the Stoa at Athens *c.*300 BC.

REFERENCES

Alesse, F. (1994), *Panezio di Rodi e la tradizione stoica* (Naples).
——(2000), *La stoa e la tradizione socratica* (Naples).
Algra, K. (1996), with P. W. van der Horst and D. T. Runia (eds.), *Polyhistor. Studies in the History and Historiography of Ancient Philosophy* (Leiden).
——(1999), with J. Barnes, J. Mansfeld, and M. Schofield (eds.), *The Cambridge History of Hellenistic Philosophy* (Cambridge).
Allen, G. W. (1979), 'Walt Whitman and Stoicism', in MacMillan (1979), 43–60.
Annas, J. (1992), *Hellenistic Philosophy of Mind* (Berkeley and Los Angeles).
——(1993), *The Morality of Happiness* (Oxford).
——(1995), 'Reply to Cooper', *Philosophy and Phenomenological Research*, 55: 600–10.
——(1999), *Platonic Ethics Old and New* (Ithaca, NY).
Arnold, E. V. (1911), *Roman Stoicism* (Cambridge).
Arnold, M. (1883), *Essays in Criticism* (New York).
Barnes, J. (1997), *Logic and the Imperial Stoa* (Leiden).
Barbour, R. (1998), *English Epicures and Stoics: Ancient Legacies in Early Stuart Culture* (Amherst, Mass.).
Beattie, M. (1979), 'Henry James: "The Voice of Stoicism"', in MacMillan (1979), 63–75.
Becker, L. (1998), *A New Stoicism* (Princeton).
Beebe, J. (1992), *Integrity in Depth* (College Station, Tex.).
Billerbeck, M. (1978), *Epiktet: von Kynismus* (Leiden).
——(1979), *Der Kyniker Demetrius: Ein Beitrag zur Geschichte der frühkaiserzeitlichen Popularphilosophie* (Leiden).
——(1996), 'The Ideal Cynic from Epictetus to Julian', in Branham and Goulet-Cazé (1996), 205–21.
Bobzien, S. (1998), *Determinism and Freedom in Stoic Philosophy* (Oxford).
Boge, H. (1973), *Griechische Tachygraphie und Tironische Noten* (Berlin).
Bonhöffer, A. (1890), *Epictet und die Stoa* (Stuttgart).

Bonhöffer, A. (1894), *Die Ethik des stoikers Epictet* (Stuttgart), trans. by Stephens (1996a).

——(1911), *Epictet und das neue Testament* (Gieszen).

Boter, G. (1999), *The Encheiridion of Epictetus and its three Christian Adaptations* (Leiden).

Boudouris, K. J. (1993) (ed.), *Hellenistic Philosophy*, 2 vols. (Athens).

Bowen, A. C., and Todd, R. B. (forthcoming), *Physics and Astronomy in later Stoic Philosophy: Cleomedes' Meteora (The Heavens)* (Berkeley and Los Angeles).

Bowersock, G. (1969), *Greek Sophists in the Roman Empire* (Oxford).

Branham, B., and Goulet-Cazé, M.-O. (1996) (eds.), *The Cynics: The Cynic Movement in Antiquity and its Legacy* (Berkeley and Los Angeles).

Braund, S. M., and Gill, C. (1997) (eds.), *The Passions in Roman Thought and Literature* (Cambridge).

Brennan, T., and Brittain, C. (forthcoming) (trans.), *Simplicius: Commentary on the Manual of Epictetus* (London).

Bruner, J. (1990), *Acts of Meaning* (Cambridge, Mass.).

Brunschwig, J., and Nussbaum, M. C. (1993) (eds.), *Passions and Perceptions: Studies in Hellenistic Philosophy of Mind* (Cambridge).

Brunt, P. (1973), 'Aspects of the Social Thought of Dio Chrysostom and the Stoics', *PCPhS*, 199: 9–34.

——(1975), 'Stoicism and the Principate', *Papers of the British School at Rome*, 43: 7–39.

——(1977), 'From Epictetus to Arrian', *Athenaeum*, 55: 19–48.

Bulloch, A. (1993), with E. Gruen, A. A. Long, and A. Stewart (eds.), *Images and Ideologies: Self-Definition in the Hellenistic World* (Berkeley and Los Angeles).

Butler, J. (1896), *Collected Works*, ed. W. E. Gladstone (Oxford).

Clarke, M. L. (1971), *Higher Education in the Ancient World* (London).

Colardeau, T. (1903), *Étude sur Epictète* (Paris).

Cooper, J. M. (1995), 'Eudaimonism and the Appeal to Nature in the Morality of Happiness', *Philosophy and Phenemonological Research*, 55: 587–99.

——(1996), 'Eudaimonism, the appeal to Nature, and "Moral Duty"', in Engstrom and Whiting (1996), 261–84, repr. in Cooper (1999), 427–48.

——(1999), *Reason and Emotion: Essays on Ancient Moral Psychology and Ethical Theory* (Princeton).

De Lacy, P. (1943), 'The Logical Structure of the Ethics of Epictetus', *Classical Philology*, 38: 112–25.

Descartes, R. (1931), *The Philosophical Works of Descartes*, ed. E. S. Haldane and G. R. T. Ross (Cambridge).

Dihle, A. (1982), *The Theory of the Will in Classical Antquity* (Berkeley and Los Angeles).

Dill, S. (1905), *Roman Society from Nero to Marcus Aurelius* (London).

Dillon, J. (1996), *The Middle Platonists*, rev. edn. (London).

——and Long, A. A. (1988) (eds.), *The Question of 'Eclecticism': Studies in Later Greek Philosophy* (Berkeley and Los Angeles).

Dobbin, R. (1991), 'Prohairesis in Epictetus', *Ancient Philosophy*, 11: 111–35.

——(1998), *Epictetus Discourses Book I* (Oxford).

Döring, K. (1979), *Exemplum Socratis* (Wiesbaden).

——and Ebert, T. (1993) (eds.), *Dialektiker und Stoiker* (Stuttgart).

Douglas, A. E. (1995), 'Form and Content in the *Tusculan Disputations*', in Powell (1995), 197–218.

Dragona-Monachou, M. (1976), *The Stoic Arguments for the Existence and Providence of the Gods* (Athens).

——(1978–9), "Ἡ προαίρεσις Ἀριστοτέλη καὶ στὸν Ἐπίκτητο', *Philosofia*, 8–9: 265–310.

Dreiser, T. (1999), *Sister Carrie* (Modern Library edn.; New York). First published 1900.

Dyck, A. (1996), *A Commentary on Cicero's* De Officiis (Ann Arbor).

Edelstein, L., and Kidd, I. G. (1972). *Posidonius*, vol. i: *The Fragments* (Cambridge, 1972; 2nd edn., 1989).

Edwards, P. (1967) (ed.), *The Encyclopaedia of Philosophy* (New York).

Engstrom, S., and Whiting, J. (1996) (eds.), *Aristotle, Kant, and the Stoics* (Cambridge).

Everson, S. (1991) (ed.), *Companions to Ancient Thought: 2 Psychology* (Cambridge).

Fine, G. (1999) (ed.), *Oxford Readings in Philosophy: Plato 2: Ethics, Politics, Religion, and the Soul* (Oxford).

Foucault, M. (1986), *The Care of the Self*, trans. R. Hurley (New York).

——(1988), *Technologies of the Self: A Seminar with Michel Foucault*, eds. L. H. Martin, G. Gutman, and P. H. Hutton (Amherst).

Frede, M. (1986), 'The Stoic Doctrine of the Affections of the Soul', in Schofield and Striker (1986), 93–112.

——(1997), 'Euphrates of Tyre', in Sorabji (1997b), 1–11.

——(1999a), 'On the Stoic Conception of the Good', in Ierodiakonou (1999), 74–94.

——(1999b), 'Stoic Epistemology', in Algra (1999), 295–322.

Fuentes Gonzalez, P. P. (1998), *Les Diatribes de Télès* (Paris).

Gaussen, A. C. C. (1906), *A Woman of Wit and Wisdom: A Memoir of Elizabeth Carter* (London).

284   *References*

Gerson, L. P. (1990), *God and Greek Philosophy: Studies in the Early History of Natural Theology* (London).

Gill, C. (1983), 'Did Chrysippus Understand Medea?', *Phronesis*, 28: 136–49.

——(1988), 'Personhood and Personality: The Four *personae* Theory in Cicero, *De officiis* I', *Oxford Studies in Ancient Philosophy*, 5: 169–99.

——(1990*a*), 'The Human Being as an Ethical Norm', in Gill (1990*b*), 137–61.

——(1990*b*) (ed.), *The Person and the Human Mind: Essays in Ancient and Modern Philosophy* (Oxford).

——(1993), 'Panaetius on the Virtue of Being Yourself', in Bulloch (1993), 330–53.

——(1995) (ed.), *The Discourses of Epictetus: The Handbook, Fragments*, with translation by R. Hard (London).

——(2000*a*), 'Stoic Writers of the Imperial Era', in Rowe and Schofield (2000), 597–611.

——(2000*b*), 'Protreptic and Dialectic in Plato's *Euthydemus*', in Robinson and Brisson (2000), 133–43.

Gleason, M. (1995), *Making Men: Sophists and Self-Presentation in Ancient Rome* (Princeton).

Gourinat, J.-B. (1996), *Premières leçons sur le Manuel d'Épictète* (Paris).

——(2000), *La Dialectique des stoïciens* (Paris).

——(forthcoming), 'Le Socrate d'Epictète', *Philosophie antique*, 1 (Paris).

Green, P. (1993) (ed.), *Hellenistic Culture and Society* (Berkeley and Los Angeles).

Griffin, M.(1976), *Seneca: A Philosopher in Politics* (Oxford).

——(1984), *Nero the End of a Dynasty* (London).

——(1986), 'Philosophy, Cato and Roman Suicide', *Greece & Rome*, 33: 64–77, 192–202.

——(1996), 'Cynicism and the Romans: Attraction and Repulsion', in Branham and Goulet-Cazé (1996), 205–21.

——, and Barnes, J. (1989) (eds.), *Philosophia Togata: Essays on Philosophy and Roman Society* (Oxford).

Hadot, I. (1996), *Simplicius: Commentaire sur le Manuel d'Epictète* (Leiden).

Hadot, P. (1987), *Exercices spirituels et philosophie antique* (Paris), trans. by M. Chase, *Philosophy as a Way of Life: Spiritual Exercises from Socrates to Foucault*, with introduction by A. Davidson (Oxford, 1995).

——(1992), *La Citadelle intérieure: Introduction aux 'Pensées' de Marc Aurèle* (Paris), trans. by M. Chase, *The Inner Citadel: The Meditations of Marcus Aurelius* (Cambridge, Mass., 1998).

——(2000), *Arrien: Manuel d'Epictète* (Paris).

Halbauer, P. O. (1911), *De Diatribis Epicteti* (Leipzig).

Hankinson, J. (1995), *The Sceptics* (London).

Hawley, J. (2000) (ed.), *Writings of the Bluestocking Circle, 1738–1785*, ii. *Elizabeth Carter* (London).

Hense, O. (1905), *C. Musonius Rufus: Reliquiae* (Leipzig).

Hershbell, J. (1986), 'The Stoicism of Epictetus', *ANRW* ii. 36.3, 2148–63.

Higgins, J. (1994), *Thunder Point* (New York).

Hijmans, B. L. (1959), *Askesis: Notes on Epictetus' Educational System* (Assen).

Holford-Strevens, L. (1988), *Aulus Gellius* (London).

Hock, R. F. (1991), '"By the Gods, It's my One Desire to see an Actual Stoic": Epictetus' Relation with Students and Visitors in his Personal Network', *Semeia*, 56: 121–42.

Ierodiakonou, K. (1999) (ed.), *Topics in Stoic Philosophy* (Oxford).

Inwood, B. (1985), *Ethics and Human Action in Early Stoicism* (Oxford).

——(1996), *'L'Oikeiosis* sociale chez Epictète', in Algra (1996), 243–64.

——(2000), 'The Will in Seneca the Younger', *Classical Philology*, 95: 44–60.

——and Donini, P. (1999), 'Stoic Ethics,' in Algra (1999), 675–738.

——and Gerson, L. P. (1997), *Hellenistic Philosophy. Introductory Readings*, 2nd edn. (Indianapolis); 1st edn., 1988.

Irwin, T. (1979), *Plato Gorgias* (Oxford).

Jagu, A. (1946), *Epictète et Platon: Essai sur les rélations du stoicisme et du platonisme à propos de la morale des entretiens* (Paris).

Jocelyn, H. D. (1982), 'Diatribes and Sermons', *Liverpool Classical Monthly*, 7: 3–7.

Jones, C. P. (1978), *The Roman World of Dio Chrysostom* (Cambridge, Mass.).

Kahn, C. (1988), 'Discovering the Will: From Aristotle to Augustine', in Dillon and Long (1988), 234–60.

Kamtekar, R. (1998), 'ΑΙΔΩΣ in Epictetus', *Classical Philology*, 93: 136–60.

Kaster, R. (1988), *Guardians of Language: The Grammarian and Society in Late Antiquity* (Berkeley/Los Angeles).

Kidd, I. G. (1988), *Posidonius*, vols. 2 (i) and 2 (ii): *The Commentary* (Cambridge).

——(1996), *Posidonius*, vol. 3: *Translation of the Fragments* (Cambridge).

Klauser, T. (1962) (ed.), *Reallexicon für Antike und Christentum*, vol. v (Stuttgart).

Kraut, R. (1979), 'Two Conceptions of Happiness', *Philosophical Review*, 88: 157–97.

——(1983), 'Comments on Gregory Vlastos, "The Socratic elenchus"', *Oxford Studies in Ancient Philosophy*, 1: 59–70.

Laks, A. and Schofield, M. (1995) (eds.), *Justice and Generosity: Studies in Hellenistic Social and Political Philosophy* (Cambridge).

Lawson, L. A. (1979), '*The Moviegoer* and the Stoic Heritage', in MacMillan (1979), 179–91.

Lebell, S. (1995), *Epictetus: The Art of Living: The Classic Manual on Virtue, Happiness, and Effectiveness* (San Francisco).

Leibniz, G. W. (1989), *Philosophical Essays*, ed. and trans. R. Ariew and D. Garber (Indianapolis).

Long, A. A. (1971a), 'The Logical Basis of Stoic Ethics', *Proceedings of the Aristotelian Society*, 71: 85–104; repr. with a postscript as ch. 6 of Long (1996a).

——(1971b) (ed.), *Problems in Stoicism* (London; repr. 1996).

——(1975–6), 'Heraclitus and Stoicism', *Philosophia*, 5–6: 132–53; repr. as ch. 2 of Long (1996a).

——(1978), 'Dialectic and the Stoic Sage', in Rist (1978), 101–24; repr. as ch. 4 of Long (1996a).

——(1982a), 'Epictetus and Marcus Aurelius', in T. J. Luce (ed.), *Ancient Writers* (New York), ii. 985–1002.

——(1982b), 'Soul and Body in Stoicism', *Phronesis*, 27: 34–57; repr. as ch. 10 of Long (1996a).

——(1983), 'Greek ethics after MacIntyre and the Stoic community of reason', *Ancient Philosophy* 3, 184–97, repr. as ch. 7 of Long, 1996a.

——(1986), *Hellenistic Philosophy: Stoics, Epicureans, Sceptics*, 2nd edn. (London); 1st edn., 1974.

——(1988), 'Socrates in Hellenistic Philosophy', *Classical Quarterly*, 38: 150–71; repr. as ch. 1 of Long (1996a).

——(1989), 'Stoic Eudaimonism', *Proceedings of the Boston Area Colloquium in Ancient Philosophy*, 4: 77–101; repr as ch. 8 of Long (1996a).

——(1991), 'Representation and the Self in Stoicism', in Everson (1991), 101–20; repr. as ch. 12 of Long (1996a).

——(1993a), 'Hierocles on *oikeiosis* and Self-Perception', in Boudouris (1993), i. 93–104; repr. as ch. 11 of Long (1996a).

——(1993b), 'Hellenistic Ethics and Philosophical Power', in Green (1993), 138–56.

——(1996a), *Stoic Studies* (Cambridge; paperback repr. Berkeley and Los Angeles, 2001).

——(1996*b*), 'The Socratic Tradition: Diogenes, Crates, and Hellenistic Ethics', in Branham and Goulet-Cazé (1996), 28–46.

——(1997), 'Stoic Philosophers on Persons, Property-Ownership, and Community', in Sorabji (1997*b*), 13–32.

——(1999), 'Stoic Psychology', in Algra (1999), 560–84.

——(2000), 'Epictetus as Socratic Mentor', *Proceedings of the Cambridge Philological Society*, 46: 79–98.

——(2001), 'Ancient Philosophy's Hardest Question: What to Make of Oneself?', *Representations*, 74: 19–36.

——and Sedley, D. N. (1987), *The Hellenistic Philosophers: The Principal Texts in Translation with Philosophical Commentary*, 2 vols. (Cambridge).

—— ——(2001), *Les Philosophes hellénistiques*, trans. J. Brunschwig and P. Pellegrin, 3 vols. (Paris).

Lutz, C. (1947), 'Musonius Rufus: The Roman Socrates', *Yale Classical Studies*, 10: 1–147.

MacIntyre, A. (1967), 'Pantheism', in Edwards (1967), v. 31–5.

——(1981), *After Virtue* (London).

——(1988), *Whose Justice? Whose Rationality?* (Notre Dame, Ind.).

MacMillan, D. J. (1979) (ed.), *The Stoic Strain in American Literature* (Toronto).

MacMullen, R. (1966), *Enemies of the Roman Order* (Cambridge, Mass.).

McPherran, M. (1996), *The Religion of Socrates* (Ithaca, NY).

Manning, C. E. (1986), 'Stoicism and Slavery in the Roman Empire', *ANRW* ii. 36.3, 1518–43.

Mansfeld, J. (1999), 'Theology', in Algra (1999), 452–78.

Marshall, J. (1998), *Descartes's Moral Theory* (Ithaca).

Mignucci, M. (1999), 'The Liar Paradox and the Stoics', in Ierodiakonou (1999), 54–70.

Millar, F. (1965), 'Epictetus and the Imperial Court', *Journal of Roman Studies*, 55: 141–8.

——(1977), *The Emperor in the Roman World* (London).

Moraux, P. (1973–84), *Der Aristotelismus bei den Griechen von Andronikos von Rhodos bis Alexander von Aphrodisas*, 3 vols. (Berlin).

Morford, M. P. O. (1991), *Stoics and Neostoics: Rubens and the Circle of Lipsius* (Princeton).

Nussbaum, M. C. (1994), *The Therapy of Desire: Theory and Practice in Hellenistic Ethics* (Princeton).

Oates, W. J. (1940), *The Stoic and Epicurean Philososophers* (New York).

Oestreich, G. (1982), *Neostoicism and the Early Modern State* (Cambridge).

Oldfather, W. A. (1925–8), *Epictetus: The Discourses as reported by Arrian, the Manual, and Fragments* 2 vols., (London and Cambridge, Mass.).

——(1927), *Contributions toward a Bibliography of Epictetus* (Urbana).

——(1952), *Contributions toward a Bibliography of Epictetus. A Supplement*, ed. M. Harman (Urbana).

Pascal, B. (1995), *Pensées and Other Writings*, trans. H. Levi (Oxford).

Pembroke, S. G. (1971), 'Oikeiosis', in Long (1971*b*), 114–49.

Powell, J. G. F. (1995) (ed.), *Cicero the Philosopher* (Oxford).

Rand, B. (1900), *The Life, Unpublished Letters and Philosophical Regimen of Anthony, Earl of Shaftesbury* (London).

Repici, L. (1993), 'The Stoics and the elenchos', in Döring and Ebert (1993), 253–69.

Rist, J. M. (1969), *Stoic Philosophy* (Cambridge).

——(1978) (ed.), *The Stoics* (Berkeley and Los Angeles).

Robinson, T. M., and Brisson, L. (2000) (eds.), *Plato: Euthydemus, Lysis, Charmides* (St Augustin).

Rowe, C., and Schofield, M. (2000) (eds.), *The Cambridge History of Greek and Roman Political Thought* (Cambridge).

Rutherford, R. B. (1989), *The Meditations of Marcus Aurelius: A Study* (Oxford).

Sandbach, F. H. (1971), '*Ennoia* and *prolēpsis*', in Long (1971*b*), 22–37.

——(1975), *The Stoics* (London).

Saunders, J. (1955), *Justus Lipsius: The Philosophy of Renaissance Stoicism* (New York).

Schenkl, H. (1916) (ed.), *Epicteti Dissertationes ab Arriano Digestae*, 2nd edn. (Leipzig).

Schofield, M. (1991), *The Stoic Idea of the City* (Cambridge).

——and Striker, G. (1986) (eds.), *The Norms of Nature: Studies in Hellenistic Ethics* (Cambridge).

Schweingruber, F. (1943), 'Sokrates und Epiktet', *Hermes*, 78: 52–79.

Sedley, D. N. (1989), 'Philosophical Allegiance in the Greco-Roman World', in Griffin and Barnes (1989), 97–119.

——(1993), 'Chrysippus on Psychophysical Causality', in Brunschwig and Nussbaum (1993), 313–31.

——(1999), 'The Ideal of Godlikeness', in Fine (1999), 309–28.

Seidler, M. (1983), 'Kant and the Stoics on Suicide', *Journal of the History of Ideas*, 429–53.

Sharples, R. W. (1996), *Stoics, Epicureans, and Sceptics: An Introduction to Hellenistic Philosophy* (London).

Sihvola, J. and Engberg-Pedersen, T. (1998) (eds.), *The Emotions in Hellenistic Philosophy* (Dordrecht).

Slings, S. R. (1999), *Plato Clitophon* (Cambridge).

Sorabji, R. (1997a), 'Is Stoic Philosophy Helpful as Psycho-Therapy?', in Sorabji (1997b), 197–210, with reply by B. Williams, 211–13.

——(1997b) (ed.), *Aristotle and After* (Institute of Classical Studies, suppl. 68; London).

——(2000), *Emotion and Peace of Mind: From Stoic Agitation to Christian Temptation* (Oxford).

Souilhé, J. (1948–65), *Epictète: Entretiens*, 4 vols. (Paris).

Spalatin, C. (1975), 'Matteo Ricci's Use of Epictetus' *Encheiridion*', *Gregorianum*, 56: 551–7.

Spanneut, M. (1962), 'Epiktet', in Klauser (1962), 599–681.

——(1969), *Le Stoicisme des pères de l'église* (Paris).

Stadter, P. (1980), *Arrian of Nicomedia* (Chapel Hill, NC).

Starr, C. G. (1949), 'Epictetus and the Tyrant', *Classical Philology*, 44: 20–9.

Stephens, W. O. (1996a), *The Ethics of the Stoic Epictetus* (New York); translation of Bonhöffer (1894).

——(1996b), 'Epictetus on how the Stoic Sage Loves', *Oxford Studies in Ancient Philosophy*, 14: 193–210.

Stockdale, J. (1993), *Courage under Fire: Testing Epictetus's Doctrines in a Laboratory of Human Behavior* (Hoover Institute, Stanford).

Striker, G. (1983), 'The Role of *oikeiosis* in Stoic Ethics', *Oxford Studies in Ancient Philosophy*, 1: 145–67; repr. as ch. 13 of Striker (1996b).

——(1990), '*Ataraxia*: Happiness as Tranquillity', *Monist*, 73: 97–110; repr. as ch. 9 of Striker (1996b).

——(1991), 'Following Nature: A Study in Stoic Ethics', *Oxford Studies in Ancient Philosophy*, 9: 1–73; repr. as ch. 12 of Striker (1996b).

——(1996a), 'Criterion of Truth', in Striker (1996b), 22–76.

——(1996b), *Essays on Hellenistic Epistemology and Ethics* (Cambridge).

Tarrant, H. (2000), *Plato's First Interpreters* (Ithaca, NY).

Taylor, C. (1989), *Sources of the Self* (Cambridge, Mass.).

Van der Waerdt, P. A. (1994) (ed.), *The Socratic Movement* (Ithaca, NY).

Vlastos, G. (1983), 'The Socratic Elenchus', *Oxford Studies in Ancient Philosophy*, 1: 27–58.

——(1991), *Socrates. Ironist and Moral Philosopher* (Cambridge).

——(1994a), Repr. of Vlastos (1983) with revisions, in Vlastos (1994b), 1–38.

——(1994b), *Socratic Studies*, ed. M. F. Burnyeat (Cambridge).

Westerink, L. G. (1970), *Olympiodorus: In Platonis Gorgiam Commentaria* (Leipzig).

290   *References*

White, N. P. (1983) (trans.), *Epictetus: The Handbook of Epictetus* (Indianopolis).

Wirth, T. (1967), 'Arrians Errinerungen an Epiktet', *Museum Helveticum*, 24: 149–89, 197–216.

Wirzsubski, C. (1950), *Libertas as a Political Ideal at Rome during the Late Republic and Early Principate* (Cambridge).

Wolfe, T. (1998), *A Man in Full* (New York).

Xenakis, J. (1969), *Epictetus Philosopher Therapist* (The Hague).

Zanker, P. (1995), *The Mask of Socrates* (Berkeley and Los Angeles).

Zanta, L. (1914), *La Renaissance du Stoicisme au XVIe siècle* (Paris).

INDEX OF PASSAGES CITED

GENERAL INDEX

The names of modern scholars are included here only where their views are mentioned in the main text or discussed in the notes. Many terms not indexed here may be found listed in the *Glossary*.